HYPNOSIS, DISSOCIATION AND SURVIVORS OF CHILD ABUSE

HYPNOSIS, DISSOCIATION AND SURVIVORS OF CHILD ABUSE

Understanding and Treatment

Marcia Degun-Mather

John Wiley & Sons, Ltd

Other Wiley Editorial Offices

John Wiley & Sons Inc., 111 River Street, Hoboken, NJ 07030, USA

Jossey-Bass, 989 Market Street, San Francisco, CA 94103-1741, USA

Wiley-VCH Verlag GmbH, Boschstr. 12, D-69469 Weinheim, Germany

John Wiley & Sons Australia Ltd, 42 McDougall Street, Milton, Queensland 4064, Australia

John Wiley & Sons (Asia) Pte Ltd, 2 Clementi Loop #02-01, Jin Xing Distripark, Singapore 129809

John Wiley & Sons Canada Ltd, 6045 Freemont Blvd, Mississauga, Ontario, L5R 4J3, Canada

Wiley also publishes its books in a variety of electronic formats. Some content that appears in
print may not be available in electronic books.

Library of Congress Cataloging-in-Publication Data

Degun-Mather, Marcia.
  Hypnosis, dissociation, and survivors of child abuse : understanding and
treatment / Marcia Degun-Mather.
      p. ; cm.
  Includes bibliographical references and index.
  ISBN-13: 978-0-470-03254-1 (cloth : alk. paper)   ISBN-13: 978-0-470-01945-0 (pbk. : alk. paper)
  ISBN-10: 0-470-03254-5 (cloth : alk. paper)   ISBN-10: 0-470-01945-X (pbk. : alk. paper)
  1. Adult child abuse victims–Rehabilitation.   2. Adult child abuse
victims–Mental health.   3. Hypnotism.   I. Title.
  [DNLM: 1. Hypnosis. 2. Memory. 3. Child Abuse–psychology.
4. Dissociative Disorders–therapy. 5. Stress Disorders, Post-Traumatic–therapy.
6. Survivors–psychology.   WM 415 D319h 2006]
  RC569.5.C55D44 2006
  616.85′822390651–dc22   2006010698

British Library Cataloguing in Publication Data

A catalogue record for this book is available from the British Library

ISBN-13 978-0-470-03254-1 (hbk)   978-0-470-01945-0 (pbk)
ISBN-10 0-470-03254-5 (hbk)   0-470-01945-X (pbk)

Typeset in 10/12 pt Palatino by SNP Best-set Typesetter Ltd., Hong Kong
Printed and bound in Great Britain by TJ International, Padstow, Cornwall
This book is printed on acid-free paper responsibly manufactured from sustainable forestry
in which at least two trees are planted for each one used for paper production.

CONTENTS

ABOUT THE AUTHOR

Marcia Degun-Mather is a Consultant Clinical Psychologist in private practice, and a lecturer and supervisor on the Diploma Course in Applied and Clinical Hypnosis for qualified health practitioners at University College London. She is an Associate Fellow of the British Psychological Society, and Fellow of the Royal Society of Medicine (Hypnosis and Psychosomatic Medicine Section). She has worked as a clinical psychologist in the mental health service of the NHS for 40 years. During this time she was made Head of the Psychology Department of Warley Psychiatric Teaching Hospital in Brentwood, Essex, where she worked and pioneered, with the help of a few colleagues, the first professional Hypnosis Training Workshops for health professionals which included a mix of psychologists, doctors and psychiatrists. She was also a founder member of the British Society of Experimental and Clinical Hypnosis.

She has contributed to two authoritative books on the application of hypnosis in psychotherapies, namely *Hypnosis: Current Clinical, Experimental, and Forensic Practices* edited by M. Heap (Croom Helm 1988), and *Hypnotherapy: A Handbook* edited by M. Heap and W. Dryden (Open University Press 1991). Her specialist interests in the mental health field are Post Traumatic Stress Disorder (simple and complex), eating disorders, and psychosexual dysfunctions. The application of hypnosis in the psychological treatment of these problems is the subject matter of her teaching on the Diploma Course at University College London. Before retiring from the NHS in 2003, she was Lead Psychologist of the Eating Disorder Service in North East London Mental Health Trust for 6 years. In her private practice now, she covers a wide range of psychological problems, many of which are the result of childhood trauma, abuse or neglect.

ACKNOWLEDGEMENTS

I would like to thank my ex-colleague and friend, Geraldine Tollinton, clinical psychologist who specialised in the field of mental health for children and families, and who spent some of her career as a team member of the much respected trauma centre in Ipswich; the Suffolk Child Sexual Abuse Treatment Service for abused children and their families, which was led by the dedicated clinical manager, Jenny Grinsted. Geraldine had a keen interest in the topic of this book, and, in over-viewing the chapters, her advice and experience were invaluable.

I am also indebted to two other colleagues, Ann Williamson and Geoff Ibbotson, both medical doctors, who are on the National Councils of the British Society of Medical and Dental Hypnosis and the British Society of Experimental and Clinical Hypnosis, and who both use clinical hypnosis in the field of trauma. They have contributed to Chapter 4 with some of their effective hypnotic interventions.

I am grateful to Professor David Oakley, Director of the Hypnosis Unit at University College London, Psychology Department, with whom I have run workshops on the topic of this book over several years. He originally supported the idea that the material of the workshops, and our successful clinical therapeutic work could provide a good basis for a book. Some of the material in this book inevitably reflects his interests and his ideas.

Last but not least, I appreciate the help given by the librarians of the Library of the North East London Mental Health Trust in accessing much of the relevant literature requested.

INTRODUCTION

This book is mainly written for mental health practitioners who work with either children or adults or both and who have a special interest in trauma, particularly interpersonal trauma, starting in childhood. Practitioners who assess and treat survivors of such trauma and abuse and are qualified in this field will be aware of the various and different approaches in understanding and treating this client group. This book focuses on the role of the hypnotic state both in understanding trauma responses and in facilitating recovery. Readers may or may not be qualified to use hypnosis professionally in clinical practice, or they may be interested in learning more about hypnosis and its role in psychotherapy. In either case, it is hoped this book will stimulate the interest of a reader with a professional background.

While there are theoretical and practical chapters in the book, those readers who would like to commence the practice of hypnosis in this field but have no professional training in it should seek appropriate training first.

The original intention to write this book was stimulated by the successful workshop on the topic presented at the annual conference of the British Society of Experimental and Clinical Hypnosis at Sheffield University in 1997. It was during the late 1990s that hypnosis had fallen into disrepute as a therapeutic intervention for post-traumatic stress disorder and other disorders in the field of trauma, largely because of the 'false memory' controversy. Hypnosis was targeted as a procedure responsible for creating false memories of childhood abuse. Depending on how hypnosis is used it can be a very effective tool for resolving trauma, as indeed was shown in the two world wars. The effectiveness of hypnosis in trauma survivors was noted by Pierre Janet who was one of the first medical doctors to understand and use hypnosis for his patients at the end of the nineteenth century.

The purpose of the Conference workshop was to put the record straight on the value of hypnosis in treating survivors of trauma, and on how not to create false memories. As a result of the Workshop, the National Council of the British Society of Experimental and Clinical Hypnosis decided to draft therapeutic guidelines for treating traumatised clients with hypnosis, and also without hypnosis (this is discussed in Chapter 1). In the few years following, these guidelines have been used successfully by practitioners. There has been a general trend to appreciate the need for safe and effective interventions in the field. The British Psychological Society produced a document on Recovered Memories (which had been considered by some to be false memories). The Royal College of Psychiatrists also produced guidelines, as did the American Society of Clinical Hypnosis.

The time has perhaps come to explain more to practitioners in general of the role and value of hypnosis for survivors of childhood trauma and abuse when it is used safely. Some prejudice or misunderstanding of hypnosis still remains, particularly in this area of past memories of childhood occurrences.

The main aim of Chapter 1 is to provide a full understanding of the hypnotic state and how relevant that is to understanding the clinical presentation of the traumatised client.

Chapter 2 is an attempt to explain the role of the hypnotic state of dissociation in producing the symptoms of post-traumatic stress disorder. Hypnosis has a role in survival of the person at the time of the trauma in order to prevent too much shock. Hence the person often has amnesic gaps in the recall of what happened.

Chapter 3 gives more information on dissociation, and an overview of the different forms of child abuse and the long-term consequences.

Chapter 4 is the beginning of the practice of applied hypnosis with such survivors. A number of hypnotic interventions are described and considered for different purposes and stages in the therapy.

Chapter 5 gives a fuller account of the complete therapeutic procedures in phase-oriented therapy. These procedures are both hypnotic and non-hypnotic and can be applied in all three phases of the therapeutic journey.

Chapter 6 consists of illustrations of the therapeutic work carried out with four different clients.

The application of hypnosis proves to be quite flexible and innovative and often client-led. Controlled trials to assess the efficacy of applied hypnosis in trauma cases are much required to provide scientific evidence. This has also been expressed by others in the field of trauma. Safe and effective hypnotic interventions are called for. It is hoped the contents of this book go some way to meet this need.

1

HYPNOSIS AND MEMORY

GENERAL ORIENTATION

This introductory chapter first tackles briefly what hypnosis is in relation to some modern theories, and then the relationship between hypnosis and memory processes. This clearly has a lot of relevance to the clinical field, particularly the field of childhood trauma and adult survivors. The complex issues arising from this will be highlighted here, but addressed in more detail in later chapters.

Initially, it is important to answer two questions concerning hypnosis. Firstly, should hypnosis be considered as a form of treatment in its own right, or as an adjunct to other treatment approaches? Secondly, if it is an adjunct, how effective is it in that capacity?

Hypnotherapy vs Adjunctive Hypnosis

There are two main approaches to the use of hypnosis in the treatment of psychological problems. The first is that hypnosis can form the basis for a distinct form of treatment in its own right. That is, there is a separate form of treatment – 'hypnotherapy' – which is distinct from other forms of treatment in the same way that homoeopathy, aromatherapy, reflexology and acupuncture are separate and distinct from orthodox medicine. It follows from this view that 'hypnotherapy' can be taught independently as a lay discipline and practised by individuals who have no other professional qualification. At present there is no form of control or regulation concerning the practice of 'hypnotherapy' and very little in the way of agreement as to what constitutes its rational base. The other view is that hypnosis should not be seen as a form of treatment or therapy in its own right (Oakley, Alden & Degun-Mather, 1996; Spiegel & Spiegel, 1978). Hypnosis from this perspective is seen as an adjunct, providing an enabling context for the delivery of recognised therapeutic interventions. It can be used as easily and effectively with cognitive-behavioural methods as it can with psychodynamic and other approaches. If hypnosis is simply a means of enhancing the effectiveness of a range of already established treatments and therapies its use cannot be separated from the therapy or treatment it supports.

By way of analogy, the advent of anaesthetics as an adjunct to surgery did not create a separate discipline of 'anaesthesiosurgeons', nor did it remove the need for orthodox surgical skills and training. By the same token the use of the labels 'hypnotherapy' and 'hypnotherapist' on their own to refer to the adjunctive use of hypnosis, though widespread even among professional psychologists, is misleading and many have argued that it should be abandoned (e.g. Vingoe, 1987). As Kirsch, Lynn and Rhue (1993) pointed out, if the term 'hypnotherapy' is to be used to refer to adjunctive use of hypnosis in accepted psychological treatments, the therapy should be identified by labelling the procedure as 'psychodynamic hypnotherapy', 'cognitive-behavioural hypnotherapy', 'eclectic hypnotherapy' etc. However, this is cumbersome and continues to blur the boundary between 'hypnotherapy' as a separate treatment modality and hypnosis as an adjunct to orthodox psychological treatment.

On balance one would argue that the terms 'hypnotherapy' and 'hypnotherapist' should be reserved for the activities of lay practitioners. This book is not about 'hypnotherapy' but about the adjunctive use of hypnosis in the psychological treatment of adult survivors of child abuse. It is directed primarily to psychologists who wish to learn how they might incorporate hypnosis into their professional work with survivors of childhood abuse and to anyone who wishes to know more about the effects of childhood trauma and how hypnosis may be used to facilitate their treatment.

If hypnosis is an adjunct to treatment, incorporating hypnosis can only be as effective as the selected treatment approach permits. Hypnosis allied to poor treatments will produce poor outcomes. Equally though, one might anticipate that good treatments can be made even better with the adjunctive use of hypnosis. Thus the first requirement for the aspiring practitioner must be to learn to become competent in their own professional activities. Good practitioners then need to learn how to incorporate hypnosis into their practice if they are to take full advantage of what it has to offer (Gibson & Heap, 1991). To return to the analogy with anaesthesia – just as anaesthesia is now available as an adjunct to all surgeons so adjunctive hypnotic procedures should be available to all psychologists to assist them in their work.

How Effective Is Hypnosis as an Adjunct?

There is a great deal of clinical opinion, published and otherwise, proclaiming the effectiveness of hypnosis in therapy. It is certainly the belief of myself and colleagues that adding hypnosis to our practice as clinical or counselling psychologists has enhanced substantially our effectiveness as therapists. However, clinical opinion is no substitute for systematic investigation. From what has been said above it is clearly inappropriate to compare treatments described as 'hypnotherapy' with other forms of treatment. What is needed ideally is a comparison of identical treatments delivered either alone or within a hypnotic context. Fortunately a few such studies exist. In the area of psychological treatments a recent meta-analysis (Kirsch, Montgomery & Sapirstein, 1995) looked at 18 studies in which cognitive-behavioural therapy alone was compared with the same therapy with hypnosis as an adjunct. The presenting problems included pain, insomnia, anxiety, phobias and obesity. The analysis indicated a substantial enhancement in treatment outcome if hypnosis was used adjunctively. Clients receiving hypnosis with a cognitive-behavioural treatment showed greater improvement than at least 70% of those receiving the cognitive-behavioural therapy on its own.

This study also provided evidence that the differential effect in favour of the hypnotic treatment increases over the follow-up period. This may be related to the fact that clients are usually taught self-hypnosis and are encouraged to continue in its use once the formal period of therapy is complete. Kirsch et al. (1995) concluded, not surprisingly perhaps, that instruction in the use of hypnosis should be included routinely as a part of training in cognitive-behavioural treatments. In the specific case of the use of hypnosis with survivors of childhood trauma there are as yet no systematic group studies or experimental single case reports and one has to rely on traditional case material (see Cardena, 2000). While this is an unsatisfactory state of affairs there is a wealth of such case material and Cardena lists three reasons to suspect that hypnosis will in due course be proven to be an effective adjunct to trauma treatments generally (Cardena, 2000). If it is accepted that hypnosis is an effective adjunct then it is worth looking further into its nature.

What Is 'Hypnosis'?

A definition

There have been many attempts at defining hypnosis. The following is a useful working description from a report prepared by a Working Party of British Psychologists for the British Psychological Society (1995).

The term 'hypnosis' denotes an interaction between one person, the 'hypnotist', and another person or people, the 'subject' or 'subjects'. In this interaction the hypnotist attempts to influence the subjects' perceptions, feelings, thinking and behaviour by asking them to concentrate on ideas and images that may evoke the intended effects. The verbal communications that the hypnotist uses to achieve these effects are termed 'suggestions'. Suggestions differ from everyday kinds of instructions in that they imply that a 'successful' response is experienced by the subject as having a quality of involuntariness or effortlessness. Subjects may learn to go through the hypnotic procedures on their own, and this is termed 'self-hypnosis'. (British Psychological Society, 1995)

To understand hypnosis and hypnotic procedures it is important to distinguish two basic elements – *trance* and *suggestion* (Heap & Aravind, 2002a).

Trance

A central issue in the history of hypnosis (and of mesmerism before that) has been whether we need to hypothesise a special state of mind, or even a special altered state of brain functioning, in order to explain the phenomena we observe in hypnosis. That is, is the hypnotic subject in a unique 'altered state of consciousness' or 'trance', induced by the hypnotist. This is the so-called 'strong' version of the 'trance' concept, and is the one which has been challenged more recently by 'non-state' or 'sociocognitive' theories of hypnosis which emphasise the role of social and interpersonal factors in shaping and maintaining the hypnotic experience.

While theories of hypnosis continue to change, the terminology in common use still reflects the original, largely 'special state' view of hypnosis, adopted by practitioners such as James Braid (1795–1860), who gave us the term 'hypnosis'. So modern practitioners will report that they 'induce' hypnosis and 'deepen' it, that people are 'in hypnosis' or 'under' it, that they are 'hypnotised' and are 'brought out' at the end . . . Those who are strongly non-state in their theoretical orientation may put 'hypnosis' and state-related terms in quotation marks when they write them or add a disclaimer (for example, 'the subject was 'hypnotised' – whatever that means'). In accordance with common usage the process of initiating hypnosis will be referred to as 'induction' and attempts to enhance the hypnotic experience are referred to as 'deepening' procedures.

Whichever side one may take in the theoretical debate, the term 'trance' can still be helpful when thinking about hypnosis if one uses it in a 'weaker' sense, that is, if the term is used as in everyday language to denote a 'state of mind', such as being happy or sad, interested or bored, attentive or disinterested. To be useful one needs an operational definition of the term 'trance' and the one I have found helpful is as follows:

'Trance' is a particular frame of mind characterised by:

(i) focused attention
(ii) disattention to extraneous stimuli
(iii) absorption in some activity, image, thought or feeling.

In this sense the word 'state' in everyday terms is one of being 'entranced' and people can, and do, enter this 'entranced state' spontaneously. Common examples of 'everyday hypnosis' include being 'lost in thought' or day dreaming; being absorbed in a sporting activity, reading, or listening to music; driving for long distances and not recalling the route taken; and becoming deeply engaged in meditation or relaxation procedures. In all of these instances absorption is a key feature. It is also common for time distortion to occur in these everyday examples – usually the passage of time is underestimated.

Time underestimation is also a frequent accompaniment of 'hypnosis' (Naish, 2001). When asked after a 25–30 minute experience of hypnosis to estimate how long it has been since they first closed their eyes individuals often say '5–10 minutes' and are surprised when they are invited to check against the clock. It is important to note that the list of trance characteristics given above does not include either physical or mental 'relaxation'.

Hypnotic experiences can be created, and typical hypnotic phenomena can be demonstrated in subjects who are both physically active – cycling on exercise bikes for instance – and who are in a state of enhanced mental alertness (Banyai & Hilgard, 1976; Fellows & Richardson, 1993). In an attempt to make the procedure more compatible with clinical settings, a more recent description of an active-alert induction procedure involves suggestions for increased mental awareness, accompanied by repetitive up and down movements of the right hand.

Hypnotic procedures can be seen as attempts to formalise this process of 'entrancement' and intensify it. Potential hypnosis subjects are given a series of instructions which, if they follow them, are intended to assist them in achieving a trance state. The instructions are so worded as to encourage:

1. *Focused attentions* (subjects may be asked to stare at an external object – so-called 'eye fixation' – or to pay close attention to the hypnotist's voice);
2. *Disattention to the surroundings* (subjects are asked for instance to put any sounds in the room 'to the back of their minds'); and
3. *Absorption in an inner mental world* (subjects may be invited to engage themselves in imagery of being in a garden perhaps and then descending a flight of steps).

If we keep these attentions in mind, hypnotic scripts seem a lot less mysterious, and of course they provide a framework for making up our own scripts.

Some people, so-called 'high hypnotisables', are able to achieve the desired state quickly, either spontaneously or through a hypnotic procedure; others take longer.

Hypnotic procedures are generally facilitated by:

1. Encouraging the subject to be non-analytical in their thinking, to 'let go' to focus on the experience and not the process.
2. Increasing the subject's motivation and willingness to actively involve themselves with the hypnosis procedures.
3. Raising subject's expectancies of a positive outcome.

The trance can be 'deepened', that is to say, the client or subject experiences a detachment from reality and more absorption in their inner processes (whatever they have focused on), and they become more responsive to suggestions either of their own or the hypnotist's. As this is a purely subjective experience, the measurements of 'depth of trance' are the subject's self-reported ratings.

Suggestion

'Hypnotic suggestion' is a communication from the hypnotist to subject, which is intended to modify or change the feelings, thoughts, behaviours or images of the subject. Hypnotic suggestions are different from other kinds of suggestions, as they have specific characteristics. As stated in the definition of hypnosis above: 'Suggestions differ from everyday kinds of instructions in that a "successful" response is experienced by the subject as having a quality of involuntariness or effortlessness.' The subject then responds to the suggestion in an involuntary manner. For example, if the suggestion is given that the subject will feel their eyelids getting heavy and closing, then they close their eyes and report that this did not feel deliberate and voluntary on their part. They closed their eyes involuntarily. The act of closing their eyes was dissociated from their awareness and control. Likewise, when a suggestion is made that one arm will feel lighter and lighter and rise up, the response of the arm rising is also reported by the client afterwards as having felt like an involuntary movement. Changes in perception and feelings can be produced by suggesting to the subject appropriate imagery. For example, the suggestion can be given that the client can imagine putting their hand into a bucket of ice and feeling the hand go numb. This change in feeling is usually verified by the subject. The suggestion can be multi-modal.

For example 'ideomotor suggestions' can be given by requesting the subject to extend one arm and imagine that it is made of steel and getting very hard and stiff. The subject responds to the idea ('ideo') of stiffness of the arm. In order to test or 'challenge' the subject's response, another suggestion is given to try and bend the arm. The subject's response to this is usually to be unable to bend the arm until the hypnotist suggests that the arm 'returns to normal'. Apart from producing alterations in perceptions and feelings, suggestions can be given to alter or change the subject's experience of time and memory. Suggestions can be made to go back in time to an earlier event in the subject's life (age regression). The recall may contain accurate recollections, but also some fantasies which are not historically accurate. Suggestions to move forward into the future (age progression) will also produce scenes which are complete fantasy. Both of these suggestions (age regression and age progression) can be used therapeutically (see Chapter 4). Some hypnotic suggestions can produce changes in the physiological responses of the subject. By increasing the arousal level of the subject through suggestion, changes can occur in the heart rate and respiration rate. Similarly the hypnotic image of the hand in the ice bucket can produce a reduction of the temperature of the hand.

'Suggestibility' or 'susceptibility' is a relatively stable personality trait, and individuals differ in the degree to which they are responsive to hypnotic suggestions. There may also be observed individual differences in the degree to which the person is responsive to the various kinds of suggestions such as ideomotor, visual or auditory imagery etc. There are measures of hypnotic susceptibility which usually consist of a number of suggestions which cover the different modalities, as well as suggested recall of the past. The scores are based on ratings of the subject's responses to the items. Most of the susceptibility scales have a high degree of test-retest reliability. The most commonly used Susceptibility Scale used in the UK is the Creative Imagination Scale (Wilson & Barber, 1978).

It is important to understand that hypnotic suggestibility or susceptibility is very different from other kinds of suggestibility. Eysenck and Furneaux (1945) discovered two different kinds of suggestibility. The first is called primary suggestibility, that is the tendency to respond to suggestions of 'unwilled' acts, such as swaying posturally or blushing or ideomotor type responses as described above. Secondary suggestibility is the label they gave to a tendency to be credulous, gullible, and easily persuaded.

Two other kinds of suggestibility have since been identified and viewed as different from either primary or secondary suggestibility. Interrogative suggestibility (Gudjonsson, 1992) is the tendency, when under authoritative pressure from an interrogator, to give seemingly expected replies to leading questions. This scenario might be produced by questioning from the police; or in a clinical context, with a vulnerable, uncertain client being pressured by a practitioner's leading questions. Placebo suggestibility is the tendency for some clients to show therapeutic changes after they have taken a substance which they are led to believe is medicine, when in fact it is a placebo (or non-medicine). This phenomena has been considered to be related to hypnotic suggestibility, but there is no sound evidence for this.

Although there are debates about trance and the meaning of trance in relation to hypnosis as mentioned earlier, suggestibility is widely accepted as an important factor in hypnosis. The issues surrounding the word 'trance' will be addressed in the next section on the main theories of hypnosis. However, recent research has shown how suggestibility is related to the two other factors of hypnosis, namely absorption and reduced critical thought, which have already been mentioned as part of the 'trance'. A study was carried out by Brown, Antonova, Langley and Oakley (2001) to analyse the effect of absorption and reduced critical thought on suggestibility in the hypnotic context. Forty-five participants were presented with a suggestibility assessment prior to receiving a simple hypnotic induction (relaxation). They then received *one* of the following: *either* further relaxation instructions *or* instructions to become absorbed *or* instructions to reduce critical thought. This was then followed by a second suggestibility assessment. Groups were then compared with each other for their objective and subjective suggestibility score change (pre- and post-hypnotic intervention). The results showed that there was a significantly larger suggestibility increase in those who had received instructions to become absorbed, and also in those who received instructions to reduce critical thought. In both these groups, the suggestibility increase was significantly greater than for those who received just further relaxation instructions. It is apparent from these findings that absorption, a state of extremely focused attention and reduced critical thought may be important features of hypnosis. Although these two features are associated with 'trance', as we understand it, one cannot jump to the conclusion that this infers hypnosis with its suggestibility-enhancing effects must be an altered state of consciousness. It merely shows how these components of hypnosis mentioned under the heading of 'trance' are closely interwoven.

MODERN THEORIES OF HYPNOSIS

As mentioned earlier in this chapter, there are two main theories of hypnosis, generally referred to as the 'State' and 'Non-state' theories. The debate between the two schools of thought addresses the issues of whether or not hypnosis is an altered state of consciousness, and what are the essential components, both internal (within the subject) and external (within the situation, that is context and procedures) which lead to what is recognised as 'hypnotic responding'. A brief résumé of the present state of the art is as follows.

'State' Theory of Hypnosis or Neodissociation Theory

As stated earlier, the origins of this theory go back to the nineteenth century and classical theories of dissociation put forward by Pierre Janet and Morton Prince. At that time the interest in dissociation was fuelled by the emergence of psychopathological conditions such as multiple personalities. Although the modern theory of neodissociation has stemmed from the classical theory, the new and modern theory relating to the understanding of hypnosis does not have the same assumptions as the classical theory. Ernest Hilgard (1991) was the first to develop the theory of neodissociation based on his research into hypnotic phenomena. Through his research he concluded that there was a loss of familiar associative processes in most phenomena of hypnosis, such as the inability to bend one's arm after the hypnotic suggestion of stiffness, that is, loss of normal voluntary control. This can be conceived as dissociative, as indeed can all the other hypnotic responses which are felt to be involuntary by the subject.

The particular experiment which seemed to confirm this dissociation in hypnosis was his study of hypnotic analgesia. He took 20 students selected for their high hypnotisability and suggested hypnotic analgesia before they put their hand and forearm into circulating ice water. The subjects then reported either no pain or little pain with a rating of 2 out of 10 (10 being the critical level at which they wanted to withdraw their hand). However, they simultaneously reported by pressing an automatic key (similar to automatic writing) that the real pain was rated as rising up to a mean of 8. It seemed there was another part of them that knew the extent of the pain, Hilgard called this the 'hidden observer'. The two different reports from the subjects provided some evidence of a split in consciousness between the overt (conscious) level and the covert (subconscious) level. It seemed to confirm a process of dissociation.

Hilgard elaborated on the assumptions arising from this theory. Firstly there are subordinate cognitive systems which have some autonomy function. These systems are interactive, but occasionally under certain circumstances may become isolated from each other. The unity of total consciousness perhaps does not exist. There are, for example, lapses in consciousness in the control of well-learned habits, such as driving a car, reciting the alphabet, etc. As these habits are over-learned, they can continue with a minimum of conscious control. Secondly there must be some sort of hierarchical control that manages the interaction between these structures. The third assumption is that there must be some sort of monitoring and controlling structure. Hilgard called this the 'executive ego' or 'central control structure', which plans, monitors and manages functions that are required for thoughts and actions involving the whole person.

Hilgard discovered in his hypnotic analgesia experiment, that some highly hypnotisable subjects were able to reduce the pain but did not produce the 'hidden observer' phenomena. Later Lawrence and Perry (1981) also found that there were two kinds of highly hypnotisables, one with and one without the hidden observer. When Lawrence and Perry age regressed the two groups to age five, one group became totally absorbed in the experience of being a child, while the other group was convinced of being a child again, but in addition retained the presence of an adult observer. This observer was like the 'hidden observer' as it knew all that was happening and the contexts too. The authors called this an experience of duality – being both a child and an adult. The subjects who had this duality experience in age regressions were also the same ones who experienced the hidden observer in the pain experiments. This phenomenon can be used very therapeutically in cases of childhood trauma (see Chapter 4).

The neodissociation theory of hypnosis has been closely linked with modern cognitive psychology, particularly with models of memory, and the distinctions between procedural and declarative knowledge (Kihlstrom, 1984) (see also the 'Different kinds of memory' section below on implicit and explicit memory, pp. 18–19). Further neurological studies to be mentioned at the end of the section would seem to support the dissociation hypothesis of Hilgard. Although his theory is considered a 'state' theory, he has expressed reservations on this term. He preferred to call hypnosis 'the hypnotic condition' because this allowed for partial dissociations; he did not see hypnosis as an all-or-nothing change from a normal waking condition.

Non-State Theory of Hypnosis: A Sociocognitive Approach

This approach has more recent origins in the 1950s. Initially T.X. Barber (1969) started research to discover the social-psychological antecedents of hypnotic behaviour. Barber and his associates (Barber, Spanos & Chaves, 1974) examined a wide range of suggested behaviours in a control group of subjects following no preliminary procedure of any kind. These behaviours included age regressions, hallucinations, amnesia, pain reduction etc. When they administered a hypnotic procedure to the same subjects, there was only a small increment in responsiveness to the same suggestions. Task motivation instructions with no hypnotic procedure produced just as large an increment in responsiveness to suggestions as did the hypnotic induction procedures. Sarbin (1950) also rejected the idea that hypnosis was an altered state of consciousness. He believed that people, like actors, adopt certain social roles, and their interventions in the hypnotic context are guided by the information concerning this particular role. For Barber and his associates, and Sarbin, hypnotic responding is goal-directed behaviour and is context-dependent. It also depends on the subject's willingness to adopt a hypnotic role, and what they understand is expected in that role. It may also depend on the subject's ability to imagine and their experiences. According to the socio-cognitive perspective, hypnotic behaviour appears to be unusual, not because it has unusual causes, but because the hypnotic role calls for unusual behaviours. The hypnotic situation also legitimises it.

Much research has been carried out to support some of these views, including analysis of the wording and interpretation of hypnotic suggestions which might produce the feeling of involuntariness in the response (Spanos, 1991, p. 331). It has also been contested that the differences between high and low hypnotisables in producing pain reduction in hypnosis might reflect differences in the attitude, motivation, expectations and interpretations of the two groups. For the socio-cognitive theorists, 'the goal of research [in hypnosis] should not be to isolate an hypnotic essence but to integrate hypnotic responding into a more general theory of social action', according to Spanos (1991, p. 355).

Two other factors contributing to hypnotic responding have been considered of great importance, that is expectations and beliefs of the subject. Kirsch (1990) has pointed out that in the early days of 'mesmerism', the patients of Mesmer went into a 'crisis' which seemed like convulsive seizures, during which they cried, shrieked and laughed. This was considered to be the essence of mesmerism, but was at least partly due to the fact that it was in line with the behaviour of Mesmer's first patient who had a hysterical disorder. This led to the popular belief that convulsions would follow a successful magnetisation, as mesmerism was then called. Kirsch maintains that a variety of changes of behaviour are interpreted as a 'trance', when they are experienced in a hypnotic context. People are then led to believe that they will be able to experience these suggested effects when they are hypnotised. A number of studies have been carried out to confirm the role of expectancy in hypnotic responding (Kirsch, 1991).

Martin Orne in the 1960s carried out research to investigate hypnotic phenomena and ascertain whether social compliance played any part in their production. He took two groups of subjects; one group were highly hypnotisable, and the other group were low hypnotisables. The first group, the high hypnotisables, were administered a hypnotic induction procedure with deepening, given suggestions to hallucinate, and to age regress. Amnesia was also suggested, and post-hypnotic suggestions were given. The low hypnotisables were asked to simulate hypnosis according to their various preconceptions about it. When comparing the responses of the two groups, Orne concluded that many of the hypnotic behaviours could be faked or simulated. However, there were some essential differences between the simulators and the 'reals', namely the 'reals' (those who were hypnotised) tended to accept illogicalities and irrationalities, whereas the simulators clung to logicality, consistency and realities.

For example, when the hypnotised subjects received the suggestion to hallucinate someone sitting in a chair and then to describe what they saw, they would describe the back of the chair the 'person' was leaning against, as though this person were transparent. The simulators just described the seated 'person'. Furthermore, the post-hypnotic suggestions were carried out by the hypnotised subjects outside the experimental set-up, whereas the simulators confined their responses to the experimental room. When questioned afterwards, the two groups also showed differences in their subjective experiences. The 'reals' maintained there was a compelling quality in the behaviour they carried out, and also an involuntariness in their behaviour, so they felt it was out of their voluntary control. Orne concluded that if the subjects' behaviours fail to reflect an alteration in their subjective experience, then they fail to reach a meaningful criteria of hypnosis. He maintained that although the simulators behaved in a similar way to the 'reals', it does not mean the behaviours are mediated by the same mental processes.

Orne observed that hypnotised subjects are willing to mix the experiences of the real world with the experiences suggested by the hypnotist in a very uncritical fashion. He called this 'trance logic', the unquestioning acceptance of illogicalities. However, it is important to note that some of the behaviours which had been generally considered to be dependent on the prior induction of hypnosis were successfully carried out by the simulators; for example, simulators could be suspended between two chairs with just the head and feet supported. Orne's work has shown that there is a role for social compliance or what he called the 'demand characteristics' of the situation. Some 'hypnotic behaviours' can be produced by compliance. Issues of compliance and role-taking are important but not sufficient to explain the perceptual distortions, hallucinatory experiences and alteration of memory (Orne, 1962).

Graham Wagstaff, a non-state theorist, has admitted to having been influenced by the work of Martin Orne (although Orne was a supporter of the State Theory). Wagstaff has also taken up the sociocognitive approach of Spanos, Barber and Sarbin. However, he highlights the importance of compliance, belief and expectancy in hypnotic responding. Compliance is inevitably linked to expectancy. He argues that if compliance plays an important part in the subjects' responses then these will also depend on what the subjects perceived to be expected of them. In this respect, expectations must have a crucial role in their responses too. The expectations are also determined by the subject's belief. If they believe that they will experience an altered state in hypnosis, then they will expect it. If, however, they do not experience this expected altered state, then they will believe they were not hypnotised. Conversely, if subjects believe hypnosis will just make them feel relaxed and comfortable and they experience this in hypnosis, then they will believe they were hypnotised, and their expectations will be met. Terms like 'hypnotic state', Wagstaff also considers are not appropriate today and should be replaced by other terms which include 'conformity', 'compliance', 'belief', 'attitudes', 'expectations', 'attention', 'concentration', 'relaxation', 'role enactment' and 'imagination'. All these are important to consider when investigating the phenomena. For more information on the theories of hypnosis, and the research carried out by the theorists mentioned, the book recommended to the reader is *Theories of Hypnosis: Current Models and Perspectives*, edited by S.J. Lynn and J.W. Rhue, 1991.

In a recent article, Stanley Krippner (Krippner, 2005) has expanded on the nature of hypnosis and hypnotic phenomena by taking a much broader perspective, inviting the reader to look at cross-cultural studies of native healing. In this brief overview of ideas and approaches, there are many variations in what he calls hypnotic-like procedures. He concludes we cannot assume that Western hypnotic models represent universal processes. There are of course some overlaps in the factors already mentioned such as 'expectancy' facilitating responsiveness, and the role played by imagination. However, he points out, hypnosis is a multifaceted phenomenon and requires explanation at multiple levels. He considers the social and cultural context in which hypnosis occurs has often been overlooked. He also rightly mentions that many investigators have stopped seeing hypnosis as a state and refer to the 'domain of hypnosis' which has the dimensions of altered state, expectation and suggestibility and the hypnotic relationship (Brown & Fromm, 1986). The domain of hypnosis could also include cognitive distortions, imagery, 'trance logic' and dissociation (Evans, 2000). The hypnotic domain has many different times and places and contextual differences. Kihlstrom (2003) has also considered hypnosis to be a multifaceted phenomena requiring explanation at multiple levels.

Recent Neurological Findings in Hypnosis Research

This research has been directed to establish whether or not there are changes in brain functioning during hypnosis, and whether or not the results would warrant the label of an 'altered state of consciousness' (ASC). The definition of an ASC according to Tart (1972) is 'a qualitative alteration in the overall pattern of mental functioning such that the experiencer feels that his (or her) consciousness is radically different from the normal way it functions'. Extensive research into the cause and effects of altered states of consciousness (Viatl et al., 2005) has shown that they can be brought about by compromised brain structure, transient changes in brain dynamics (disconnectivity) and neurochemical and metabolic processes. Altered brain functioning and conscious experience can also be the result of environmental stimuli, mental practices and techniques of self control. Hypnosis is one area covered by Viatl et al. (2005) in their review of the psychobiological research of altered states of consciousness (ASC).

In highly hypnotisable subjects there appears to be some frontal lobe inhibition in hypnosis (Gruzelier, 2000; Gruzelier & Warren, 1993; Kallio, Revonsuo, Hamalainen & Gruzelier, 2001). There was found to be impaired letter fluency (left frontal) but not category fluency (left temporal) in high hypnotisables, but not low hypnotisables. Hypnosis would appear to be associated with inhibition of the left dorsolateral prefrontal cortex (Gruzelier, 1998). In a more recent study by Farvolden and Woody (2004) memory tasks which are known to be a function of the frontal lobe, together with other memory tasks which are not related to the frontal lobe functioning, were administered to two groups of subjects; they were high hypnotisables and low hypnotisables. The 'highs' performed significantly less well than the 'lows' on the memory tasks related to frontal lobe functions, that is free recall, proactive interference and source-amnesia tasks. On the other memory tasks not involving the frontal lobe, there was no significant difference between 'highs' and 'lows'.

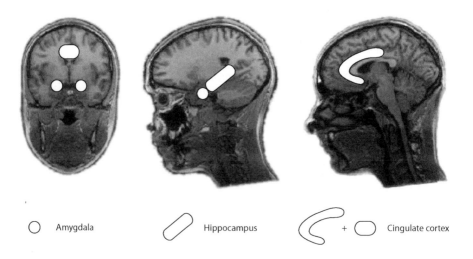

○ Amygdala   ⬭ Hippocampus   ⟨ + ○ Cingulate cortex

Figure 1. Parts of the brain highlighted by research into memory and hypnotism.

Other investigators have studied hypnotic analgesia and also discovered the involvement of the anterior cingulate cortex. This is a part of the brain receiving somato-sensory and emotional information. The ACC is also considered to be a critical interface between emotional and attentional systems in the frontal area. It is also involved in differentiating between reality and imagination or fantasy. In some studies of hypnotic analgesia, both highs and lows have been presented with a painful stimulus without suggested analgesia (control condition) and then again after the hypnotic suggestion of analgesia. The EEG activity localised in the ACC area predicted exactly the intensity of the pain ratings in the control condition.

This relationship between EEG and pain ratings remained unchanged by hypnosis for the 'lows', but was totally changed in the highs following the hypnotic analgesia. (Croft, Williams, Haenschel & Gruzelier, 2002). Therefore, there appears to be no coherence between somato-sensory and frontal brain areas during hypnotic analgesia. This would indicate a breakdown in the connection between the brain areas involved in analysing somato-sensory aspects of the stiumuli input and areas organising the behavioural responses to them. The conclusion would be a dissociation between sensory input and later higher order processing. (Crawford, Knebel & Vendemia, 1998; Friederick et al., 2001). This would be consistent with the neodissociation theory hypothesised by Hilgard. Hypnosis affects integrative functions of the brain and induces alteration or breakdown in communication between subunits within the brain responsible for conscious experience.

Gruzelier (2005) has confirmed from his studies that there is changed activity in the frontal areas during hypnosis and a de-coupling between the anterior cingulate cortex and the dorsolateral prefrontal cortex. Furthermore, he has reported in the highly hypnotisables, differences in their focused attention and absorption during hypnosis compared with their usual absorption when reading a book. The difference is shown by their electrodermal orienting responses. Their hypnotic focusing of attention in hypnosis is also shown to be different from those who simulate hypnosis, and those who are low hypnotisables. Other neurophysiological changes in hypnosis in the highly hypnotisables can distinguish it from the effects of relaxation (such as changes in the alpha and theta activity on the EEG, and other features (Williams & Gruzelier, 2001). Gruzelier's conclusion is that with the findings of neuroscience we can see how unconscious processing can determine behaviour. This changed activity in the frontal areas in hypnosis confirms that information not processed consciously can dictate our actions.

To appreciate further the brain structures involved in the regulation of states of consciousness, the reader is directed to the book *The Feeling of What Happens: Body, Emotion and the Making of Consciousness* by Antonio

Damasio (2000). Rainville and Price (2003) have further shown that changes in brain activity in these structures involved in basic representation of body-self and the regulation of states of consciousness are produced by hypnotic procedures. These structures include the brain stem nuclei, the thalamus and the anterior cingulate cortex. These provide the foundations of consciousness. Damasio (2000) states that consciousness is dependent on brain structures which are involved in representation and regulation of body states and functions. From what has been said so far, it follows that hypnosis modifies the basic aspects of consciousness regulation. Rainville and Price (2003) found in their study that changes in relaxation-mental ease and in absorption were associated with changes in brain activity which was consistent with the involvement of these brain structures and the regulation of consciousness, and also body-self representation. The authors of this article however consider that while their findings contribute to an understanding of hypnosis, they are not sufficient to view it as an altered state of consciousness.

Naish (2001) who has studied the phenomena of time distortion in hypnosis as referred to earlier in this chapter in relation to the concept of 'trance', has stated that alterations in the anterior cingulate cortex produced by hypnosis could well be responsible for time misperception of hypnotic subjects. Since the anterior cingulate cortex (ACC) is involved in differentiating between the real and imaginary, then hypnosis impacts on this part of the brain which is involved in reality testing. Misjudgement of time in hypnosis by a hypnotised subject could be one result of this loss of reality testing. Patients who have damage to the ACC have also a problem of not being able to distinguish between imagined and real events.

The evidence so far in the field of neuropsychology and neurophysiology would seem to support the view of hypnosis being an altered state of consciousness. Whether or not this will settle the debate between the 'state' theorists and the 'non-state' theorists of hypnosis remains to be seen. From the present author's viewpoint, both theories have evidence to support them based on scientific investigations. The two positions are not incompatible. The sociocognitive model is looking at the social influences, the attitudes, expectations and belief systems which can 'set the scene' to bring about or contribute to these internal changes which inevitably involve brain changes. The so-called 'hypnotic-like procedures' are many and varied and are very much dictated by culture and beliefs. Furthermore, there are other kinds of procedures which can also produce changes in the brain, which might be classified as altered states of consciousness (Viatl et al., 2005) but would not be labelled as 'hypnotic-like procedures'.

There are many levels at which hypnosis and hypnotic phenomena can be investigated. According to Spiegel 'Multilevel explanations are an absolute necessity in understanding human mind/brain/body phenomena because we are both neurally-based and social creatures who experience the world in mental phenomenal terms' (Spiegel, 2005, p. 32).

With regard to the remit of this book, more emphasis has perhaps been placed on the neurological investigations since these can have more relevance to the next few chapters concerning the neurological psychological findings in trauma cases, and the therapeutic role of hypnosis.

ON MEMORY

Memory and forgetting are not 'all-or-nothing' phenomena. Forgetting is not a total failure to remember. Remembering also does not imply total recall, as though everything has been completely recorded on a video. Memory is a selective process, and also a reconstructive process. It is selective in that certain aspects of experience are retained and others are discarded. Therefore, only certain parts of an experience undergo consolidation and become part of long-term memory. Much depends on how we encode information, and this will determine what and how we remember. If we process the meaning of the information which we are exposed to, or which we are trying to learn then a fuller memory of it will be consolidated. The next step, the act of recall or retrieval, is a reconstructive act. That is to say that first the memory is triggered by a cue and part of it is recalled, which then leads to recall of other parts of the memory or other specific memories. This recall also depends on our schema; that is a model of the world around us is based on past experience. Events and information happen within a context for which we already have a schema or script. This gives us a framework within which we can recall certain elements of the event. These schemata can facilitate memory, but can also be responsible for inaccuracies and distortions. Bartlett (1932) demonstrated how people often use their own view of the world to distort what they have heard. Schemata can also bias people's recollections. Partial information recalled can also modify the picture of what has happened and contributes to the reconstructive nature of the act of retrieval. Perceptual biases and selective attention always influence memories and the way in which they are recalled.

State Dependent Memory

During the process of learning, associations are made and play an important part in what is remembered later. We may attempt to think of the associations and context in which we learned the information to assist in our recall. If we learned it sitting on a beach or indoors we might find that returning to that same environment would facilitate recall. On the other hand the internal context of our learning information can be equally important, that is, the mood or emotion we were experiencing at the time. The elicitation of the same mood in which we experienced an event or learnt information can increase the recall of the memory. In clinical practice, this can be seen when memories of childhood abuse return when the person's circumstances in some way reflect the past situation in which they were abused (e.g. their own child reaches the same age when they were abused).

Emotion and Memory

Emotional states can also affect memory as it has been shown in psychiatric patients who are depressed (Burbach & Borduin, 1986). These authors found that the validity of retrospective information obtained from depressed patients and their families was questionable. Depression can distort memory and perception.

The frontal lobes are the main centre for memory and the retrieval process. Also involved in the consolidation of memory is the brain structure known as the hippocampus which is bilateral in the medial temporal lobes. Stress can have a detrimental effect on the function of the hippocampus due to high levels of glucocorticoids in conditions of prolonged stress. This anti-stress hormone leads to cell death in the hippocampus in such conditions of stress (Sapolsky et al., 1990). Adult survivors of child sexual abuse have shown a 17 per cent reduction in the left hippocampus volume (Stein et al., 1997).

Highly emotional arousing events can cause what is known as 'flashbulb memories' as the events are recalled with great detail and clarity, and the memory is reported to be very vivid. Examples of such events are President Kennedy's assassination and the Challenger space shuttle disaster. In one study students were asked to write down what they were doing at this time when they heard the news. Three years later the same students were asked to recall the same event and circumstances. Eleven out of 44 recalled every detail incorrectly, where they were and what they were doing. When shown the original record they gave three years previously which was only 24 hours after the disaster, some said the original report must have been inaccurate! Emotion may enhance a memory but this does not imply the memory was accurate (Conway, 1995). Emotional experiences can be mis-recalled and sometimes may be forgotten completely. The brain structure involved in the enhancement of memory of emotional events is the amygdala. This structure in the limbic area is also implicated in traumatic memories which are dis-cussed in the next chapter.

Different Kinds of Memory

It may now become apparent that there are two different kinds of knowledge and memory which involve different parts of the brain. Explicit memory is memory of the knowledge we have which is conscious and which we can express verbally and declare. This knowledge is called declarative knowledge. Implicit memory is related to knowledge we have of which we are not consciously aware. It cannot be declared or verbalised. Implicit memory is present at birth and is behavioural, perceptual, emotional and somatosensory, and is involved in the learning of skills and in conditioning and associations. This knowledge is called procedural knowledge and does not involve conscious awareness.

The neural structures involved in these two kinds of memory are inevitably different. Explicit memory (relating to declarative knowledge) is mediated by the hippocampus (sometimes called the cognitive map) where meaning is found for information received; and the prefrontal area is also involved. The brain then stores these experiences as part of permanent memory, known as cortical consolidation. Autobiographical memory is explicit memory; it is also sometimes called episodic memory which is knowledge of specific events at different times. Another part of explicit memory is what is called semantic memory which is to do with knowledge of different topics or subjects such as philosophy and mathematics. Explicit memory has also been called narrative memory.

Implicit memory is not processed in the same way and does not involve consciousness. The amygdala which is part of the limbic system is implicated in the processing of sensory information before it reaches the hippocampus. It is therefore outside conscious awareness, and it has no narrative. It is at this level that traumatic memories are processed, and these often present as 'body memories', for which the subject has no explanation or meaning, and over which there is no conscious control (see next chapter), they are fragmented memories too. Attachment experiences during the early development of childhood are also encoded in implicit memory. Children below the age of two years have implicit memory but do not have a narrative or autobiographical memory. As language develops after this age and the child is able to use language to communicate, then autobiographical memory starts to develop. The sense of self, social interaction and language combined together create autobiographical memory.

Conditioning (both classical and operant) take place from birth and are part of implicit memory. They are evident in behavioural and enactive memories and do not involve conscious awareness, unlike verbal explicit memory. Verbal memory often contains errors and distortions, whereas implicit memories reflect exactly what has been learned or what has happened. Trauma memories or behaviour memories even from an early age can be a 'literal mirroring' of the traumatic event (Terr, 1988).

ON HYPNOSIS AND MEMORY

Hypnotic Recall in a Clinical Setting

At the beginning of the twentieth century, the work of Breuer and Freud (1895) followed by laboratory experiments provided some evidence for the use of hypnosis to enhance recall of remote memories (Hull, 1933, pp. 111–27). The belief that hypnosis could aid in the recovery of lost memories was generally accepted. However, we have now learned more about the effects of hypnosis on memory. We know that a person relinquishes normal reality monitoring and also responsibility for their behaviours in hypnosis. This might motivate a person to add new information to a memory report. Furthermore, their involvement in fantasy in hypnosis may also cause them to include some of these imaginations into the memory report. Thirdly, the increase in suggestibility in hypnosis and the willingness to put aside any critical judgements may make it even more difficult for the hypnotised person to distinguish between true memories and the fantasised details they had added. This combined with the belief that hypnosis produces accurate recall could make the person convinced that it was all true memories they had reported. It is also possible for a person to be in hypnosis and deliberately distort their recollections, perhaps to show their willingness to co-operate (Orne, 1961). It is perhaps even more likely that the vividness of recollections in hypnosis convinces the hypnotised person that the recalled material is absolutely true. It is unfortunate that there is a common misconception that hypnosis elicits only the truth and not lies, and produces increased accuracy.

Nonetheless, hypnosis has been used successfully to retrieve some lost memories in cases of psychological trauma, and it is shown to be still beneficial for this purpose up to the present day. It is also now appreciated that many disorders, particularly dissociative disorders, have symptoms and characteristics similar to hypnotic phenomena. These are also associated with hypnotisability (Spiegel & Spiegel, 1978). The use of hypnosis in their treatment, particularly psychogenic amnesia became an obvious choice (see next chapter). Hypnosis provides access to ideas and emotions blocked from conscious awareness. However, it might still hold that hypnotically recovered memories may be a mixture of fact and fiction. This in no way detracts from the therapeutic value of the recollections.

Hypnosis probably facilitates memory, not only by creating vivid images but also by enabling the re-instatement of the same context in which the recalled event was first encoded. Reconstructing the contextual cues present during encoding helps the process of retrieval. The person's mood at the time of encoding may also be recreated and thereby facilitate recall. Accessibility of a memory is improved when the mood state at retrieval is the same as the mood state at acquisition (Bower, 1981; Clark, Milberg & Ross, 1983). This is known as state-dependent memory (see next chapter).

Pierre Janet had considerable success with his patients when using hypnotic age regression to elicit unconscious memories and emotions. Sometimes if the memories were too distressing for the patient, he would deliberately change the memory into something which was psychologically more tolerable. Since this was therapeutically beneficial, he was not concerned that this was not historically accurate.

In fact there is now experimental evidence that in hypnotic age regressions, the hypnotised person does not literally relive earlier stages in their life with behavioural, psychological and physiological responses appropriate to those stages. There are no changes in the EEG which would indicate a literal revivification of an earlier stage of childhood (McCranie et al., 1955). In a well-known study by Martin Orne (1951), he age-regressed subjects and discovered that there was a mixture of adult with childlike responses when they were subjectively feeling they were a child again. One subject who was regressed to six years old was asked if he knew the time. He responded by looking at a hallucinated watch on his wrist, which he is unlikely to have worn at that age. Other anomalies were also seen in other subjects. Some would write in childlike writing, but spell complex words accurately such as 'psychological'. Orne described their drawings as 'sophisticated oversimplifications' (p. 215). However, it is common for hypnotised age-regressed subjects to claim that they relive an earlier event rather than just imagining it or thinking about it. In a study by Perry and Walsh (1978), they found that 50% of highly hypnotisable subjects who had been age-regressed to childhood, reported the experience of being both child and adult simultaneously or in alternation. In a later study, Lawrence and Perry (1981) found that subjects who experienced this kind of duality in age-regressions also reported experiencing the 'hidden observer' phenomena in the cold-pressor pain experiment by Hilgard (see section on theories). Those subjects who did not experience the duality in age regression, also did not experience the hidden observer effect. These two hypnotic experiences indicate a tendency to dissociate, a feature of some highly hypnotisable subjects.

These findings would suggest that one cannot accept as totally accurate the statements of hypnotically regressed subjects. The factors to remember are that there may be confabulation, and there are risks of creating pseudo-memories. Knowing the beliefs of the hypnotised person are important, as well as the beliefs of the hypnotist, within a clinical setting the briefing of the client is vital; and also the knowledge and understanding of the hypnotist of how to minimise the risks of false memories are essential (see next section). However, this does not imply that hypnosis should not be used in reconstructing memory for therapeutic benefit, and introducing a new perspective on the events the clients have recalled, as described by Janet. Erickson and Rossi (1980) reported a case called 'February Man'. This was a case of a woman who was pregnant and afraid she would not make a good mother because of her own childhood experience which was devoid of love. The February Man was a fictitious entity introduced by Erickson and who was responsible for altering the way in which this woman perceived and recalled her past history, emphasising the positive features rather than the negative ones. There was no creation of false memories as Erickson only changed the emphasis and restructured the affect attached to her veridical memories. Reframing is not the same as implanting a false memory.

An important feature of hypnosis in the therapeutic setting where recall of post-traumatic events is needed is in the eliciting of intense emotions of which the client had previously been unaware. Insight from the memories together with the experiences of the intense emotions can be greatly beneficial and enable resolution of the trauma. The hypnotic abreaction which is spontaneous may be a result of the state-dependent memory which is so easily produced through hypnosis, as previously mentioned. Hypnosis also diminishes anxiety and fear with suggestions of relaxation, and this might make it easier for the client to think about and recall events. Furthermore, if hypnosis is an altered state of consciousness involving the anterior cingulate cortex, it is part of implicit memory which involves emotional and somatosensory memory, where intense emotions are stored, and body memories related to trauma. Hypnosis then could be considered the ideal tool for resolving post trauma (see next chapter). It has been noted by Kolb (1988) that altered states of consciousness, whether induced by hypnosis or drugs are very effective in trauma cases as they shed important light on the motivations that are behind the actions taken in the fully conscious state.

Hypnotic Recall in Laboratory and Forensic Settings

Some of the research in this area of hypnotic recall also has important relevance for clinicians. In some investigations, hypnotised and non-hypnotised controls were presented with films or slide sequences of criminal acts or accidents, and then asked to recall what they saw (Sanders & Simmons, 1983; Sheehan, Grigg & McCann, 1984; Yuille & McEwan, 1985). A common finding was that the memories of the hypnotised group were less reliable, although these same subjects were more confident that they were accurate. This obviously has vital forensic implications. Furthermore, it has been reported that in some legal cases, leading questions to a hypnotised witness can elicit inaccurate information in which the witness firmly believes (Orne et al., 1988, p. 41). It has been found that if subjects are presented with subtle misinformation following the viewing of a film or slide, this incorrect post-event information is more easily elicited than the originally perceived details, when the subjects produce later memory reports.

Putnam (1979) carried out the same experiment but added leading questions which implied that something happened (but in fact did not happen). The hypnotised group responded significantly more often in the direction of the misleading question, and so were more frequently incorrect. Sheehan et al. (1984) introduced misleading information following a hypnotic induction with two groups, one highly hypnotisable and the other relatively unhypnotisable but simulating hypnosis. The hypnotised group showed greater integration of the false information into their memory reports than did the simulators. They also found that the highly hypnotisable introduced far more details in their reports, both accurate and inaccurate. This was both inferential and peripheral information. The consequence of the more detailed memory report is that it creates far greater credibility. Whether it is the hypnosis or the high hypnotisability of the subjects that serves to encourage this kind of reporting of information is not known. It might be the combination of both.

However, a study by Rainer (1983) involved a similar procedure except that misleading information was given to both groups in the waking condition before hypnosis was introduced to the first group and simulation for the other group. Then misleading information was given after hypnotic induction for the first group, and after the simulation of hypnosis for the other group. The only condition showing greater acceptance of false information was when false information was given in hypnosis rather than out of it, although it was statistically significant. Dywan and Bowers (1983) compared the memory for pictures in two groups of subjects, hypnotised and not hypnotised. In the hypnotised group there was increased accuracy of recall and also an increase in inaccurate information. However, not all highly hypnotisable subjects show evidence of pseudo memories or false information, and some subjects show it even though they are not hypnotisable. There are obviously individual differences in those who accept false information, and it has been suggested (Sheehan et al., 1984) that this phenomenon needs to be explained in terms other than the tendency for hypnosis to produce memory distortion. The conclusion is that (a) there is some evidence for greater susceptibility to misleading information in hypnosis when this is introduced deliberately; (b) there is both increase in memory accuracy and memory inaccuracy in hypnosis; and (c) distortions in memory occur outside hypnosis as well as within hypnosis.

Confidence in their reported information (whether accurate or inaccurate) is very high in the highly hypnotisables. This was found by Dywan and Bowers (1983) and also by Sheehan et al. (1984). Another observation of researchers has been that accuracy may stay constant with subjects across the condition of hypnosis and waking states while confidence may vary, but on the whole there is no relationship between accuracy and confidence in hypnosis. Most of these laboratory experiments with hypnosis would discourage the use of hypnosis in a forensic setting. With regard to a clinical setting, they offer pointers to what a therapist should and should not do, such as not to offer leading questions, nor expect total veridical truth. As an adjunct in psychotherapy, particularly in cases of past trauma and some dissociative disorders, hypnosis has been shown to be an invaluable therapeutic tool. There are several reasons why this should be the case in spite of investigations showing confabulation and inaccurate information being readily accepted by hypnotised subjects.

Firstly, the autobiographical memories recalled in a clinical setting are often very meaningful experiences associated with intense emotions, which may be inaccessible to conscious awareness and unacceptable to the client. Laboratory experiments do not address this kind of recall. Very personal or traumatic experiences are for obvious reasons not elicited in the laboratory. Secondly, the therapist is interested in the meaning of these experiences for the client rather than their historical accuracy. It is not the role of the therapist to challenge the details of the memories to discover whether or not they are accurate. Thirdly, this kind of doubting would jeopardise the treatment, and the therapist would not expect a client to invent fictitious memories deliberately. Fourthly, the context of psychotherapy is very different from the forensic setting, also the laboratory. The aim of the therapist is to help the client to work through their version of history, which may involve valid memories mixed with confabulation and fantasy. Often the main purpose is to facilitate the 'reconstruction' of their history, as stated earlier. There is in fact no need in the clinical situation to verify the truth or falsity of hypnotically recalled memories, as it is so often just as effective to deal with the client's fantasies as it is to address the realities which are documented (Orne et al., 1984).

An important advantage of hypnosis in psychodynamic therapy is the ease with which a client can alter their memories, and accept both the re-experiencing of events as memories, and the different perspective of the events which they see. In fact this can happen without hypnosis but less time and effort is required by using hypnosis. The historical accuracy of events is less important than the manner in which the clients express and understand them and also deal with them. It would therefore seem that the attributes of hypnosis which make it an invaluable therapeutic tool are also big obstacles in the forensic field. This fact has to be appreciated by therapists, particularly if they have a client who is called to be a witness in court proceedings relevant to their particular problem. Judges can refuse to accept the testimony of witnesses if hypnosis has been used in their treatment.

The following points would summarise the findings of research into hypnosis and memory:

- Hypnosis facilitates the normal reconstructive processes of memory. Confabulations and fantasies may be incorporated into the memory. External influences such as leading questions may also affect the memory report.
- The hypnotised person does not discriminate between accurate and inaccurate information recalled, and they have confidence in what they recall, regardless of whether it is accurate or not.
- The increase in memory production during hypnosis might be partly explained by the relaxed state of hypnosis and absence of critical judgement. As shown in the previous section on hypnosis, it seems to be an altered state of consciousness in which fantasy and reality are not distinguished. So information that a person might normally question or feel uncertain about, and thus would not mention, might be confidently included in recall during hypnosis.
- Hypnotic age regression involves the suggestion that a person will relive an experience that may not be consciously recalled. This is not a literal revivification of the past time-frame in childhood. The memory is influenced by adult information and knowledge. There can also be confabulation and responses to environmental cues from the hypnotist and internal cues from the person's own beliefs.
- There are obvious concerns about hypnosis used in a forensic setting. The conclusion of Orne and his colleagues is that 'hypnotically induced memories should never be permitted to form the basis for testimony by witnesses or victims in a court of law' (Pettinati, 1988, p. 284).
- Hypnosis has great therapeutic benefit in a clinical setting. It allows the client to reconnect with lost memories and emotions. As it is relaxing at the same time it minimises the pain, normally experienced by clients when remembering traumatic events. The accuracy of the memory is not as important as it would be in a court of law. Moreover, the release of emotions facilitated by hypnosis is a major benefit for the client. Also the client's own idiosyncratic view of events which might include confabulations or distortions needs to be known by the therapist in order to help modify them. The cognitive restructuring offered by therapy changes the perspective of the client, as well as changing the memory to some extent. This would be unacceptable in a legal setting but contributes greatly to the healing process in a clinical setting.

FALSE MEMORY ISSUES

Recent Causes of False Memories

In the early to late 1990s, there was an outbreak of adults who claimed to recover memories of being sexually abused as a child. There were many cases, especially in America, of adults accusing their parents of having sexually abused them as children and taking them to court. It was the large number of cases which cast doubt on the validity of these allegations. This is not to say that there were not some adults among them who genuinely had recovered memories after a long period of dissociative amnesia (see Chapter 2). There had to be other reasons for such an epidemic of allegations. Many other adults came forward to claim they had been falsely accused of having abused their grown-up children. This triggered the setting up of the False Memory Syndrome Foundation in America and the British False Memory Society in Britain. These organisations were created to support the families and parents who believed they had been falsely accused by their grown-up children. In retrospect, I understand there was some difficulty in identifying genuine cases of false accusations and screening out those with other agendas such as enquirers and those seeking cover knowing their guilt.

However, one of the real causes for such an epidemic of false accusations was the therapeutic movement in the USA in which therapists were considering child sexual abuse to be the explanation for a whole range of symptoms in their disturbed clients. The clients who may have had no memory of CSA, would be encouraged to believe it and pursue the 'memory work' suggested by the therapist, thus having a false memory implanted. A book, *The Courage to Heal* written by Bass and Davis (1988) who had recovered their memories in therapy, also encouraged readers to follow their path of memory recovery. They stated, 'If you are unable to remember any specific instances [of abuse] but still have a feeling that something abusive happened to you, it probably did' (Bass & Davis, 1988, p. 21). Therapists would also use leading questions and hypnosis in order to unlock past memories of the client, which they believed were suppressed.

This is a misuse of hypnosis. As we have seen, hypnosis is valuable in reconstructing memories which we know exist, but if it is used to try to elicit memories which we (including the clients) do not know exist, then it is highly likely to produce false memories. With repeated probing and leading questions plus hypnosis, clients can be led to believe that certain events happened when they did not. Biased therapy and misuse of hypnosis have certainly been largely responsible for false memories. This misuse of hypnosis has been termed 'Recovered Memory Therapy' (RMT). It includes guided imagery, relaxation, regression work, dream analysis and even drugs such as sodium amytal (Perry, 1995). 'Memories' produced in this kind of way have rarely been corroborated independently. The argument that accuracy of recall is not so important to the clinician as it is in a forensic setting has certainly been taken too far in this case. Inaccuracies are not the same as total fantasy or total falsehood. It is, however, not surprising that the FMSF and the BFMS started and continue to question the validity of repression and dissociation. In the words of Campbell Perry 'as well as asking whether such "recovered" memories are true, we need to ask whether such mental mechanisms are possible' (Perry, 2000, p. 126). In this review of dissociation in relation to false memories, Perry does mention that there is more scientific evidence of dissociation than repression (see Chapter 3).

Even to the present day, the FMSF do not believe in Dissociative Identity Disorder or Multiple Personality Disorder (the most extreme form of dissociation). Members of the FMSF and BFMS consider this disorder to be iatrogenic (produced by therapy) and not a genuine mental disorder. Piper (2004) concludes from his review of the literature that DID is best understood as culture-bound and often an iatrogenic condition. However, there is evidence to the contrary as well (see Chapter 3), and it seems that again bad therapy can be responsible for this dismissal of DID as a genuine mental disorder. In some cases DID has been linked to recovered memory therapy, and also to the belief of some clients that they were abducted by aliens.

The incidence of hypnosis being used in cases reporting alien abduction was stated in one study as 31% (Bullard, 1987). However, of those reports which rated high in amount of information, hypnosis had been used in 70%. In another study (Rodeghier et al., 1991) abduction experients were no more responsive to hypnotic suggestion than the general population. Regardless of hypnotisability, the hypnotic context might be enough to influence the person. There does not appear to be any relationship between psychopathology and Alien Abduction Experiences (AAE). There have been concerns that suggestive psychotherapeutic procedures could create these false memories, and professional organisations in the mental health field such as the American Psychological Association and the American Society of Clinical Hypnosis (Bloom, 1994) have cautioned members against practices which might produce false memories.

Besides suggestive therapy, other factors which may be a cause of AAEs have been found, such as fantasy proneness and certain sleep disorders. Media influences and expectancies might also contribute (Cardena, Lynn & Krippner, 2000). Hypnosis being used for past life regression can certainly be responsible for the creation of false memories. The premise of the therapy is that traumas that occurred in a previous life can influence the person's present life. Some of the details of events reported from past life regressions are historically accurate, although the subject claims not to have had previous knowledge of any of it. This can, however, be attributed to cryptoamnesia or forgetting the source of information which they have learned in the present life.

Spanos (1996) viewed PLEs as socially constructed accounts, details of which could often be found in books, television and the media. There are, however, different cultures and religions which believe in reincarnation, but this does not necessarily imply that they believe hypnosis would help them retrieve memories of past lives. Some people, both children and adults, can have spontaneous experiences which they describe as past life experiences. If some of these PLEs can be verified historically, then the question arises whether this is chance, coincidence, a cultural construction or represents veridical 'memories' consistent with a reincarnation hypothesis (Cardena et al., 2000). Spanos et al. (1991) found that hypnotic past life regressions were related to the subject's belief in reincarnation, as well as fantasy proneness and hypnotisability.

Creating False Memories without Hypnosis

The well-known experiment involving a teenager and his brother (Garry, Loftus & Brown, 1994) is often quoted as evidence that false memories can quite easily be created without hypnosis. A 14-year-old boy called Chris was given four summaries of childhood events by his brother Jim. Three of these were actual events in his childhood and the fourth one was false. This was an incident in a shopping mall, where Chris was supposedly lost. Jim repeated false details about this non-existent event. Two weeks later, Chris remembered details that Jim had told him, but was dismayed when he was told that it was false and had never happened. The parallel between this experiment and the implanting of false memories in therapy (albeit not deliberately sometimes) does not seem justified. Children often do get lost while out shopping, and are warned about it. So they have a pre-existing schema first. The story of getting lost in the shopping mall was completely plausible and highly likely to occur. It is probably less likely that a client who had no memory of childhood abuse would be convinced (without hypnosis) by a false statement from a therapist that it had happened. Nonetheless, false memories can be created in a clinical setting without hypnosis, and there are a number of risk factors involved.

Gudjonsson and Clark (1986) explored the individual differences that may determine whether or not misinformation is accepted and believed by subjects being interrogated. While the findings apply more to police interrogations, they also have some relevance to clinical interviewing. They found several of their hypotheses confirmed. There were three components of suggestibility in those who accepted misinformation: uncertainty about the right answer to the interviewer; interpersonal distrust in the interviewer and expectation that the interviewer should know the right answer. The degree of suggestibility also depended on the person's coping strategies; and if they had poor memory and low intelligence they were more likely to be suggestible. Low self-esteem, anxiety proneness, lack of assertiveness and fear of negative evaluation enhance suggestibility.

Negative feedback can also affect the interviewee's mood and heighten suggestibility. In fact, those who wanted to avoid any criticism which they thought might make them stupid would give the answer they thought was required whether right or wrong. Gudjonsson (1984, 1992) has considered this kind of suggestibility, which he calls interrogative suggestibility is different from hypnotic suggestibility or even misinformation suggestibility. While interrogative suggestibility includes misinformation suggestibility, it is a much broader concept as there are the additional factors of interpersonal pressures in a closed social interaction, and the demand for a response. Interrogative suggestive influence which consists of leading questions with strong positive or negative feedback can be responsible for creating false memories, particularly in the context of uncertainty and high expectation of definite answers.

Within a clinical setting, if the client is highly hypnotisable and is asked leading questions about abuse then they are open to suggestive influences.

Highly stressful conditions in the interview can make the client more vulnerable to giving a false memory.

If the therapist has wrong assumptions about memory, then they may contribute to producing a false memory in the client.

Social and interpersonal influences can also be at the root of false memories. The book by Bass and Davis (1988) has already been mentioned. Self-help groups for survivors of abuse have also been found to contribute to false memories. A potential client may decide to attend these groups, and hearing the histories of the other members, they may then begin to believe the same might have happened to them, particularly if they are not certain about their own past. Friends and the media might also play a role in creating a false memory in a client and again particularly if they are uncertain about what caused their present difficulties.

Memory and False Memory Issues

The following important points regarding memory in relation to false memory issues should be considered by all clinicians:

- Memory is reconstructive rather than reproductive, and it is better for central details rather than peripheral details.
- There is more than one memory system in humans.

- Some of the information recalled will be accurate and some inaccurate.
- Suggestion, expectancy and post event misinformation can lead to false memories, especially if the person is very hypnotisable and is high on interrogative suggestibility; and if the person is uncertain about events and/or anxious and stressed, they will be more vulnerable.
- Most of the research into memory and false memories has been done in the laboratory or experimental situations. The findings may therefore not be applicable to trauma memory. There is growing evidence that traumatic memory is processed differently from narrative memory.
- Traumatic events can be partially or wholly forgotten, and then recalled later. These are not false memories. There is some evidence that these recovered memories reflect events that really happened and corroborative evidence has been found (see Chapter 2).
- The beliefs and assumptions of the therapist play an important part in influencing the client, and this can inadvertently create a false memory.

Hypnosis, Memory and False Memory Issues

The following points regarding hypnosis and memory in relation to false memory issues are important for any clinician intending to use hypnosis for recall:

- Hypnosis does not make memory more accurate, nor less accurate.
- Hypnosis may facilitate certain procedures which are already used to improve recall such as contextual re-instatement and repeated retrieval.
- Hypnosis does facilitate access to traumatic memories and helps in the process of memory integration in a safe way (see next chapter).
- Hypnosis may increase the confidence of the client and the therapist in believing all the material recalled is completely accurate. Prior warning of this effect can reduce the possibility of its occurrence.
- Hypnotic age regressions are not a literal return to an earlier stage of physical and psychological development. The material recalled in hypnotic regression may be both accurate and inaccurate historically. However, the productivity of information elicited in hypnosis may be greater than it would have been without hypnosis.

GUIDELINES FOR CLINICAL PRACTICE

Standards of Care with Possibly Traumatised Clients

These guidelines are based primarily on: the American Society of Clinical Hypnosis Guidelines on Clinical Hypnosis and Memory (1994); the British

Psychological Society Report on Recovered Memories (1995); the British Society of Experimental and Clinical Hypnosis Guidelines; Brown (1995); a collection of papers published by Conway (1997); and Williams (1995).

The following guidelines apply to all clinicians whose work brings them into contact with survivors of trauma and abuse. Hypnosis can be expected to facilitate both good and bad practices in therapy as we have seen; and views have been widely expressed about the role of hypnosis in creating false memories. It is, therefore, essential that therapists who employ hypnosis in their work should be particularly mindful of good clinical practice.

Concerning the nature of therapy

Classic abreaction and the use of memory recovery techniques as a main focus of treatment are contraindicated. What is desirable is a phase-oriented treatment approach with three main stages:

1. *Stabilisation*: management of intrusive re-experiencing symptoms, and developing coping strategies and skills;
2. *Systematic uncovering*: a graduated process of integrating memories and associated effect related to the trauma into consciousness, using primarily free recall and secondarily memory integration methods;
3. *Post integrative self-development*, such as new social competences and self-esteem.

Concerning the dangers of false memory production in therapy

The likelihood of creating false memories is reduced if the following points are adhered to:

- The client gives informed consent following discussion of what is known from current research about the nature of human memory, and an explicit statement that not all memories recovered in treatment are accurate. All memory is reconstructive, and the therapist cannot confirm or disconfirm the accuracy of what is recalled.
- The therapist recognises a duty to both the client and community. Clients should not be encouraged to cut off from family or friends or sue as a part of therapy, even when abuse memories are corroborated, as this is rarely beneficial therapeutically, and is arguably not part of the therapist's role.
- The risks are assessed, especially with clients with post-traumatic stress symptoms but an absence of an identifiable stressor or memories of abuse. Risks which are commonly identified include:

    ○ high hypnotisability;

    ○ high interrogative suggestibility (where interpersonal pressure is added to post-event suggestion);

    ○ deep involvement with self-help trauma groups or their literature.

- The therapist assesses their own beliefs and biases about possible trauma and its treatment, especially when assessing new clients. The belief that trauma is the primary cause of most psychological problems, and that memory uncovering is the primary treatment, is likely to create conditions conducive to the development of false memories in the client. Uncritical acceptance that trauma did not occur is as unjustifiable as lightly accepting statements of trauma as fact. A careful and thorough diagnostic assessment is necessary, free from assumptions and biases. After the assessment, the therapist should treat the condition presenting, and not the condition suspected.

- If the decision is made to pursue therapy for trauma, and with hypnosis for memory integration, the therapist should explain how hypnosis can be used, and engage in an educational process about hypnosis. Then the client can give informed consent for hypnosis. In the case of known traumatic events, hypnosis can be used to facilitate processing of the memories. With or without hypnosis the memory integration may be contaminated by fantasy, as described earlier.

- The therapist is aware of current memory research and its relevance to clinical settings.

- The therapist is aware of the role of suggestion in memory distortion and does not use persuasive techniques or interrogative methods, but adopts a more egalitarian and permissive approach.

- In order to help the client recover memories, it is best to use free recall rather than hypnosis and guided imagery, or structural enquiry or leading questions.

- Anxiety, distress, and uncertainty about the course of therapy are kept to a minimum.

- If the client remains uncertain about what happened in the past, they need to be helped to tolerate ambiguity rather than be pushed to remember more.

When all these factors are considered and appreciated by the therapist, it is worth remembering that the role of the therapist is to help the client to resolve the issues presented whether they be trauma or other issues. If this involves some fantasies and some inaccuracies at times in the process of resolution, the aim is not to have complete historical accuracies at all times, but to bring about therapeutic changes which enable the client to move on in a positive way. The safe remembering hypnotic procedures described in this book (see Chapter 4) contain safeguards minimising any creation of false memories.

The False Memory Controversy

The False Memory Societies in the USA and in Britain have created aware-ness among clinicians of the dangers and risks of producing false memories in therapy, and are perhaps largely responsible for speeding up the research in the field of trauma and trauma treatment. The guidelines in trauma treat-ment have also been instigated by therapists' concern of these risks. There is now a wealth of research in the psychoneurology of trauma, and a range of safe therapeutic approaches. However, there remain areas of contention for both these Societies regarding the therapies and the concepts on which they are based. While it is beyond the remit of this book to address all the issues in detail, some general points should be made.

One of the main areas of contention between the False Memory Societies and therapists has been the defence mechanisms of repression and dissocia-tion. Repression is an 'all or nothing' concept, that is to say the person blocks out the complete memory of certain events in their personal history. Trau-matic dissociation can also cause partial memories only. These will be dis-cussed in more detail in chapter 2. There is evidence for this traumatic dissociation to be part of the implicit memory and out of conscious control, as described earlier in this chapter. Some advocates of the False Memory Society have argued that victims of extreme trauma remember the trauma only too well (McNally, 2003; Pendergrast, 1996) and consider that it is a contradiction in terms to state that 'intrusive recollections [flashbacks] of a trauma might count as amnesia for the trauma' (McNally, 2003, p. 172). This seems to be a misunderstanding of trauma memories which are only partial memories and not a product of declarative explicit memory. There is also failure to recognise that although some traumatised persons do indeed have declarative or narrative memories of what has happened to them, this is not always the case; many others experience fragmented traumatic memories without a narrative.

There are also contentious issues regarding the two memory systems, that is implicit memory and explicit memory. Both Pendergrast (1996) and McNally (2003) criticise the claims of Bessel van der Kolk (2000b) that trau-matic memories which are implicit memories can be transcribed into a nar-rative form, once the person starts talking about them, and they become part of explicit memory. This is a part of the therapy used by many clinicians. According to McNally (2003, p. 179) it is not possible to translate or recode fragments of implicit memory into a narrative form, and if it were possible the translation would be reconstructive and not reproductive.

First, no one would deny that the 'translation' is reconstructive, since all explicit memory is reconstructive, as described earlier in this chapter. However, McNally continues to question the nature of implicit memory. The somatosensory information in implicit memory store, such as bodily

sensations are considered by McNally to be 'foreign to cognitive neuroscience of memory'. He states that implicit memory tasks do not reflect an
implicit memory system in the brain. In his own words, there is 'no underlying psychobiological unity'. In view of the neurological findings so far, and
mentioned earlier, this view could be contended. Certainly there is room for
a healthy debate especially in view of the clinical and neurological findings
of patients who have recovered from post-traumatic stress disorder following this therapy of 'translation' (see next chapter). However, no one is claim-
ing that research should not continue in order to understand more of the
various reactions to trauma and the processes involved. One cannot assume
a unitary model of memory, as some false memory advocates tend to do. The
work of Kihlstrom (1994) is consistent with the hypothesis that traumatic
memories do exist and have an effect outside conscious awareness; they have
an impact on the patients' thoughts and actions without their being aware.

Amnesia for traumas is also questioned by the False Memory Societies.
They still do not generally accept that repression and/or dissociation can be
responsible for failure to remember traumas of the past. Instead this has
been referred to as 'failure to think about the trauma' (McNally, 2003, p. 183).
There have in fact been many studies of survivors of child sexual abuse, and
in all the studies so far there have been cases who claim to have forgotten
the abuse and later to have recovered the memories (see next chapter).
Studies have also shown that therapy in many cases was not responsible
for the memory recovery and moreover there has often been corroborative
evidence. Recovered memories of abuse have mostly been found to be no
more and no less accurate than continuous memories (Williams, 1995). This
does not convince false memory advocates who believe that ordinary forgetting or 'failure to think about trauma' are sufficient to explain the phenomena of dissociative amnesia. It is certainly true that some survivors of child
abuse have stated that they pretended it never happened, or that it happened
to someone else. This in itself could lead to dissociating or blocking everything out successfully. I believe we have to accept the complexity and variety
of responses to trauma and their long-term effects, which may also vary
considerably.

Lastly, but not least, the forms of trauma treatment now with the three
phases and guidelines are not a form of Recovered Memory Therapy (RMT)
which is what is considered by the False Memory Societies. Reconstruction
of narrative memory in the context of the three stages is an appropriate
therapeutic goal. This is not the same procedure as RMT as no pressure is
put on the client to recall, and no suggestions are given to facilitate recall.
Brown et al. (1998) have also pointed out that hypnotic procedures and
imagery do not contribute to pseudo-memories as long as they are combined
with free recall and warnings, but they can increase the amount of information without a significant increase in errors. It is the combination of hypnosis

with suggestive interviewing along with interrogative techniques which increases the memory distortion rate. It would also seem that the false memory advocates may have gone too far in the demands regarding the assessment and treatment approaches. They have suggested that clinicians should not enquire about childhood abuse, and that the focus should be on present life problems and never about past recollections, nor about dissociative states (Brown et al., 1998). These demands reflect their serious concern about the possibility of the therapists creating Dissociative Identity Disorder, the most extreme form of dissociation. There is no evidence that this psychiatric disorder can be suggested or that therapists have a role in its emergence. The understanding of dissociative alters or ego-states will be covered in later chapters.

The understanding of the role of hypnosis and dissociation in cases of survivors of child abuse, both in their psychopathology and also in their effective treatment will hopefully help therapists and clinicians. Although there may be a lot more to learn about dissociation and defence mechanisms, many clients have benefited from the therapy based on these concepts we have learned so far.

2

THE NATURE OF TRAUMA MEMORY WITH PARTICULAR REFERENCE TO EXPERIENCES FOLLOWING CHILDHOOD ABUSE

DEFINITION OF TRAUMA

Trauma has been defined in DSM-IV (American Psychiatric Association, 1994) as an event which a person experiences or witnesses which involves 'actual or threatened death or serious injury or a threat to the physical integrity of self or others'. The response to the event inevitably has elements of fear, helplessness and horror. Trauma has also been defined by Spiegel (1996) as 'the experience of being made into an object or thing; the victim of someone else's rage or nature's indifference'. It is an overwhelming experience when for a brief period of time the person traumatised loses control of the body, and is helpless. It is outside the range of usual human experience.

The immediate reactions to such events may include shock and numbing, fear of dying, anger regarding whoever or whatever caused the event, and even guilt or shame that they (the victim) were not able to do something more to prevent or avert the losses and consequences. Subsequently there are often sleep problems, disruption in the daily routine of work, and loss of appetite. The person may resort to alcohol or drugs to control their emotional states.

There are three recognised symptom clusters which may emerge and persist after a month or more, and which meet the diagnostic criteria of post-traumatic stress disorder (DSM-IV, 1994) (otherwise referred to as PTSD).

1. Experiencing intrusive mental activity in the form of flashbacks to the event (visual or auditory or even kinaesthetic) and thoughts, memories or daydreams and nightmares, all resulting in preoccupation with the event.
2. Numbing of responsiveness and inability to experience a wide range of emotions (both positive, affectionate etc. and sometimes negative). There is also a sense of detachment from everyday events, and an inability to focus on the present. Detachment and emotional numbing help the person to reduce the pain of the traumatic memories. It is the result of dissociation or repression which also can produce amnesic gaps in their memory of the event. Conscious and deliberate avoidance of situations or people who remind them of the event can also happen. Many clients who suffer from PTSD experience an alternation between periods of having flashbacks and other intrusive thoughts and images of the trauma on the one hand, and periods of numbing and detachment on the other.
3. The third symptom cluster relates to a state of hyperarousal and hypervigilance. The person has an exaggerated startle response, outbursts of irritability, poor concentration and sleep difficulties. They usually experience anxiety and panics, but may also become depressed.

MAIN THEORIES OF PTSD

Dissociative Theory

Dissociation is defined by DSM-IV (1994) as 'a disruption in the usually integrated functions of consciousness, memory, identity or perception of the environment'. Janet (1907) was the first to recognise dissociation and develop dissociation theory which proposes that dissociation is a defence mechanism which prevents a person being overwhelmed by fear when faced with a traumatic event; it reduces the adverse emotional effects. As a result of dissociation, there is emotional detachment, impairment of memory and perceptual changes (Cardena & Spiegel, 1993). The person may have only partial memory of the traumatic event; and a complete memory of the event is not accessible.

LEARNING THEORY

Behaviour therapists draw upon learning theory to explain the symptoms of PTSD. The traumatic event, an unconditioned stimulus (UCS) evokes fear, the unconditioned response (UCR). The UCS is associated with cues present at the time of the trauma, and so becomes conditioned stimuli (CS). For example, a victim raped in a dark alley may become fearful of the dark. Darkness, a conditioned stimulus (CS), then elicits a conditioned emotional response (CER), fear. Through stimulus generalisation, other related stimuli are conditioned. The rape victim for example may begin to fear all alley-ways. This is higher order conditioning.

The link between CS and CER does not extinguish over time because the victim avoids the cues in order to reduce anxiety (operant conditioning). The victim also avoids thinking of the trauma, so does not learn from the event.

The dissociation at the time of the trauma may also reduce exposure to aspects of the trauma, and later dissociation may prevent exposure to reminder cues. Amnesia may also be the result of diverting attention away from the trauma. There may also be an invalidating environment when the victim is ignored when communicating emotional experiences. Failure to reinforce expression of internal states can lead to disruption in normal development in children who have been traumatised.

Information Processing Theories

1. Fear network theory

Learning theory does not explain the intrusive symptoms of PTSD. Foa, Steketee and Rothbaum (1989) based their theory of PTSD on the work of Lang (1979) who considered that emotional information was held in memory as a network containing information on stimuli which elicit the emotion; responses to the stimuli, such as cognitions, behaviours and physiological responses; and also the meaning of the stimuli and responses. Foa et al. (1998) also considered that a traumatic experience could lead to the forma-tion of a fear network with similar information on what should be avoided and what was threatening. They believe that the intrusive symptoms of PTSD are the result of activation of the fear network by reminders of the trauma. Although these are undesirable symptoms, the view of Foa et al. (1998) is that nonetheless activation of the fear network is necessary to process and resolve the traumatic material. Repetitive and prolonged expo-sure to traumatic memory in a safe environment results in extinction of the fear, and changes in the fear structure. It also reduces the avoidance strate-gies, which are no longer necessary. Furthermore, with reduction of fear the person modifies their cognitions and self-statements regarding the event, and new information is introduced.

2. Social cognitive theories

Horowitz (1986) suggested that the impact of trauma on the person's belief system needed to be addressed. Adjustments have to be made to reconcile the traumatic event with the person's previous beliefs. There is a psychological need for new incompatible information to be integrated with existing beliefs. The focus is more on the content of cognitions and meanings of the trauma for the person, rather than the mechanism of fear maintenance. In Horowitz's view, trauma information is kept active in memory until the processing is completed by integrating new information.

When intrusive flashbacks and nightmares occur and intense feelings become overwhelming, psychological defence mechanisms take over. The person then experiences numbing and avoidance. They oscillate between the two phases of intrusion and avoidance until information about the trauma is processed.

Janoff-Bulman (1992) has also emphasised the importance of the cognitions and beliefs of the person. The basic assumptions a person has about themselves and the world are shattered. There are three major assumptions which people may have which could be easily shattered. The first concerns personal vulnerability, e.g. 'I am less likely than others to experience misfortune'. The second concerns the meaningful nature of the world, e.g. 'the world is predictable, controllable and fair'. Lastly the perception of one's self may be 'I am worthy, competent and good.' If these beliefs are destroyed by the trauma then there is cognitive disintegration and anxiety. Recovery involves the reconstruction of fundamental core beliefs and producing equilibrium. This can be done by re-interpreting the event and reducing the gap between prior beliefs and new beliefs. Re-evaluating the trauma may be done by assessing benefits which could arise from it, such as learning something from it by being stronger. There can be a problem if the trauma is seen to confirm negative beliefs about self. Several areas of cognition might be disrupted or confirmed i.e. safety, trust, power, esteem and intimacy. Core beliefs are most important and if disrupted can lead to PTSD.

There may be over-accommodation of new information from the trauma, such as believing never to trust anyone again. This is obviously an attempt to prevent future traumas. These over-accommodated emotions interfere with natural emotions evoked by the event such as fear and anger, and therefore prevent the processing of the emotions and beliefs. Emotional expression and release are needed for the trauma memory to be processed fully. Once the feelings are accessed, they can dissipate a little to allow the challenging of core beliefs and cognitions.

The psychodynamic approach to trauma contains most of the components of the social cognitive theories. In addition, psychodynamic theorists consider that themes may emerge after the trauma which reactivate conflicts from the person's earlier developmental periods in their life, which have not been resolved. These may be issues to do with attachment, danger and protection (Marmar et al., 1995). The person's psychological functioning regresses and they may repeat earlier maladaptive relationship patterns, which also may be re-enacted in the therapeutic relationship.

Hypnosis, Dissociation and PTSD

One factor in common with all these theories is the role of dissociation in the face of trauma. As stated earlier, dissociation is a lack of normal integration of thoughts, feelings and experiences into the stream of consciousness and memory (Bernstein & Putnam, 1986). Janet (1907) was one of the first to observe that intense emotion precipitated by trauma can cause amnesia, loss of narrative memory and intrusive visual images and somatic complaints. He believed intense arousal interfered with information processing. He recognised that the intrusive images and perceptions had 'a life' of their own and were unrelated to any narrative, that is they seemed to be dissociated from their context of the actual historical event. He also understood that dissociation was part of the hypnotic state which in the case of trauma protected the person psychologically.

In recent times trauma specialists have come to recognise the link between the hypnotic state and responses to trauma. In 1990, Spiegel and Cardena noted the similarity between hypnotic phenomena and the symptoms of PTSD, and also the efficacy of hypnosis as a tool in the treatment of PTSD (Spiegel & Cardena, 1990). Spiegel (2003) noted 15 studies of psychological reactions within the first month following a major disaster report. There was a high prevalence of dissociative symptoms, which included depersonalisation, derealisation, amnesia and numbing. Depersonalisation consisted of out-of-body experiences or detached from the body, feeling of watching oneself as in a dream. Derealisation involved feeling the surroundings were unreal or having dreamlike experiences, including transient hallucinations. There were also degrees of impairment of memory and concentration and in some cases total amnesia for the event. Numbing, loss of interest and inability to feel deeply about anything were common. An inability to feel pain has also been reported by survivors of torture.

Other authors have commented on the similarity of dissociative symptoms and hypnotic phenomena. Bliss (1986) described the traumatised person as switching off the experience and feeling as if they are no longer present. One part of the mind is detached from the other part of the mind experiencing the event, rather like the 'hidden observer'. Bliss calls this 'self-generated hypnosis'. Judith Herman (1996) describes the hypnotic state in trauma as attention being narrowed and perceptions altered. Peripheral detail, context and time sense fall away, as attention is focused on central details of the immediate present. With extremely narrowed attention people experience perceptual distortions including insensitivity to pain, time slowing down, amnesia and depersonalisation and derealisation. Peritraumatic dissociation (or dissociative symptoms immediately following the trauma) has been found to predict the development of PTSD (Shalev et al., 1996). Numbing particularly is a good predictor of PTSD, together with depression. Children who have experienced multiple trauma are most likely to use dissociation and this may include spontaneous episodes of trance (Terr, 1991).

The Three Components of Hypnosis and PTSD

Spiegel (2001) has also drawn parallels between the three components of the hypnotic state and the three symptom clusters in the diagnosis of PTSD as follows:

1. Absorption is a tendency for narrowing the attention and being highly focused, so that awareness of the peripheral detail and context is lost. Those who are highly hypnotisable have frequent occurrences of this kind of experience. When a trauma survivor is having flashbacks, this is what happens to them; they lose the context and peripheral awareness, as they are so focused on the perceived threat.
2. Dissociation is probably complementary to absorption as perceptions, actions and memories which would normally be in conscious awareness occur outside consciousness. This can happen in hypnosis when, following a suggestion of arm levitation, the arm rises without the awareness or voluntary control of the subjects. Similarly in the case of source amnesia, a person may be given information in the hypnotic state and remember it afterwards, but not be able to recall when, where and from whom they learned it. In trauma the experience is suddenly discontinued by the fear, loss of control and the focus of attention being narrowed, thus parts of the event are lost. Similarly in the case of numbing, there is a disconnection with relevant emotions, and enjoyment of pleasurable activities is lost.
3. Suggestibility in hypnosis is the tendency to respond readily to cues that are given. Similarly traumatised people who are focused on one thing only will respond in an automaton-like fashion to various cues, without thinking what they are. For example, a soldier with PTSD may jump with fear when a car backfires, although he is not on the battlefield. Again this is linked to the narrowing of attention.

If the state of mind of a traumatised person is an altered state of consciousness like hypnosis, then it follows that the encoding, storing and retrieval of information will be affected (Spiegel, 2001). Encoding will be influenced by the narrowing of attention. For example, the victim of an assault may remember the blade of the knife but not the contextual features of the attacker and the surroundings. Storage of information is also affected by the blocking off or dissociation of certain emotions. Dissociation of emotions impedes cognitive and affective processing. Heightened arousal can influence both the storage and retrieval of traumatic memories. If the information was stored in a state of fear or other strong emotion, then it will best be retrieved in that same state (state-dependent memory, as discussed earlier in Chapter 1). Spiegel also holds that state-dependency involves the dissociation state itself.

Thus the three stages of memory may in the case of a traumatic event be influenced by the altered state of consciousness of the trauma victim, in a similar way as the memory of a hypnotised subject. Spiegel's hypothesis can be seen in Table 2.1.

These trauma memories are stored and retrieved in a fragmented form devoid of the context. These are episodic or procedural memories, part of implicit memory. They are segregated from associative networks involved in memory processing in the brain. Due to the narrowing of focus of attention, the range of associations will be limited. Dissociation which segregates the sets of associations is bound to impair memory storage and retrieval. In the next section the neurological basis for this phenomenon will be discussed further.

The similarities between the hypnotic dissociative state and the trauma responses and symptoms would make a strong case for using hypnosis to access trauma memories and to facilitate their retrieval and further processing; state-dependent memory necessary for this procedure can be easily accessed with hypnosis. Herman et al. (1989) found that patients with borderline personality disorders with a history of child abuse had high scores on the Dissociative Experiences Scale. There is also a link between

Table 2.1 Spiegel's hypothesis on three stages of memory in a traumatic event

	Hypnosis (components)		Memory (stages)
1.	Absorption	affects	Encoding
2.	Dissociation	affects	Storage
3.	Suggestibility	affects	Retrieval

hypnotisability and a history of punishment in childhood (Hilgard, 1970). A strong relationship exists between trauma, dissociation and hypnotisability in the clinical populations (Whalen & Nash, 1996). As Spiegel (2003) states 'hypnotic and dissociative phenomena clearly affect and are influenced by memory processing during and after trauma, and would therefore be crucial elements of the psychotherapy of traumatic reactions' (Spiegel, 2003, p. 82).

THE NEUROBIOLOGY OF TRAUMA MEMORY

The Processing of Information

The parts of the brain relevant to understanding processing are as follows.

The brain stem and the hypothalamus are involved in the regulation of internal homeostasis such as heart rate and respiration. This part of the brain is mature at birth. The hypothalamus also regulates body temperature, hydration, essential nutrition and rest. It is part of what is called the limbic system which is the centre of instincts and reflexes.

The limbic system is considered the survival centre and regulates the autonomic nervous system (ANS) with its two branches, the sympathetic nervous system (SNS) and the parasympathetic nervous system (PNS); the latter governing the digestive and excretory functions (survival on an everyday basis), and the former governing functions necessary in the face of threat and danger, involving muscle and visceral responses to stress, such as fight, flight and freeze.

Two other areas of the limbic system are vital in processing information, namely the amygdala and the hippocampus. These are two structures which lie on opposite sides of the brain within the limbic system. The amygdala is on the right side and the hippocampus on the left side.

Sensory information coming from all parts of the body first goes to the thalamus which is part of the mid brain, and also has two parts which flank the limbic system. The information from the thalamus is then passed to the amygdala which evaluates its emotional significance. The role of the amygdala is to transform sensory stimuli into emotional and hormonal signals. The amygdala processes and stores emotional reactions. From the amygdala information is then passed to the hippocampus which then processes it to make sense of the experience; that is, to categorise it and give it meaning. This information will then go to the pre-frontal cortex to integrate the experience and to plan action. The function of the frontal lobes in general is to act as a supervisory system for the integration of experiences. It allows for reflective thought and action.

It is important to know that the amygdala is mature at birth, but the hippocampus develops later between the second and third year of life. This explains what we call infantile amnesia. Before the development of the hippocampus, experiences are processed through the amygdala which stores emotional and sensory information only. So experiences of early childhood cannot be accessed in any narrative form. They have only been stored as emotions and sensations at an unconscious level, part of implicit memory. The full functioning of both the amygdala and the hippocampus are required later for processing life events.

The Processing of Traumatic Events

In the case of trauma the limbic system does not respond in the same way as it would for normal everyday events. In threat or danger the hypothalamus activates the sympathetic branch (SNS) of the autonomic nervous system (ANS) producing heightened arousal so the body is ready for the action of fight or flight. The hormones released are epinephrine and norepinephrine, and the heart rate and respiration increases and blood flows to the muscles. If fight or flight are not possible, then the limbic system will activate the parasympathetic branch (PNS) of the autonomic nervous system (ANS) in order to produce tonic immobility (freeze response). In the case of overwhelming trauma the cortisol, which is released to halt the alarm response when necessary, is in fact not sufficient to do this and the limbic system continues to activate the ANS to prepare for fight, flight or freeze. In the case of animals facing threat, the SNS activates fight or flight, but if the animal gets trapped it will 'freeze' or 'play dead' when it loses muscle tone and also loses sense of pain.

In these traumatic circumstances, the SNS remains activated and so does the PNS in order to produce the immobility. There would appear to be an imbalance in the automonic nervous system (ANS). However, there is a biological purpose for this, since an animal who appears dead often does not attract the interest of the predator. When the predator departs, the apparently dead animal will often get up and shake itself violently in order to release all the energy which has been built up. Humans do not do this, and it has been suggested that we may continue to dissociate in the face of trauma which then produces PTSD (Scaer, 2001). However, the freeze response is certainly seen in humans, particularly in cases of rape when the victim may go limp and not be able to resist. This seems a dissociative state but it is not followed by the shaking response as in animals.

In PTSD the SNS remains constantly high, and the person is unable to deal with the additional stresses of everyday life. It has been found in cases of PTSD, that the serum cortisol levels are low. Cortisol is a hormone which can shut off biological reactions of stress when the stress has terminated. The cortisol levels in PTSD appear too low to fulfil this function (Resnick et al., 1997).

As a result of the overwhelming experience of trauma and the heightened arousal, there is a failure in the central nervous system to process the sensory information fully. As described earlier, traumatic memories are mostly in the form of sensory flashbacks and are not integrated into declarative memory so contain very few if any narrative elements. The complete processing of information as described above does not take place. The integration of experience breaks down.

Research using neuroimagery has thrown light on the neurological changes which take place in clients with PTSD and which explain their symptoms of intrusive mental activity or flashbacks. Rauch et al. (1996) studied patients with PTSD using position emission tomography (PET scan). These clients were required to read detailed scripts of the traumatic experiences they had lived through. The PET scan revealed in all cases that there was heightened activity in the right hemisphere of the brain specifically in the amygdala, the insula and the medial temporal lobe, which are all areas most involved in emotional arousal. There was at the same time a significant *decrease* of activity in the left inferior frontal lobe, and Broca's area which is responsible for translating experiences into language. After therapy using EMDR (eye movement desensitisation reprocessing), the same procedure was repeated on the same patients. The PET scan then revealed activation of the left side of the brain and Broca's area, suggesting that the neurological changes in PTSD can be reversed.

These results are not surprising, since the amygdala which is involved in the emotional evaluation of incoming stimuli has been overstimulated in the face of trauma. Le Doux (1992) in his research observed that over-activation of the amygdala produces emotional and sensory impressions that are based on fragmentary information rather than complete perceptions of the event. Memories of the event are therefore stored as somatic sensations. Traumatic events are therefore stored in implicit memory (unconscious memory). This information is not passed through to the hippocampus which would categorise and make meaning of it, because the hippocampus is affected by the stress hormones which have been released. The amygdala on the other hand does not succumb to stress hormones. Due to the suppression of activity in the hippocampus there is no cognitive evaluation of the traumatic experience and the person cannot make any conscious appraisal of what to respond to. In some clients with PTSD, there may be painful bodily sensations and emotions which they cannot understand as they have no information about the context in which they arose. The explicit information is missing so they cannot make sense of the emotional and somatic symptoms. (See figure on page 14 for location of these areas of the brain.)

Traumatic memories are mostly encoded implicitly. There is a saying in the field of trauma 'The body keeps the score' (van der Kolk et al., 1996). In chronic cases of PTSD, there is some evidence for shrinkage of the hippocampus (Bremner et al., 1995; Stein et al., 1997). Animals who have decreased functioning of the hippocampus show behavioural disinhibition (Gray, 1982). They respond to incoming stimuli as though they were emergencies and they take action of fight or flight. In human beings, this could explain the problems of PTSD patients in processing arousing information and learning from experience. It has also been suggested that decreased size of the hippocampus may contribute to continual dissociation and misinterpretation of information which might or might not relate to threat. Extreme emotional arousal prevents the proper evaluation and categorisation of experiences due to the impairment of hippocampal functions.

Recent findings (Van der Kolk, 2003) have also shown that there is decreased dorsolateral frontal cortex activation in patients with PTSD. This would explain why they continue to re-experience the past trauma without full conscious awareness and control. After treatment with EMDR, it was again discovered that neurological changes could take place, and there was increased activation of the dorsolateral prefrontal cortex as a result of effective treatment. This area of the brain is responsible not only for the integration of experience and reflective thought, but also our memory of the world and self over time. Those with PTSD lose the sense of self and the sense of time with past, present and future.

From these neurological studies, one can see that there is hemisphere lateralisation in traumatic memories. The right hemisphere which develops earlier than the left hemisphere is involved in emotional communication and expression. The amygdala which evaluates the emotional significance of incoming stimuli is a part of the right hemisphere, and also part of implicit memory which encodes sensory and emotional information. This is implicated in traumatic memory. The left hemisphere which develops later is responsible for verbal communication and organises problem solving and processes information in a sequential way (Davidson & Tomarken, 1989). This is less active in PTSD. Failure of the left hemisphere has been considered by some authors (Marmar et al., 1995; Shalev et al., 1996) to be the cause of derealisation and depersonalisation in acute PTSD when there is extreme emotional arousal.

These facts help understand why early childhood trauma is particularly damaging. The child does not have explicit memory with narratives for the first two or three years. Since the memories of trauma remain in the amygdala (or implicit memory) the hippocampus, when it does start to develop, will not be activated as it should be. The reason for this is that the ongoing trauma of the past will have caused a decrease in hippocampal volume and information will not be processed fully. This will inevitably impact on the development of a sense of self and integration of experiences. The hippocampus remains vulnerable throughout maturation. The stress will inevitably decrease the hippocampal activity, stalling its development and certainly preventing the sensory information from passing through the hippocampus to the frontal cortex where it would normally be integrated, and become an explicit memory, contributing to autobiographical memory and a sense of self. This whole process would be jeopardised for the traumatised child. Other factors contribute to the complex PTSD of adult survivors of childhood abuse which will be addressed in the next section of this chapter.

Summary and Conclusions on the Nature of Traumatic Memory

There is strong evidence from psychological and neurological research that traumatic memories are encoded and stored differently from ordinary autobiographical memory. There are neurological disconnections in the brain which prevent traumatic material being processed in the normal way. Normally information from the body and senses passes through the thalamus to the amygdala (part of the limbic system) which evaluates the emotional significance. It is then passed on to the hippocampus which makes meaning of it and then to the prefrontal cortex which integrates the experience and plans action. A sense of self is also developed in this area of the brain.

In the case of overwhelming traumatic experiences, the amygdala becomes overstimulated and the traumatic information does not go beyond the amygdala to the hippocampus. The information is stored in sensory-motor modalities, and the fragmented traumatic memories remain as sensation, emotions or involuntary movements without any context or meaning. Some authors have described this as primary processing of information without the essential secondary processing which would involve the cognitive evaluation in the hippocampus and the integration of the experience in the prefrontal cortex (Straker, Watson & Robinson, 2002). The stress hormones activated by the autonomic nervous system which in turn are activated by the limbic system are responsible for this disconnection. These stress hormones debilitate the function of the hippocampus. Furthermore, the cortisol levels drop so that there is failure in stalling the extreme stress signals. It becomes a chronic condition.

The lack of meaning and integration of experiences have serious implications, particularly for childhood trauma. The concept of self is developed in the prefrontal cortex where all experiences are integrated. If information does not get processed through the hippocampus to the frontal areas, then the sense of self is disrupted. In traumatised children, the later development of the hippocampus could be compromised.

The dissociative symptomatology of PTSD which includes depersonalisation, derealisation and amnesia has been considered to be the result of the inactivated hippocampus (Van der Kolk, 2003) or in the terms of Straker et al. (2002), the disconnection of brain function and absence of secondary processing.

This division between primary and secondary processing would seem to reflect the difference between implicit memory and explicit memory. It also implies the cause of dissociation in PTSD.

Neurological Link between Hypnosis and PTSD

As Spiegel (2001) has pointed out that just as there is the parallel between the symptoms of PTSD and the components of hypnosis, similar parallels can be found in the neurological findings of trauma and the hypnotic state. Vermetten and Bremner (2004) noted that neuroimaging studies of hypnotic processes revealed similar patterns of brain activity as those seen in studies of emotional recall. The heightened physiological arousal can produce the narrowing and intensification of attention characteristic of the hypnotic state. Vermetten and Bremner (2004) also consider dissociation involves the ability to segregate and encode experience into separate psychobiological processes as occurs in the response to trauma. They have observed that traumatic experiences mobilise hypnotic responses which include the dissociative symptoms of numbing, freezing, feelings of involuntariness, loss of self agency, and time distortion, derealisation and analgesia, and out-of-body experiences; and the authors believe these hypnotic response patterns should be taken into account when analysing brain correlates of trauma disorders.

Hypnotic ability can be both an asset and a drawback; since, on the one hand, it is a defence mechanism which has a protective purpose, but on the other hand it can become maladaptive when it leads to dysfunctions and psychopathology.

In addition to the neurological findings in PTSD patients so far discussed, Vermetten and Bremner (2004) highlighted further research findings which make a neurological link between hypnosis and traumatic recall (that is imagined or real re-exposure to a traumatic event). There are similar neurological changes in the same brain structures involved in hypnosis and traumatic recall. In hypnosis there is frontal lobe inhibition and inhibition of the left dorsolateral prefrontal cortex, similar to the disconnection found in PTSD. The anterior cingulate cortex (ACC) is also involved in both hypnosis and traumatic recall. As mentioned in the previous chapter this area of the brain is the interface between the emotional and attentional systems in the frontal areas, and processes attention, executive functions and episodic memory. It is involved in the cognitive induction of emotional responses, and differentiates between images of reality and of fantasy. ACC activation occurs in the event of traumatic stimuli and inhibits feelings of fearfulness when there is no more external threat. Failure of activation of the ACC leads to increased fear when it is not contextually appropriate, and is responsible for hyperarousal or exaggerated emotional responses, as seen in PTSD. Likewise in hypnosis there is a breakdown in the connection between the brain area analysing somatosensory stimuli input and the areas organising behavioural responses to them, and a loss of discrimination between reality and fantasy. In both traumatic recall and hypnosis there is a dissociation between sensory input and higher order processing.

Vermetten and Bremner (2004) make the point that individuals with trauma-related psychopathology such as PTSD alternate between states of consciousness in which they re-experience the trauma, and they use their hypnotic capacity to block pain, alter time perception and modify emotional responses. They are in fact the most highly hypnotisable clients in the psychiatric population. The hypnotic responsivity is responsible for the changes in connectivity of the brain structures and the psychopathology. Nonetheless this same hypnotic capacity can be a great asset when employed therapeutically. What creates the splits can heal the splits (Brende, 1985).

Adult Memories of Child Abuse, Dissociative Amnesia and Recovered Memories

Dissociative amnesia in adult life following childhood trauma has been documented in the literature and defined as 'an inability to recall important personal information, usually of a traumatic or stressful nature that is too important to be explained by ordinary forgetfulness' (American Psychiatric Association, DSM-IV). Delayed recall for all or parts of the trauma has also been recorded (Van der Kolk, 1996) in cases of natural disasters, accidents, kidnapping, torture and war-related trauma. In a general population study by Elliott and Briere (1995) the authors found that amnesia occurred in a proportion of victims after any traumatic event, no matter what kind. Total amnesia for child sexual abuse (CSA) has been found to be quite high in adult survivors of this kind of abuse. It can also be found in adult survivors of other kinds of childhood abuse, although this has not been so comprehensively researched. There are special features of ongoing childhood trauma which do not necessarily apply in cases of single event trauma in adult life. As Terr (1991) has pointed out, the child is exposed repeatedly to overwhelming experiences in which the perpetrator is often an adult figure in a caring role, on whom the child may be emotionally and physically dependent. Thus there is a betrayal of trust in the adult who should be the nurturer but becomes the abuser. The child needs to survive and may not have access to another adult figure who believes what has happened and is psychologically available to rescue the child.

Terr considers cases of rape and other single traumatic events to be Type I trauma and child abuse to be what she calls Type II trauma where the caregiver is the abuser. This produces a scenario of continuous traumatisation where no escape is possible. The traumatised child remains helpless over a period of years. From a common-sense point of view this might seem to make a case for hyperamnesia rather than amnesia if the experiences are repeated and reinforced. However, research shows in a substantial number of cases, the opposite is true. Loftus et al. (1994) found 19% of survivors of child sexual abuse had experienced total amnesia and Williams (1994) found 38% of survivors of CSA had similarly had amnesia for it. In the first study by Herman and Schatzow (1987), out of 53 female survivors of child sexual abuse who were in therapy, 36% of them had always remembered the abuse in detail, while the remaining 64% had some degree of amnesia for the sexual abuse at some periods of their lives. About 36% of this latter group had mild to moderate amnesia, that is, they claimed that they had always been aware that it happened but recently recovered more memories of it; 28% of the group reported that there had been a period of time when they had no memory for the sexual abuse at all, but it later came into their conscious awareness.

In these instances of recovered memories, the women often developed post-traumatic stress symptoms and in most cases the women were keen to obtain corroborative evidence for their memories; 74% of them were successful in obtaining such evidence to substantiate their own reports. In another study in Holland (Ensink, 1992), differences were found between a group of sexually abused women who were amnesic and a group who had continuous memories for CSA; the former were more likely than the latter to report time loss and flashbacks, characteristics typical of trauma memory. Percentage rates for those survivors of CSA with degrees of amnesia and those with continuous memory seem to vary slightly. Cameron (1994, 1996) found that a total 35% of 60 female survivors of CSA had continuous memories, 23% had partially forgotten and 42% had completely forgotten the abuse for some time between 15 and 20 years. Some authors conclude that complete amnesia is rare and that remembering abuse is more common (Loftus, Polensky & Fullilove, 1994). However traumatic memory is not an all-or-nothing phenomenon (Brown, Scheflin & Hammond, 1998).

There are at least three categories of post-traumatic memory: (1) continuous recall (no amnesia) but delayed understanding; (2) partial amnesia and delayed recall; and (3) total or profound amnesia with delayed recall. Brown et al. (1998) criticise surveys which do not include such distinctions. They also fairly point out that the False Memory Debate does not include these considerations, nor the complexity of trauma memory (as mentioned in Chapter 1). (For a fuller, fair and unbiased view of this controversial field, see Brown et al. (1998)).

There is considerable evidence that recovered memories or delayed recall can be corroborated. More than half of CSA survivors can corroborate their memories, both continuous memories and recovered memories (Brewin & Andrews, 1998; Brewin, Andrews & Gotlieb, 1993; Widom, 1997). In a recent study (Fivush & Edwards, 2004), 12 women survivors of CSA were asked to provide narratives of their abuse and discuss their experiences of remembering and forgetting the abuse. As in many other reported cases of CSA, there were periods when they were unable to recall their abuse. There were other periods when they felt they had never forgotten the abuse. There appeared to be three groups of survivors in this sample. One group had continuous memories and said they never forgot the abuse. Another group had continuous memories but could not remember details of it and tried hard to remember some of it. A third group experienced recovered memories when memory for the abuse seemed to come flooding back after a long period of having forgotten it.

There seem to be many memory responses to childhood trauma, forming a continuum from total recall to total forgetting, rather than a dichotomy of those who remember and those who forget. The narratives of these survivors also differed in terms of their coherence. Five out of six women who had continuous memories produced coherent narratives of the abuse in contrast to those with recovered memories who gave incoherent narratives. Fivush and Edwards (2004) warn that remembering and forgetting is much more complex than has previously been considered and we should start conceptualising remembering and forgetting as a dynamic fluid process.

The varieties of response to trauma and the different kinds of remembering and forgetting seen in survivors of childhood trauma can also be explained by Spiegel's model discussed in the earlier part of this chapter. In an altered state of consciousness which is like hypnosis, memories are stored differently and there are a limited range of associations due to narrowness of focus. The strong effect can influence storage and retrieval of information. It is also necessary for the person to be in a similar dissociative state before they can retrieve the information (state-dependent memory). In trauma the process of memory storage is discontinuous. This would explain the 'on-off' quality of dissociative amnesia according to Spiegel (2003). Dissociation can isolate memories by separating them from common associative networks. This makes retrieval more difficult. Hypnotic and dissociative phenomena affect and are influenced by memory processing (Spiegel, 2003).

Not all survivors of child abuse have dissociative amnesia, so other factors must operate, which will now be discussed.

FACTORS LEADING TO MEMORY LOSS AND DELAYED RECALL OF CHILD ABUSE

There has not only been controversy about dissociative amnesia for traumatic events and a lack of full understanding of this, but also concern about the nature of recovered memories and the reasons for this delayed recall. Common belief is often that recovered memory is produced by the therapist suggesting to a client in therapy that she/he could have suffered psychological symptoms as a result of childhood trauma and this suggestion is taken as fact by the client. Since most clients in the surveys were in psychotherapy at the time this could be a plausible explanation and in some cases might be so. However, studies which have been designed to investigate both predictors of memory loss and also causes of memory recovery would suggest that this is not a full and adequate explanation. Demand characteristics in the clinical context, or in other words, pressures within the therapeutic situation, do not seem to be largely responsible.

Predictors of Amnesia

Terr (1991) showed that repeated trauma of long duration was more likely to result in amnesia. Herman and Schatzow (1987) showed that young age of onset of the sexual abuse, its duration and the degree of violence used were all related to amnesia in the victim with later delayed recall. Briere and Conte (1993) also investigated factors predicting amnesia for CSA. Again the age of onset, duration of the abuse, degree of violence (extent of the injury and fear of death), the number of abusers, and also severity of current symptoms were all related to amnesia for CSA with later recovered memories. They conclude that amnesia for abuse appears to be a common phenomena in survivors of CSA. Elliott and Briere (1995) examined delayed recall of CSA among a random sample of 505 from the general population; 42% of those who reported CSA maintained they had periods of memory loss. Those who had delayed recall reported more use of threats of harm by the perpetrators at the time of the abuse than did those with continuous recall. Greater symptomatology was also found among those with recovered memories of recent origin. These symptoms included heightened intrusions, avoidance responses and tension reduction behaviours. Cameron (1994, 1996) found that significant predictors of amnesic periods in those who reported child abuse were: young age of onset, severe symptoms, multiple abusers, multiple acts of sexual violence and a natural parent as abuser. Presence of amnesia for CSA also seems to be related to dissociative symptoms (Ensink, 1992) as measured by the Dissociative Experiences Scale (DES).

The issue of whether recovered memories after periods of amnesia are true or false memories has been a highly controversial issue. Both retrospective and prospective studies have been carried out to try and validate or otherwise the veridicality of recovered memories. Retrospective studies have been designed to find corroborative evidence that the abuse occurred in the past. Prospective studies were designed to establish from follow-up data, whether or not children who had medical records of abuse in the past and had now reached adulthood had had any periods of amnesia or had continuous memory of the abuse.

With regard to retrospective data in the Herman and Schatzow study (1987) 74% of the 53 women in psychotherapy with reported CSA were able to provide corroborative evidence for the abuse (40% from perpetrators and 34% from siblings or others). Mostly the survivors themselves had wished to see evidence for their reported and/or recovered memories. Those who had recovered memories presented with PTSD symptoms at the time they recovered them. In a study of 170 students in Canada (Belicki et al., 1994), 41 reported a history of child sexual abuse; 64 reported no abuse and 9 reported physical abuse. Of those who reported CSA, 55.4% reported they had forgotten the abuse for some period of time. Corroborative evidence for the abuse did not differentiate between those who had experienced amnesia and those who had continuous memories. The differentiating factors between having had disrupted memory and those who had continuous memory were the greater number of repeated episodes of sexual abuse, the combination of physical and sexual abuse, and abuse by a family member in the former group (i.e. those with disrupted memories).

In another retrospective study by Kristiansen et al. (1995) out of 113 women aged 18–57 with abuse histories, 51% had experienced partial or total amnesia for the abuse; 49% had continuous memories. Corroborative evidence was available for 62% of the total sample. Women with continuous memories were more likely to have evidence of the abuse, but 45% of those who had recovered memories after periods of amnesia could also provide corroborative evidence.

In a prospective study, Williams (1994, 1995) questioned 129 women with medical records of sexual abuse and physical injuries. These women were originally part of a research study on the consequences of abuse. It was 17 years after this study that Williams interviewed them. Thirty-eight per cent of the women were amnesic for the CSA or failed to report it and 32% said they had never been abused. A remaining 16% of these reported there had been a time when they had forgotten the abuse. Those women who had forgotten and had recovered their memories later had an equal number of discrepancies between their reports in the present and the past documentation as did those who had always remembered. Those with recovered memories were more likely to have been younger at the time of abuse and less likely to have received support from their mothers. Williams concludes that 'recovered memories of child sexual abuse reported by adults can be quite consistent with contemporaneous documentation of the abuse and should not be summarily dismissed by therapists, lawyers, family members, judges or the women themselves' (Williams, 1995, p. 670).

An interesting feature of this study is the fact that those with recovered memories were younger at the time of the abuse and had age ranges from 2–12 years while those with continuous memories were never younger than 3 at the time of the abuse. In view of what has been stated earlier, namely that explicit narrative memory is not likely before the age of 3 due to the slow maturation of the hippocampus, those with recovered memories would be some of those who had had infantile amnesia and not dissociative amnesia (an argument put forward by Pope and Hudson, 1995). However, the incidence of amnesia did not differ significantly between those whose abuse started at 3 and those whose abuse started at age 4–6 years.

One cannot therefore argue that infantile amnesia is the total explanation for amnesic periods. Yet again Williams confirmed the findings that amnesia and subsequent recovered memory was significantly related to incestuous abuse and the closeness of the relationship with the abuser. The general conclusion seems to be that recovered memories can in many instances be corroborated and that they are not more inaccurate than continuous memories. Furthermore, retrospective studies also suggest that the memories are mostly accurate in terms of a general gist though the details may not be, and in this it is similar to continuous memory (Brewin et al., 1993).

Psychological mechanisms involved in delayed recall are not known exactly and there are different interpretations of what happens psychologically when amnesia of long duration (e.g. 15–20 years or longer) occurs. Herman and Schatzow (1987), for example, consider that it is 'massive repression'. However, it can be understood as a form of dissociation or dissociative amnesia as Briere and Conte (1993), and Spiegel (2003) believe. In some cases neither repression nor dissociative amnesia may be the reason for memory loss.

There is some evidence to suggest that avoidance and intentional efforts not to think about the past could be alternative ways of coping. In a study of 553 students, Melchert (1996) found that those who reported emotional and sexual abuse in childhood (18%) and also those who reported physical abuse (21%) reported there was a time when they had no memory for the abuse. They were then asked to decide whether they had unconsciously blocked out the memory or whether they had just avoided the memory at the time, but could have remembered it, if they had wanted to. Most of them indicated they had blocked out the memory unconsciously, but half of these actually believed that the memory might have been available had they not been avoiding it.

Andrews et al. (2000) consider that there are a number of possible mechanisms involved in forgetting trauma. They first mention the two different kinds of memory of emotion-laden events; one is the autobiographical memory (explicit memory) and the other implicit memory, based on lower level perceptual processing. There is evidence for survivors presenting with both. Andrews et al. (2000) suggest that forgetting may include not only disruption to encoding but also disruption to the retrieval of adequately encoded memories.

Fivush and Edwards (2004) in their study found that abused women who deliberately tried to block out their memories from conscious awareness for a period of time, nonetheless reported that they had a kind of awareness that the abuse had happened. Four women said they had disturbing feelings of uncertainty about their memories. Although they had no doubt that the abuse occurred, they maintained the memory had a surreal quality. In trying to keep their experiences out of conscious awareness, they had memories which had lost associative connections to other experiences and to the self. This is reminiscent of hypnotic experiences, and may be a product of self-generated hypnosis.

It would seem from the literature that recovered memories following amnesia are largely valid and accurate although the mechanisms to explain the memory loss are not fully understood and may be varied in kind, including repression, dissociative amnesia and deliberate attempts to avoid the memories which might be available if avoidance were prevented.

There are many possible factors contributing to amnesia in CSA survivors and they all may interact. An important factor according to some authors (Freyd, 1996; Terr, 1991) is the interpersonal nature of the trauma of CSA, that is the betrayal by a very close person such as a parent in the child's life and the great sense of shame and stigmatisation which is created in the child (see next chapter). Van der Kolk, Pelcovitz et al., (1996) found interpersonal trauma produced more PTSD symptoms than natural disasters.

According to Brown et al. (1998) there are 30 studies of amnesia in CSA. Among these, there was not one study in which there was no amnesia for CSA documented. They conclude that 'amnesia for CSA is a robust finding' (p. 194). The base rates for continuous memory range from 23 to 72% and average 50% across the studies.

The Precipitants and Process of Memory Recovery

The recovery of memories of child sexual abuse is commonly produced by triggers in the environment or in dreams. Elliott and Briere (1995) found a 40% rate of full and partial amnesia for CSA in their sample. Memories were triggered by the following: an event similar to the original incident (47%);

experiencing something of a sexual nature (31%); having a dream or night-mare (30%). Nineteen per cent recovered the memory in psychotherapy. This is contrary to the belief that most repressed memories are recovered in therapy (Loftus et al., 1994). Feldman-Summers and Pope (1994) took 500 male and female psychologists at random and assessed incidence of physical and sexual abuse as a child and the incidence of those who had had periods of memory loss. They looked at the circumstances in which memories were recovered. Out of 330 who co-operated by returning questionnaires, 24/% had had physical abuse, 22% sexual abuse. Forty per cent of the total report-ing abuse had had periods of amnesia. Precipitants of recovering memories were psychotherapy and other external events. There were no significant differences between the incidence of these different triggers. Psychotherapy was sometimes associated with recovery of memory but in only 19% was it the sole precipitant. Furthermore, 70% of those who recovered memories were able to provide corroborative evidence.

In the study by Andrews et al. (2000) the authors set up telephone inter-views with 108 therapists and received 236 detailed accounts of clients recov-ering traumatic memories. Some clients had had total amnesia; some had partial memories, and others had a vague sense of suspicion. The purpose of the study was to discover triggers to recovery of the memories, the quali-ties of the recovered memories and the amount of time taken to recover them. Fifty-five per cent of 226 cases had had total amnesia; 14% had a vague sense of suspicion and 31% had partial amnesia. Eighty clients were survi-vors of CSA; 31 had experienced CSA and other forms of abuse; 19 had child maltreatment; and 32 experienced other childhood trauma. Of those clients who recovered their first memory in therapy, the survivors of CSA or CSA with other abuse took the longest time to recover the memory, that is 56 and 50 weeks respectively. Those who suffered child maltreatment or other trauma, but no sexual abuse recovered memories in 16 and 15 weeks respec-tively. The most common trigger to the memories in the therapy was a thera-peutic technique. Nonetheless this accounted for less than half of the instances of reported memory recovery. The most common triggers to recov-ered memory prior to therapy were events related to the client's children, or their children reaching the same age as the client was at the time of the supposed abuse, or situations involving physical contact with the client or physical danger to the client or other known person. Other triggers included the media, books, loss or threat of loss, someone reminded them or someone else described abuse.

The completeness of the memories was not related to degree of amnesia, but to the type of abuse recalled. Memories which were fragmented occurred more frequently in those who had suffered CSA with or without another kind of abuse (73%). Child maltreatment or abuse without CSA had a much lower rate of fragmented memories (40% and 49% respectively).

The authors concluded that the risks associated with the use of therapeutic techniques are less than anticipated. Triggers to recovered memories outside therapy were twice as many as the triggers in therapy. They suggested that therapeutic techniques may have a priming effect to recall. The time taken to recall also does not relate to degree of amnesia, but rather the nature of the abuse. It is suggested that abuse with a sexual element may produce more cognitive avoidance, and hence result in a longer time to retrieve the memory. Most of the memories recovered produced flashbacks and symptoms of PTSD. Fear and distress were the most common emotions experienced with the recovered memories. Very few autobiographical facts were produced. Once again the authors support the hypothesis that dissociation at the time of the trauma disrupted the encoding of information in memory at that time.

It is often difficult for adults to discriminate between the real and the imagined childhood events because of the lower level perceptual processing in the child (implicit memory). This may decay with time in childhood memories, but where there is greater perceptual information as in trauma, the more likely it is that the person will believe it really happened. However, corroboration was no less likely to be reported for recovered memories with perceptual reliving of the fear than for memories which did not have these features.

Recovered memories mostly do not present as explicit narrative memory, but emerge in the form of somatosensory flashbacks. These fragments of memory continue over time and are slowly integrated. This may become an incomplete narrative ultimately which may be seen as psychiatric symptoms which warrant treatment. The flashbacks which initially present are often bodily feelings, sensory experiences and emotions which do not seem to be connected to any identifiable narrative. (Kristiansen et al., 1995; Roe & Schwartz, 1996). This is consistent with the findings related earlier in this chapter concerning post-traumatic stress symptoms and the nature of traumatic memory, namely that it is implicit memory and dissociated from the normal explicit information processing system. Cameron (1996) found that those survivors of abuse who had been amnesic were more likely than the non-amnesic to report these fragmentary sensory memories. Slowly these memories became more detailed and organised. There may also be behavioural re-enactments of the trauma which precede the somatosensory flashbacks (Davies & Frawley, 1994).

Later hallucinatory-type experiences of sexual trauma may occur during the transition between waking and sleep or sleep and waking. Dreams and nightmares of the sexual abuse may then follow and even during a daytime flashback the person may suddenly re-experience some part of the abuse as though it is happening in the present. Therapy is a slow process of integrating emotions and sensations and re-associating them with events which are put together and organised into narrative form. Van der Kolk and Fisler (1995) reported that their patients who recovered memories at first experienced sensory flashbacks which they finally were able to put together in narrative form. Once this happens, the survivors of trauma lose their PTSD symptoms (Foa et al., 1995). They found continued exposure to the memories during the therapy of rape victims results in a transformation into narrative form. The narratives contain more thoughts and feelings post therapy and they become organised and less fragmented.

SUMMARY AND IMPLICATIONS

From the literature on traumatic responses to single and relatively recent traumatic events, and the trauma responses of those with recovered memories of multiple long-term child abuse of several decades ago, it is evident that symptoms of PTSD may be manifest. In both kinds of trauma cases, there can also be continuous memories. What is not understood clearly is whether memories for repeated abuse over long periods of time in childhood are stored like memories for a single event of trauma. The exact mechanisms involved in periods of amnesia in those people who have suffered years of victimisation are also not certain. It would seem there are a number of different mechanisms. Memory loss of this kind could involve repression, dissociation, failure of state-dependent retrieval, deliberate attempts to block out the memory or pretending it has not happened.

Factors predicting amnesia in survivors of child abuse are the age of onset, multiple acts of abuse, multiple abusers, threats of violence with sexual abuse, and the perpetrator being a close member of the family or in a caretaker role, and absence of an alternative supportive adult figure (Cameron, 1994). Fear is also an important emotion according to Andrews et al. (2000). In an earlier study of traumatised populations, Kuehn (1974) found that victims of crime which had caused injury to the person had less complete memories than those who had experienced a crime without injury. Personal survival and related fear are clearly major contributors.

Recently however, Vermetten & Bremner (2004) have pointed out that with long-term memory storage, memories are shifted from the hippocampus to neocortical areas where sensory impressions take place (Kim & Fanselaw, 1992; Phillips & Le Doux, 1992). They believe that this shift in long-term memory storage could mean a shift from conscious representational memory (explicit memory) to unconscious memory processes (implicit memory). The stress hormones also affect the functioning of the hippocampus which modulates the encoding of memories. The authors consider that this can explain a whole range of memory symptoms including hypermnesia, amnesia, deficits in declarative memory, delayed recall of abuse and other memory distortions.

Since effective therapy for both short-term and long-term trauma cases involves enabling the client to transform fragmented traumatic memories (implicit memory) into a meaningful narrative form (as explicit memory), accessing the implicit memory system first seems essential. Hypnosis seems to be an appropriate therapeutic tool for this task. Hypnosis can certainly be an effective tool to create state-dependent recall. Both psychologically and neurologically the hypnotic trance seems an obvious choice.

An interesting study by Barbara Lex (1979) illustrated the beneficial effect of a spontaneous and natural trance state used by Native Americans. When they return home after combat they perform rituals together, which involve rhythmical movement and focused attention which lead to trance states. According to Lex, there is right hemisphere dominance implicated in this ritual rhythmical movement and focused attention which leads to trance states. This is deliberately done to deal with the stress. Emotions are released and there is a limited capacity for language. This discharge of affect then produces a rebound effect in which the left hemisphere becomes involved. This shift in lateralisation enables the person to experience a change in mental state and they can begin to integrate and assimilate traumatic material.

While modern hypnosis or trance in our society may not be used in this ritualistic manner, the neurophysiology is the same, and a trance state can produce activation and release of emotional material (right hemisphere) which can be followed by a relaxed, calm and rational re-evaluation (left hemisphere). This ritualistic behaviour of the Native Americans is also reminiscent of the violent shaking which follows the freeze response in animals when the threat or danger is over. As Scaer (2001) points out, this response releases the nervous energy which was blocked off. This may or may not be an identical comparison. However, both Spiegel (1996) and Van der Kolk (1996) consider that bilateral stimulation of the brain is necessary to facilitate secondary processing and resolution of trauma memories.

3

THE NATURE OF DISSOCIATION AND THE LONG-TERM CONSEQUENCES OF CHILDHOOD ABUSE

DISSOCIATION

The DSM-IV definition of dissociation is 'A disruption in the usually integrated functions of consciousness, memory, identity or perception of the environment. It may be sudden, gradual, transient or chronic.'

As seen from the previous chapter, dissociation is considered to be an adaptive response to traumatisation. It has been described by Briere (1992) as a disruption in the normally occurring connection between feelings, thoughts, behaviours and memories and is seen in response to trauma, seemingly to reduce psychological distress during and after the trauma. It may be a way of allowing gradual assimilation of the traumatic information over a period of time manageable to the survivor. It may also prevent total assimilation of this material when it becomes pathological (Horowitz, 1986).

Cardena (1994) has highlighted three different ways in which dissociation has been described in clinical psychology; firstly as semi-independent mental systems that are not consciously accessible and not integrated in the persons' conscious memory or identity; secondly, as an alteration in consciousness whereby some aspects of the person's self or environment became disconnected from each other and thirdly as a defence mechanism that produces amnesia (non-organic), warding off pain and sometimes a lack of integration of the personality as in Multiple Personality Disorder or Dissociative Identity Disorder (DSM-IV; American Psychiatric Association, 1994).

Cardena considers that automatic behaviour, that is, divided attention which involves a non-conscious mental executive (Hilgard, 1986) such as driving a car while carrying out other actions simultaneously, e.g. holding a lively conversation, should not be labelled 'dissociation', as it is qualitatively different from a person in a dissociative fugue state. The term dissociation he believes is wrongly applied to the processing of stimuli that are 'consciously not accessible because of physical or attentional limitations' (Cardena, 1994, p. 18). The term should only be applied to a past or present situation where information should 'ordinarily' be accessible to the individual but is not. Cardena also argues against the use of the word dissociation to explain state-dependent learning, i.e. material learnt while in a certain mood or emotion is more easily retrieved when that mood is re-instated. There is no clear reason why forgotten material which is retrieved in this way could not be ordinarily integrated into the person's waking consciousness. He claims that this again is very different from the lapses of memory seen in Dissociative Identity Disorder which involve changes in consciousness. Putnam (1988) reports that such patients may display alterations in their psychobiological states when they shift to a different 'alter'. As Putman points out, dissociative amnesia is the inability to recall important personal information that is too extensive to be understood in terms of ordinary forgetfulness or age. The person is unable to integrate or recall consciously important information that should be accessible, particularly since it is affecting their behaviour. Cardena distinguishes this pathological dissociation from the non-pathological hypnotic experience of the 'hidden observer' phenomenon.

Lastly, Cardena gives the example of another kind of dissociation which he also believes warrants such a label; that is a gross discrepancy or disconnection between the verbal report of a subjective experience and the concurrent behaviours or physiological responses of the individual. He gives examples from pathological conditions and also hypnotic responses of normal people. In the former case a patient may report a lack of physical sensation in a part of the body for which there is no neurological or anatomical evidence of such impairment. In the second case, a person may respond to a hypnotic suggestion of *not* perceiving an object which is actually present, and report that indeed they do not see the object (trance logic). Nonetheless they will behave as though it is present by responding to it or avoiding it, e.g. walking around a chair which they have reported is not there. Hypnosis in this case seems to be a kind of controllable dissociation (Speigel & Cardena, 1990).

Cardena has clearly defined the different kinds of dissociation demonstrated in pathological states and the hypnotic state. However, some of his views do not appear to be in accordance with those of John and Helen Watkins (1997) whose Ego-state theory of personality development would appear to embrace state-dependent learning as part of a normal process of dissociation. Watkins and Watkins (1997) consider that processes of differentiation, dissociation, and integration of experiences are part of the normal development of the personality. As a result of dissociation, ego-states are formed, these are defined as 'an organised system of behaviour and experience whose elements are bound together by some common principal, and which is separated from other such states by a boundary which is more or less permeable' (Watkins & Watkins, 1997, p. 25). These ego-states can be activated by certain stimuli or situations. Their origins may be at different times in the persons' life. Watkins and Watkins consider that this is part of normal development. They give the example of normal ego-states in the case of a doctor playing 'peek-a-boo' with his two-year old child when the telephone rings. He answers it, and it is a call from a colleague asking for professional advice. Immediately the doctor accesses his medical knowledge to share with his colleague, and in so doing, his voice tone, his language and his whole demeanour change. He has shifted from one ego-state to another. After the phone call, he returns to play with his child with complete ease; he can shift from one ego-state to another, and at the end of the day remember the whole series of events without any difficulty.

The ego-states created by trauma will have boundaries between them which may not be so permeable, and amnesic barriers between the ego-states may exist, so that one ego state may have difficulty remembering what happened in a certain situation which triggered the emergence of a different ego-state. In the case of Dissociative Identity Disorder, the alters do not know about the other alters and the barriers are usually totally and not partially amnesic. There are degrees of permeability and degrees of awareness or shared consciousness of the ego-states. Their concept of dissociation is not all or nothing. They see it as a process which is on a continuum with degrees of co-consciousness between different parts of the mind and body.

Cardena on the other hand is quite clear and specific in limiting the definition of dissociation to an alteration in experience whereby there is a full disengagement or disconnection from the self and/or the environment. He would not use the term to describe an altered state of consciousness where this disengagement has not occurred, e.g. states of 'ecstasy'. Depersonalisation and derealisation are examples of dissociative experiences according to Cardena (1994). In depersonalisation, the person experiences themselves as detached from their emotions, actions or thoughts and may also feel detached from the physical body. The person may feel the thoughts and actions have a 'life of their own' and the self is 'standing back' and observing them as an outsider. In derealisation the person feels the external surroundings are not real and they have a dreamlike quality, lacking substance. The world is experienced by the person as not quite real, but they do not necessarily believe it to be unreal.

Van der Kolk, Van der Hart & Marmar (1996) consider there are three levels of dissociation. *Primary dissociation* is manifest in somatosensory fragments of memory of a traumatic event which are not integrated into a personal memory. This occurs in the context of an altered state of consciousness. *Secondary dissociation* can occur when the person is traumatised, namely a separation between the observing ego and the experiencing ego leading to depersonalisation and derealisation (such as an 'out-of-body experience'). This can protect the person from the full impact of the pain. This could be akin to Hilgard's 'hidden observer'.

Tertiary dissociation is the label given to ego-states that may develop in a severely traumatised child, each having its own identity through associated cognitions, emotions and behaviours, as in Dissociative Identity Disorder. These categories would also be recognised by Cardena as dissociation. Waller, Putnam & Carlson (1996) found evidence for two types of dissociation, namely non-pathological and pathological. The former concerns imaginative involvement or absorption, and the latter relates to amnesia, derealisation, depersonalisation and identity fragmentation.

Nijenhuis (1999) has highlighted the importance of two types of pathological dissociation, namely psychological dissociation and somatoform dissociation. Psychological dissociation presents as cognitive emotional and behavioural alterations including amnesia, depersonalisation and identity confusion. These phenomena are often associated with somatisation, and patients with dissociative disorders often report somatoform symptoms, which may meet the criteria of somatisation disorder or conversion disorder (Nijenhuis, 2000). In such cases somatoform dissociation is also present with psychological dissociation. Somatoform dissociation refers to functional losses in the body such as localised anaesthesia in parts of the body or sensory losses such as lack of a sense of touch, or auditory, gustatory or olfactory losses. Pain symptoms which appear to have no organic cause or sexual dysfunctions may be dissociative symptoms and may be due to reactivation of a traumatic memory. Somatoform dissociation is due to a failure to integrate somatic components of an experience. Somatoform dissociation and psychological dissociation are very closely related and particularly prevalent in the dissociative disorders.

Nijenhuis et al. (2001) view somatoform dissociative responses as similar to animal defence reactions to major threat. When an animal's defence manoeuvres have failed, it will freeze or show total submission to the predator and also total anaesthesia. Studies have shown that somatoform dissociation is strongly associated with a history of child physical abuse (Nijenhuis et al., 2001). They found that both somatoform dissociation and psychological dissociation were correlated with a history of physical abuse and severe sexual abuse. Severe threat to the integrity of the body seems to produce bodily numbing, analgesia and amnesia. These dissociative states may primarily represent non-integrated defensive states in a response to threat to life (Nijenhuis & Van der Hart, 1999).

Nijenhuis (2000) also reflects back to the observations of Janet who referred to *mental stigmata* which were functional losses such as loss of sensations, analgesia and loss of motor control (inability to move or speak). Nijenhuis and Van der Hart (1999) call these negative symptoms. Janet also observed *mental accident*, or 'fixed ideas', which were intrusions of dissociated emotions, thoughts or perceptions or movements, reactivations of traumatic memories. These two sets of symptoms may oscillate in the same person (as already discussed in Chapter 2). There appears to be two dissociative personalities in the same person. Whatever is not integrated in one dissociative personality or state (not sensing, not perceiving) may be prominent in the other personality or state with a complexity of feelings and sensations and motor reactions. Janet recognised both the components of reactions and functions which fail to become integrated into the whole personality (Nijenhuis, 2000).

Nijenhuis, following Janet's observations and his own, considers these two dissociative states as separate personalities in dissociative disorders. Many of these patients appear quite normal when they present with a range of negative symptoms such as amnesia and anaesthesia, and he labels them 'an apparently normal personality'. The other alternating state, which presents with defensive reactions to major threat and shows positive symptoms of trauma-related movements and pain is named the 'emotional personality'. There may be more than one ANP (apparently normal personality) and more than one EP (emotional personality) in any one dissociative disorder. Both ANPs and EPs may manifest somatoform dissociations and psychological dissociation. One phenomena is mental stigmata or negative symptoms and mental accidents or positive symptoms. The other phenomena are manifestations of psychological and somatoform dissociations (Nijenhuis, 2000). More will be discussed later about this so-called structural dissociation in relation to different diagnoses of survivors of child abuse.

Nijenhuis (1999) found that somatoform dissociation was strongly related to multiple types of trauma including physical and sexual abuse, and where there was a threat to the integrity of the body. Freezing or stilling occur in the face of threat, and analgesia and anaesthesia when the strike is about to happen. Acute pain occurs when the threat subsides. Somatoform dissociation can manifest in this case as negative somatic experiences, such as anaesthesia or positive somatic experiences such as pain and motor activity. According to Nijenhuis' model of structural dissociation, it is these animal defence mechanisms which represent 'emotional personalities' (EPs).

Waller et al. (2000) studied an unselected group of patients with mental health problems and a variety of diagnoses. They were given the Dissociative Experiences Scale (Carlson & Putnam, 1993) which measures severity of psychological dissociation; the somatoform Dissociation Questionnaire (Nijenhuis, Spinoven, Van Dyck, Van der Hart & Vanderlinden, 1997) which reflects the presence and severity of somatic features and the Child Abuse and Trauma Scale (Sanders & Becker-Lausen, 1995) which measures subjective reports of childhood emotional abuse, neglect, physical abuse and sexual abuse. Using these measures, the authors found that there was a link between different types of childhood trauma and different forms of dissociation. Severity of physical abuse was associated with somatoform dissociation but not psychological dissociation. The severity of neglect, sexual abuse and emotional abuse was linked more broadly with both kinds of dissociation. The authors conclude that somatoform dissociation which involves freezing, analgesia and learned helplessness is more likely to be related to trauma involving physical contact or physical threats. The severity of the abuse is also an important factor.

More research has been recently carried out concerning different types of dissociation in relation to different diagnoses. Several authors have considered that psychological dissociation of a pathological kind may fall into two categories. Allen (2001) and Holmes et al. (2005) define two distinct types of dissociation namely 'detachment' and 'compartmentalisation'. Detachment is the label for the more pervasive forms of dissociative symptoms, such as depersonalisation and derealisation. Compartmentalisation refers to the more 'dramatic' dissociative phenomena such as dissociative amnesia, fugue states and Dissociative Identity Disorder. Detachment is considered an altered state of consciousness with a sense of being separated from one's body or oneself (depersonalisation), or feeling separated from the external world (derealisation). Compartmentalisation would cover dissociative amnesia, and physical or neurological symptoms without an organic basis, as seen in conversion disorders such as sensory loss, pseudoseizures and what one might consider as somatoform dissociation. These phenomena of compartmentalisation are deficits in the ability to control processes or actions which would normally be controllable.

Holmes et al. (2005) consider that both forms of dissociation exist in post-traumatic stress disorder. Among the avoidance symptoms there may be an inability to recall a certain important part of the traumatic event. The memories of it are often fragmented. These memory deficits might well be the product of peri-traumatic detachment according to Holmes et al., since this would cause inadequate coding of the trauma-related information. In some instances there may be dissociative amnesia when memories are not retrievable. Where there is a retrieval deficit there is compartmentalisation. There is some evidence that detachment comprising depersonalisation and derealisation is a separate factor from amnesia or compartmentalisation (Holmes et al., 2005).

In a recent study of a sample of 1326 general population, clinical, and university participants, Briere et al. (2005) employed the Multiscale Dissociation Inventory which was developed on the basis of empirical data by Briere

(2002). This scale (the MDI) measures five factors which were significantly associated with trauma exposure, namely Disengagement, Identity Dissociation, Emotional Constriction, Memory Disturbance and Depersonalisation/ Derealisation. There were some differences shown between the types of trauma experiences and the five factors of dissociation. Those who had a previous history of sexual abuse or assault had elevations on all five factors. Those with a history of physical abuse or assault showed high scores on four factors, that is all except Depersonalisation/Derealisation. Those who had experienced accidents and disasters in the past had elevated scores on only disengagement (that is 'spacing out' or absent-mindedness). The three PTSD symptom clusters were considered separately. Re-experiencing was related to Disengagement; avoidance and numbing was associated with Identity Dissociation, Emotional Construction and Depersonalisation/Derealisation, while hyperarousal was predicted by Disengagement and Memory Disturbance. Briere et al. (2005) consider that their findings support the view of dissociation 'as a multifaceted collection of distinct but overlapping dimensions as opposed to a unitary trait' (Briere et al., 2005, p. 228). They also rightly believe that gaining more information about the specific dissociative symptoms by multidimensional assessment will enable a more focused clinical intervention. The same holds for all the other views of dissociation mentioned in this chapter.

The Origins of the Concept of Dissociation

Pierre Janet, who was a contemporary of Freud and Breuer, developed a theory of dissociation as a response to trauma. His ideas are consistent with modern basic research findings in the field of trauma, as discussed in Chapter 2. Janet believed that the intense emotions evoked by terrifying and overwhelming events interfered with memory storage. The person became helpless and incapable of taking proper action against the danger and threat to life. Memory of the events or event is disrupted and seemingly lost. In fact he believed the memory or parts of the memory were kept out of conscious awareness by dissociation as a defence mechanism. There were in his view 'fixed ideas' containing memories from the past which continue to affect mood and behaviour in the present. The traumatised person is unable therefore to create a full memory of the event and put it into narrative form. In common with modern memory theorists, he believed memory to be a creative act whereby the person can organise and categorise their experiences and thus make meaning of it. In this way the memory is assimilated and accommodated into their schemas. This memory process, Janet considered, was disrupted by traumatic experiences due to the dissociation defence.

Likewise he believed the 'narrowing of consciousness' in response to trauma was part of this dissociative process and prevented the association and linking of experiences. Nonetheless the dissociated parts of memory of the event or the 'fixed ideas' were not 'lost' and continued to affect the individuals' moods and behaviour. Hence one sees the dissociated experiences of the past re-emerge as vivid flashbacks and intrude upon the present ongoing stream of consciousness, causing disorientation and a loss of connection with the immediate environment. The person feels they are re-living the event and the sense of time changes such that the past event appears to be happening in the present.

Dissociation can generally be understood as 'altered experiences of detachment from the self or surroundings, or a lack of integration between various mental processes, or a presumed defence mechanism, which functions to ward off ongoing anxiety or pain' (Cardena, 1994, p. 27). Janet's theory of dissociation mainly concerned this phenomena; a defence mechanism.

Repression and Dissociation: from Freud and Janet to Contemporary Views

It is difficult to comprehend with our present state of knowledge whether or not there is a difference between repression and dissociation or whether they may be one and the same mental process. Repression we understand as a process implying divisions of the mind, mainly the unconscious and the conscious. Repression, according to Freud, is an unconscious process whereby conflicting impulses are suppressed and are therefore out of the conscious awareness of the individual. This is triggered by the anxiety arising from these internal stimuli or impulses. The repressed feelings or impulses may push their way back into conscious awareness in the disguised form of dreams and/or psychological symptoms. Freud, in his theory of repression, was essentially concerned with the inner conflicts of the mind and the need of individuals to defend themselves against this inner threat by the defence of repression. Repression he saw as an attempt to gain mastery over instincts and inner conflicts rather than a defence against the impact of external threat and danger. Janet's theory of dissociation was essentially concerned with survival in the face of external, environmental dangers, and a psychological escape from their overwhelming effects on the person.

According to Mollon (1996), Freud's theory of repression gained greater recognition than Janet's theory of dissociation due to a misleading impression that dissociation implied an innate weakness in the integrative powers of the mind. Repression and dissociation are assumed to be different in other ways. Repression has been referred to as a 'vertical' split between the conscious and the unconscious mind (Cardena, 1994), and dissociation to be a 'horizontal' splitting of consciousness when the person may alternate between different states of awareness.

Mollon (1996) quotes a description that Freud and Breuer gave of the mental state of Anna O, which clearly demonstrated dissociation rather than repression, that is, the appearance of 'two personalities' in the patient. However, for Breuer and Freud (1893–5) trauma was repressed and therefore forgotten. For Janet (1907) trauma was dissociated and therefore forgotten. The psychological interventions of Freud involved bringing repressed contents from the unconscious into the conscious. Janet on the other hand was intent on getting rid of the 'fixed ideas' through helping the patient to associate them with other ideas, and thus assimilate the information. This would appear to be a different process, and apparently more consonant with modern theories and practice of information processing (Mollon, 1996).

Breuer did not fail to recognise a kind of 'detachment' (dissociation) in response to trauma, when he observed that emotional shock in a traumatised person appeared to produce this state of 'hypnotism', a state of mind which feels empty or vacant.

Freud also observed what he called 'splitting'. His concept of repression was a defence mechanism whereby mental contents were excluded from consciousness, but he later developed a new concept of 'splitting' in addition to repression. Splitting was seen as a splitting of the personality, so that there were two minds or more within the same person. Freud commented that some of his patients, after recovery, stated that during their illness they felt there was another normal person inside them, like a detached spectator. He developed this concept of splitting from Janet's theory of dissociation. It was seen by him as a splitting of the ego so that two different attitudes may persist side by side throughout the person's life (Freud, 1933/1964).

Klein and Fairbairn more recently have retained the term 'splitting' and considered it a major defence as well as an organising principle of the normal mind. They also distinguish it from repression (Klein, 1952/1975). Repression does not result in a disintegration of the self, whereas splitting creates parallel units of experience not integrated. What is split off does not go underground, but moves sideways and by projection it may be seen as someone else. Splitting alters the object and the self (Tarnopolsky, 2003). Freud considered the personality to be divided into the conscious, preconscious and unconscious, or the id, ego and superego. In his opinion the secondary 'splitting' resulted in severe pathology.

Fairbairn on the other hand believed there were multiple egos originating from our experiences (both positive and negative). These splittings were the result of inevitable failures and frustrations in one's early upbringing. This is reminiscent of the Ego-state theory of Watkins and Watkins (1997). However, Fairbairn links the mechanisms of both splitting and repression in the face of trauma. For example, the child who is rebuffed, frustrated or abused introjects all that is bad into the ego. Then the child splits them up within the ego, and then represses the whole process. In this way part of the ego remains free, but is restricted by the unconscious burden of what has been introjected but not seen. These introjected experiences undermine the personality from within (Fairbairn, 1952). He refers to this as the 'internal saboteur'. In this case the Superego is seen as secondary, and not as funda-mental as the introjected bad object.

In order to survive, the child has to retain a connection with the parent, even if that parent is the abuser. For this reason the child internalises the bad experiences, and feels bad inside, rather than casting the blame on to the parent. This is also accepted by contemporary trauma specialists. Para-doxically, once this internalisation is established, the child begins a re-projection of the bad object into external figures. An external abuser is found in order to relieve the internal persecution. Fairbairn believed this phenom-enon explained the retraumatisation of many survivors, who repeatedly chose bad partners. The child, however, cannot do without the parent, so does not reject them, but attempts to control them. The concept of projective identification has continued to the present day by Feldman (1994). The concept of splitting, or dissociation has thus been incorporated into modern psychoanalytic theory.

Different kinds of repression have been outlined by Jones (1993). Freud's 'primary repression' refers to inaccessibility of experiences not linked to verbal representations (preverbal repression). Post verbal infantile repres-sion may occur when the child has reached the age of language, but cannot understand an experience, and cannot find words for it, as when a child suffers sexual abuse. This is not to say that repression may not also occur in children traumatised during a preverbal age.

Jones also refers to state-dependent repression, which is the same as state-dependent learning mentioned earlier, and considered by some to be disso-ciation. One might also question whether state-dependent learning should fall into the category of repression; if an event which occurred in a height-ened state of arousal cannot be recalled in a normal calm state of mind, but can be recalled if the highly aroused state is recreated, then is this really repressed material that is recalled?

Repression proper occurs when events or feelings etc. which were once in conscious awareness and had verbal representation came to be excluded from consciousness. This can be due to a conscious deliberate attempt not to think about it or it can be an automatic process. Conditioned repression occurs also when a thought is avoided because it is associated with pain or shame or guilt.

Perhaps all of these occurrences would fit Freud's view of repression, namely that it was a way of rejecting and keeping something out of consciousness. As yet we do not seem to know enough to be clear on this point and it is probably wiser to consider the different possibilities underlying these psychological phenomena. Mollon (1998) has usefully identified five main differences between dissociation and repression. Firstly, he considers dissociation involves an alteration in consciousness (not so in repression). Secondly, dissociation involves a splitting of consciousness but repression involves 'splitting of the mind'. Presumably he is referring here to the division between the conscious and the unconscious, or the 'vertical split'. This, however, is yet to be scientifically established, and relates to his third point that dissociation is directly observable, but the phenomenon of repression can only be inferred. Certainly in the case of recovery of memories of child sexual abuse, one infers that the memories had been repressed. As stated above, this has also been referred to as 'dissociative amnesia'. Fourthly, Mollon (1998) points out that dissociation commonly occurs in response to exogenous trauma, whereas repression occurs more as a result of internal conflicts. Fifthly, repression often gives rise to neurotic symptoms, but cannot in itself be considered a symptom; dissociation on the other hand may be a symptom as well as a defence.

This 'either-or' phenomena may not be exactly true. Although Freud considered repression as a completely unconscious mechanism, more recent research (Erdelyi 1996) suggests that there may be a conscious deliberate process of suppression which may then lead to repression or may be the same process. Erdelyi considers repression is a matter of deliberately *not* thinking about something and thinking about something else. This diminishes the presence of the avoided topic in consciousness. Conversely, deliberately focusing on a topic and bringing it continually to mind may strengthen the memory of it (hypermnesia). Erdelyi believes that suppression and repression are the same and calls it 'not thinking' which would include cognitive avoidance, selective inattention and inhibition. Not thinking about an event in this way might lead to amnesia, as a result of memories for events being 'degraded' through deliberate suppression/repression of this nature. Erdelyi also considers that 'degraded' memories may become distorted due to the person's attempts to reconstruct the memory according to intellectual or emotional needs.

All memory is in fact reconstructive, as stated in Chapter 1, but degraded memories could be particularly subject to distractions of a defensive kind such as projection, displacement and rationalisation. Reconstructive memories of abuse could not be seen as false memories in some instances, though they may be traumatic memories which have been considerably distorted. Another factor which confounds the issue is post-event information. This could be of two kinds according to Mollon (1996). Following the experience of an abusive event, a child might be forced by the abuser to pretend it never happened, and the abuser himself may show behaviour which conveys denial that the event ever happened. Secondly the child might think about it and deliberately choose to pretend it had not happened. This latter is what Mollon calls an endogenous suggestion.

Whether or not these factors explain what happens when memories of abuse have been 'forgotten', only to be recovered later in life, we are not sure. Similarly we do not know whether the memories are repressed or dissociated. However, Pope and Brown (1996) are in favour of discarding the term repression as it seems to present confusion and controversy in some scientific circles. They make the point that there is a long history of the term 'repression', and professional and popular meanings have emerged over time. The word 'repressed' is often used in place of the word 'forget', and professionals are faced with the possible mechanism of repression and the phenomenon of dissociative amnesia. Pope and Brown (1996) also consider that repression may represent other cognitive processes.

The present concern is the nature of the defence mechanism involved, and whether these might have diagnostic and therapeutic implications in survivors of child abuse. There is a need to have systematic clinical studies of 'repressive' phenomena, and experimental studies of inhibitory processes in memory which would provide more understanding of the clinical picture (Brewin & Andrews, 1997).

In a report published by the International Society for Traumatic Stress Studies (1998) entitled *Childhood Trauma Remembered*, seven unproven mechanisms by which traumatic memories may be forgotten are used (see Figure 3.1). This list contains both 'repression' and 'dissociation', and other mechanisms (mentioned already in this chapter), which researchers have variously subsumed under the headings of 'repression' and/or 'dissociation', in particular state-dependent learning and conditioned extinction. The point is well made in this report that there is no consensus regarding *how* 'forgotten' memories can later be 'recovered'.

Childhood abuse or trauma can elicit dissociation in a variety of ways as well as repression and any of the other mechanisms mentioned above.

In conclusion, the two main defence mechanisms, dissociation and repression with particular relevance to adult survivors of child abuse may be summarised as follows.

Dissociation is a process by which some traumatic experience, because it is too over-stimulating or overwhelming to be processed or repressed along the usual channels, is cordoned off, and established as a separate psychic state within the personality, creating two or more ego-states that alternate in consciousness. In different internal and external contexts, it may emerge to cause the individual to think, behave, remember and feel differently according to the context. Survivors often dissociate in this kind of way. They may also repress or suppress what has happened to them. They get on with their lives, only to have a trigger later in life to bring back the memories to consciousness. When they recover memories, they usually get symptoms of post-traumatic stress disorder.

- *Failure to encode:* A failure to create a memory at the time of the event.

- *Dissociation:* An altered cognitive state which sometimes occurs during a traumatic event, and which may interfere with the normal process for remembering (encoding, consolidation or retrieval) of such events.

- *Simple forgetting:* The fading of a memory over time (a normal phenomenon with non-traumatic memories).

- *Repression:* A theoretical psychological process hypothesised to actively prevent conscious retrieval of memories.

- *Conditioned extinction:* A laboratory phenomenon by which certain conditions can activate inhibition (or reduce the availability of previously learned behaviour).

- *State-dependent learning:* A mechanism that would explain why traumatic memories can be retrieved only when the individual is in the same emotional, environmental and neurobiological state that was present during the original traumatic event.

- *Long-term depression:* A cellular mechanism which suppresses the transmission of data from certain nerve cells to alters; this could theoretically impair the retrieval of previously accessible information.

Figure 3.1 Seven unproven mechanisms by which traumatic memories may be forgotten. *Source*: International Society for Traumatic Stress Studies (1998).

Repression is an active process by which the ego attains mastery over conflictual material. This brings about the forgetting of once familiar mental contents, whereas dissociation leads to the severing of the connection between one set of mental contents and another (Davies & Frawley, 1994). The total loss of memory for what happened in their childhood, in the case of adult survivors, may be due to the active process of repression, or it may be due to a dissociative process. More research is needed to provide the answer.

Long-Term Effects of Childhood Abuse: Various Responses and Dissociation

Before embarking on the clinical presentations of adult survivors of childhood abuse, two important issues need to be addressed. Firstly, one needs to understand what healthy development of the child and parenting involves. Secondly, one needs to know what constitutes abuse of the child. Wolfe (1999) has outlined the determinants of a healthy parent–child relationship, which includes adequate knowledge of child development including normal sexual development and experimentation: adequate skill in coping with stress related to caring for small children and ways to enhance development through stimulation and attention; making opportunities to develop normal parent–child attachment (more will be discussed on this topic later); adequate parental knowledge of home management including financial planning, meal planning and proper shelter; and to provide for necessary social and health services.

Child abuse has been classified into four major types according to the National Incidence Studies (NIS) which was conducted by the US Department of Health and Human Services in 1980, 1986 and 1993. The estimates are derived from official reports of abuse and neglect, as well as professionals who have come into contact with abused or maltreated children (Wolfe, 1999). The four categories are physical abuse, child neglect, sexual abuse and emotional abuse (or psychological abuse).

Physical abuse is the infliction of physical injury often by punching, beating, kicking, biting, burning, shaking or otherwise harming a child. The abuse can often be the result of an attempt by the parent to control the child. In addition to the physical scars, the child's psychological development is also damaged, as seen by their tendency to be disruptive and aggressive, and to have emotional and cognitive problems. *Neglect* of a child can be either physical or emotional or both. Physical neglect can involve failure to seek healthcare, abandonment, expulsion from the home and refusal to allow a runaway to return home. There may be educational neglect too, such as allowing truancy and failure to enrol the child in school when of an appropriate age. Emotional neglect means inattention to the child's need for affection, and failure to provide needed psychological care. There may be spousal abuse and stimulation to the extent, and in the manner for that culture. The child who is neglected may have physical health problems, limited growth and maybe other health conditions such as diabetes or allergies. Patterns of behaviour can include either extreme passivity or being undisciplined. Neglected children tend not to persist, and have poor impulse control, and are very dependent upon their teachers for support. If they witness domestic violence they become fearful and distressed and show somatic signs of distress, such as sleep problems, bed-wetting, headaches, stomach pains, diarrhoea and ulcers. Later they may become aggressive themselves with peers and partners, and experience low self-esteem.

Sexual abuse can involve fondling a child's genitals, intercourse which may be incestuous, rape, sodomy, exhibitionism and commercial exploitation through prostitution and all forms of inappropriate sexualised contact with a child including non-tactile contact. The development of the sexually abused child can be very seriously affected especially when it has been of long duration, and has involved the use of force and penetration, and or has been perpetrated by someone in a close relationship to the child. The physical health of the sexually abused child may suffer, for example with gynaecological problems, sexually transmitted diseases and urinary tract problems. The reactions of children to sexual abuse are affected by the nature of the assault, the age of the child when abused, the duration of the abuse, and the child's relationship to the abuser, and the responses of other close adults, such as the mother. The acute symptoms of stress include fears, anger, depression, fatigue, passivity and poor concentration. Younger children may become enuretic and have sleep problems. Sexually abused children may show sexualised behaviour such as drug use, delinquency, promiscuity or self-destructive behaviours. Their school performance is likely to suffer, and an effect on their peer relations can be expected. Unlike other forms of abuse, it is not related to parental failure to attend to developmental needs. Sexual abuse involves secrecy; it implies a breach of trust in a relationship with another, who has more power, and on whom the child is dependent. It involves intrusion and exploitation of the child's innocence.

Emotional abuse or psychological abuse refers to significant verbal threats, undermining the child's confidence and self-respect with verbal statements, and scapegoating and belittling them. There may be forms of punishment which terrify the child, or the child might be significantly rejected, isolated, corrupted or exploited. Emotional abuse is inevitably also part of all the other forms of abuse and rarely exists by itself.

Not all these forms of abuse have the same consequences in later childhood and adulthood. One person may suffer several different forms of abuse in childhood; and some symptoms such as dissociation appear as a consequence of several forms of abuse. The causes of the various types of abusive behaviour are varied although there may be certain common causes such as lack of parental bonding. Most of the studies of adult survivors were initially concerning a history of child sexual abuse, and as a result more theories have developed on this form of abuse than the other forms of abuse.

Physical abuse and neglect both physical and emotional can be addressed separately since the causes are mostly different from child sexual abuse (CSA) and they also do not involve the same factors as CSA, such as betrayal and exploitation. In cases of child physical abuse, there are factors relating to the family and the community in which they live as well as shortcomings in the parenting. Abusive parents lack skills and resources to cope with child-rearing and life stresses. The child's misbehaviour can then lead to more parental stress and more abusive behaviour from the parent in an attempt to gain some control over the child. Parental rejection and lack of affection ensues. Widom (1989) found that child abusers often had a history of child abuse themselves, and that this was a significant risk factor. Widom (1993) also found that substance abuse was common in parents who physically abused and neglected their children.

The families of physically abused children tend to interact and communicate less than other non-abusive families. The parents often report depression and low self-efficacy. They do not rely on positive teaching methods, and consider that the child deserves punishment, rationalising their way of maintaining control. They have disinhibition of aggression, and limited interpersonal skills (Wolfe, 1999). The emotional arousal of anger interferes with problem solving. This arousal may also trigger memories of their own parent's abuse, and previous conflicts with their child. Thus there are overgeneralised anger responses on the part of the parent. No evidence has been found of any specific psychiatric disorder, but a number of social and family problems are related to this pattern of behaviour, such as poverty, alcoholism, family chaos and household crowding, and social isolation. Marital conflict in the parents, and domestic violence seem to be related to violence towards the child as well. Abused women may also be less capable of responding to children's needs, and this increases the pressure on the family.

The social isolation of an abusive family is largely due to lack of adequate daycare for the child, few or no peer groups, no close friends, and no good housing. It may also be a product of poor communication. Lack of economic and family resources, residential instability and neighbourhood poverty influence the rate of child abuse more than any individual or family factor alone according to Coulton, Korbin, Su & Chow (1995). The parents' total acceptance of corporal punishment rather than learning less coercive methods of discipline must also be a major factor.

There may also be a link between Attention Deficit Hyperactive Disorder (ADHD) and child physical abuse. The child's behaviour may play a role in escalating the abuse, but it is more likely that the adult's inadequacy preceded it. There is no evidence that ADHD evokes punitive poverty.

Wolfe (1999) has a transitional model of physical child abuse. Stage one starts with poor child-rearing preparation, and a low sense of control and predictability together with stressful life events. In stage two, a conditional emotional arousal to the child's behaviour has been established, and there are multiple sources of anger and aggression, and a belief that the child's behaviour is threatening. This can cause increased pressure on the parent–child relationship, and an increase in the physical abuse. There is a habitual pattern of aggression and arousal, as the parent sees the ineffectiveness of their efforts. Stage three shows a chronic pattern of anger and abuse. There is repetition of provocative stimuli and an escalation of the parent's response, so stressful events become commonplace. There are feelings of helplessness and hopelessness in the parent who believes that increasing the intensity of the punishment is the only way to gain control and the child increases problem behaviour.

Consequences of physical abuse and neglect

Abuse and neglect disrupt the development of the child. Early mother–child bonding and attachment is crucial to the child's ability to learn to regulate emotions. Emotions serve as an internal monitoring and guidance systems to appraise events, and thereby help the child to understand their world. The abused child cannot learn to regulate the intensity of his emotions, as the child is in a world of emotional turmoil. This poor emotion regulation leads to difficulty interpreting the emotions and behaviours of others, and this in turn leads to limited ability to learn basic relationship skills. The dysregulation of emotions and lack of a secure attachment will be further addressed in a later section of this chapter on theories.

With regard to the ultimate consequences of this lack of social awareness in the physically abused child, there are problems with peer acceptance and a lack of empathy and understanding of the distress of others. In fact the child finally reacts in a similar way to the abusive parent with fear, aggression or anger. The child tends to attribute hostile intent to others, and thus they are often rejected by their peers. They do not blame their parents for their abuse but rather external events which provoked it. Herman (1992) considers that this interpretation of the abuse might be a way of trying to preserve the attachment to the parent. Minimisation, rationalisation, suppression of thoughts, denial and dissociation all absolve the abuser of responsibility. In addition to the social and relationship problems, the abused child has cognitive impairments. With the lack of language stimulation, and little encouragement to learn, their academic success has been undermined. Perez and Widom (1994) found that child abuse not only leads to intellectual under-achievement, but it becomes longterm. It has also been found that non-physically abused siblings showed the same deficit which suggests that it may have been the result of neglect rather than violence.

Abused children have many problems with their social behaviours, due to poor self-control, distractability, negative emotions and low enthusiasm. They are resistant to any directions (Wolfe, 1999). They also are difficult to manage and not very capable of building up trust. They do not relate well to peers and are often rejected by them. They are hostile to both peers and teachers, and have learned aggressive behaviour as a way of resolving interpersonal conflicts. Victims of violence often become perpetrators of violence (Widom, 1989). This cycle of violence can lead to mood disorders and antisocial behaviour. In a study by Flisher et al. (1997), 24% of youngsters with a history of physical abuse had mood disorders and depression; 31% had ADHD; over 55% had anxiety disorder, agoraphobia and generalised anxiety disorder.

Physical, emotional and sexual abuse all lead to depression, emotional distress, rejection, loss of affection, low self-esteem and hopelessness (Kaufman, 1991; Koverola, Pound, Heger & Lytle, 1993; Toth, Manly & Cicchetti, 1992). Depression is the only factor differentiating the abused from the neglected children. Low self-esteem and depression result from harsh physical and verbal child rearing. Social support is needed from mothers and peers, or it may get worse. There is also the possibility of PTSD. Physical abuse is traumatic, as it unleashes strong emotions. Few studies have looked at the incidence of PTSD in the physically abused. The traumatic impact may emerge later in life. In one study of 1200 maltreated children, 33% met the criteria for current PTSD. Child physical abuse has been linked to police arrest as a juvenile or as an adult (Widom, 1989). It has also been linked to sexual and physical violence as an adult, particularly males (Feldman, 1997). Child neglect can also lead to violence. Child physical abuse together with neglect in females is more likely to lead to violent acts. These are not inevitable consequences. The availability of a caring adult could prevent them. Some survivors have led productive lives, while others have been fraught with serious psychological distress.

Emotional or psychological abuse

This represents the core issue in the study of maltreatment. What do abuse events signify to the developing child and how does this affect the emotional and psychological growth? Starr and Wolfe (1991) maintain that psychological abuse is the critical aspect in the overwhelming majority of what appear as physical and sexual maltreatment cases. Some parents use withdrawal of love or threats of abandonment to induce guilt. Others may use humiliation and attacks on self-esteem, so the child feels restricted, over-controlled and unable to enjoy life. There is a lack of responsivity, warmth and acceptance. Extreme overprotection may also prevent the child from leading a fulfilling life. The exploitation of the child in cases of sexual abuse may prevent the child from experiencing childhood. Mothers who have low expectations of their own efficacy to control a child often display a condescending and unconvincing pattern of positive feelings towards the child, and the behaviour actually suggests powerlessness. This gives conflicting messages and confuses the child. This results in lack of responsiveness and non-compliance on the part of the child. Low expectation of self on the part of the mother is likely to lead to her kicking or beating. Conflicting messages given to the child may also be labelled 'double-bind' communication which has been considered as another source of psychological abuse.

Psychological abuse has often been a component of physical abuse, as it includes rejecting, isolating, terrorising, ignoring and corrupting all which can be seen in some scenarios of physical abuse. It has been suggested that it is the psychological element of physical abuse which is responsible for the negative sequelae seen in physical abuse cases, such as depression and low self-esteem (Zelikovsky & Lynn, 1994). These same authors carried out a study of comparison between three groups of college students: (1) those who reported childhood physical and psychological abuse; (2) those who reported psychological abuse only; and (3) those who reported neither forms of abuse (Zelikovsky & Lynn, 2002). They used a variety of measures of symptoms, questionnaires and clinical interviews to establish psychopathology, types of abuse, and also dissociative experiences and symptoms.

Those who had histories of combined abuses had received more psychiatric diagnosis than the other two groups. The prevalence of depression was also higher. The survivors of combined abuses had higher levels of dissociation than the group who only had psychological abuse. The more severe the abuse, it would seem, the greater likelihood of dissociative symptoms. This would support the idea of Bernstein and Putnam (1986) that abusive experiences are on a continuum. The authors Zelikovsky and Lynn (2002) make a distinction between dissociative symptoms and dissociative experiences. The dissociative symptoms which are pathological were more prevalent in the cases of combined abuses, whereas dissociative experiences were endorsed more in the psychological abuse only group. This latter group had also suffered major depression and had increased lifetime vulnerability to psychopathology when compared with those who had never been abused. The authors concluded that the effects of psychological abuse may be mediated by many variables including severity, the specific nature of the psychological abuse, and whether or not it is combined with physical abuse.

The Outcome of Child Abuse

A link has been found between the degree of violence shown in a delinquent offence and the degree of violence the perpetrator suffered. However, child abuse alone is not a predictor of violence as 40% of delinquent violence is accounted for by paranoid symptoms and neurological deficits (Lewis, Shanock, Pincus & Glaser, 1979). However, maltreatment in general can be a determinant of delinquency; Garbarino (1981) points out that abuse and neglect deprives a child of social relations that are normal. The child becomes isolated and is overly influenced by peer pressure to engage in delinquent acts. Those who also suffer neglect may probably come from an upbringing in poverty, and suffer the frustration of living in deprived conditions. Poverty is often linked to violence in this way (Crittenden, 1983; Straus et al., 1980).

More studies have been done on the sequelae of child sexual abuse than either child physical abuse or neglect. The long-term effects of child sexual abuse will be covered in the next subsection. It seems that CSA has a major influence on psychological functioning, even when the effects of other variables are controlled.

Most of the long-term effects of child abuse can be understood in the framework of developmental psychopathology. Abuse itself is but one of many types of disturbance in the interactions between the parents, the child and the environment. Burgess and Youngblade (1988) emphasised the development of coercive cycles of family interactions which are indications of the inability of parents to raise children competently. However, there are factors which can operate to protect the abused child. These may include the presence of a nurturing person who can give love and affection, and the way the child perceives the abuse, perhaps in believing the causes were beyond the parent's control. Social support at the time of victimisation is also important. Those who are successful in breaking the abusive cycle are likely to have had a non-abusive adult during childhood; to have had psychotherapy and a supportive relative.

Parents who were survivors of child abuse, and who managed to break the cycle of violence had greater social resources, supportive friends and were in social groups in the community. They also used agency services (Starr & Wolfe, 1991) and were in touch with their emotions relating to their abusive childhood and able to discuss their childhood experiences. Starr and Wolfe (1991) stress the importance of more longitudinal studies on adult sequelae of child maltreatment. Much attention has recently been paid to the developmental effects on the children which inevitably impacts on adjustment of the adult; and attachment theory which applies to survivors of all the forms of abuse. The sense of self and emotional expression stems from important early experiences with significant adults. Multiple interactions between the child and the caregiver shape the development of the child. There has been a move away from a more static psychopathological model of abuse. A process model emphasises the developmental model of parenting (Starr & Wolfe, 1991). The formation of a good parent–child relationship is built on consistent parental responses to the child's behaviour (see later section on Theories).

Of equal importance are the child's attributions regarding parental behaviour. If the child interprets victimisation as their own failure, they may feel helpless. If they attribute blame to the parent, their future adjustment will be worse than if they had blamed external events. A perception of control over the parent's behaviour in whatever way, even acting out, may mediate adjustment. Factors such as severity, chronicity and frequency also have to be considered in the study of attributions. With severity of abuse, attributions of blame to the perpetrator increase (Herzberger et al., 1981). Starr and Wolfe (1991) have criticised the categorisation of different forms of abuse, and the making of arbitary distinctions. This often ignores the co-occurrence of different forms of abuse and the severity.

It is evident from the research on the long-term effect of child abuse, that there is no one psychiatric condition that emerges, which one could satisfactorily label as an 'abuse syndrome' (Wenninger and Heiman 1998). In the case of survivors of child sexual abuse, many psychological disorders are manifest, but they may not be solely the result of the sexual abuse, but also the dysfunctional family, which can be the context in which the child abuse occurs. Although most of the research on long-term effects of child abuse has mainly been carried out on survivors of CSA, some of the findings and diagnoses would also be applicable to survivors of other forms of abuse, particularly in cases of combined abuses. The main disorders identified in CSA survivors are post-traumatic stress disorder, clinical depression, anxiety disorders, eating disorders (all of which can be found in survivors of other forms of abuse). Borderline personality disorders, histrionic personality disorder and Dissociative Identity Disorders are also common in survivors of CSA. There may also be dual diagnoses. Problem areas may include self-destructive behaviours, self-mutilation, substance abuse, relationship problems and psychosexual dysfunctions. These different diagnoses manifest a variety of dissociative symptoms and may be considered under the 'umbrella' heading of complex PTSD. A brief overview of some of these clinical presentations and related theories can be useful to understand this client group and to consider appropriate therapeutic interventions.

Complex Post-Traumatic Stress Disorder

There would appear to be a large proportion of survivors of CSA and some CPA who suffer symptoms of PTSD (Carlson et al., 1998). Both Carlson et al. (1998) and Finkelhor (1987) have examined the PTSD model in relation to child sexual abuse and given it credence in understanding many of the long-term sequelae of CSA. Carlson et al. (1998) differentiate between traumatic and non-traumatic abuse, the former involving physical danger and extreme emotional pain and the later involving a gradual progression from touching and fondling to more invasive behaviour by the abuser over a period of years. In the case of traumatic abuse, the child develops an expectation of danger and uncontrollability.

Even after escaping from an abusive environment, the child may still interpret neutral cues as threatening and develop avoidant behaviours. The core symptoms of PTSD and secondary symptoms arising from these are often evident. The intrusive mental activity or re-experiencing of the traumatic memories can be seen in the nightmares and increased levels of anxiety and anger. Behavioural re-experiencing may take the form of aggression towards others or self-mutilation and re-enactment (Smith & Bentovim, 1994). Horowitz (1991) has suggested that behaving like the aggressor may be a way of warding off the assault, and gaining mastery over a painful experience.

Avoidance and escape behaviours in PTSD are ways of protecting the individual from reminders of the traumatic event. Dissociation and/or cognitive avoidance is manifest in partial or total amnesia, depersonalisation and derealisation. Behavioural avoidance can be seen in being absent from home or running away from it. Emotional avoidance can sometimes be so great as to produce feelings of disconnection and detachment which can of themselves be very disturbing for the individual (Herman, 1992). This can be another reason for self-harming behaviours, i.e. an attempt to bring back feelings and stop the dissociative state. On the other hand some survivors of CSA will report that self-harm is a way of reducing the pain of flashbacks or re-experiencing of the trauma. It introduces an alternative distracting pain. It is also possible that the physical self-injury causes the release of endorphins which then has a sedative effect. Thus re-experiencing can alternate with avoidance in many ways and the clinician's task of discovering the true basis of each behaviour can be complex.

Secondary responses to these core responses of PTSD in survivors of CSA are depression, aggression to others or self, low self-esteem, disturbances in identity, guilt, shame and impaired interpersonal relationships. Depression can be the result of feeling out of control of one's environment; aggression may be in lieu of trauma-related fears or as a result of social learning and identifying with the abuser. Self-directed aggression can be an attempt to regulate affect as described above. Self-hate and self-disgust can be due to internalisation of the abuser's negative views of the child, and lead to low self-esteem. Carlson et al. (1998) have also considered low self-esteem to arise from the poor academic performance and poor cognitive and social learning which often occurs in abused children. They have difficulties in concentration from being pre-occupied with self-protection. Negative self-evaluation can disrupt the process of modelling and identification with significant others. Anti-social behaviour may also lead to negative feedback from peers, teachers and others. Furthermore, the child's realisation that other children may not have the same abusive experiences can make them feel different or 'special' in a negative sense.

Disturbances in identity and low self-esteem can also stem from the frequent experiences of dissociation. Avoidance of emotional pain through dissociation in the form of forgetting or numbing or depersonalisation can distort the sense of self (Cole & Putnam, 1992). Briere (1996) has also observed that the development of a sense of self is impaired in abused children because of excessive avoidance which impedes normal attachment processes. Re-experiencing and avoidance may lead to disconnection from family and peers as observed by Herman (1992) and this inevitably leads to problems in interpersonal relationships. There may also be no good models for healthy relationships in the child's environment.

Alexander (1992) has underlined the importance of disturbed attachments to caretakers seen in sexually abused children. They may fail to protect the child for a variety of reasons, and often in spite of the best intentions. For example, it is not uncommon for the mother of an abused child to be a survivor of sexual abuse herself and be prone to dissociating in the face of potential threat to herself or her child, thus missing important cues in the child's behaviour and in situations. This clearly affects parenting skills. Most of the clients displaying these symptoms of complex PTSD would acquire the diagnosis of borderline personality disorder. Key features of BPD are unstable interpersonal relationships, identity disturbance, impulsivity, suicidal behaviour, self-harm and affective instability, inappropriate intense anger and stress-related paranoid ideation or severe dissociative symptoms (DSM-IV, American Psychiatric Association). Some clinicians have problems with this diagnostic label and prefer it to be called a syndrome (Bell, 2002) and consider that there are clarifications that are needed regarding this whole list of criteria.

There have also been problems with the complex clinical picture of Dissociative Identity Disorder. As mentioned earlier there are discrete ego-states or alter egos who have different behaviours, different memories, demeanour and vocal characteristics. Each ego state may have amnesia for the alter states. Other dissociative features emerge too, such as periods of depersonalisation and derealisation and identity confusion. They often present with psychosomatic complaints such as gastro-intestinal problems. Somatoform dissociative symptoms are common including analgesia, somatic pain, loss of motor control, alterations in smell, taste and vision (Nijenhuis, 1999). First-rank symptoms of schizophrenia (Schneiderian symptoms) are a common experience of DID clients. They may have hallucinations or feel their body is controlled by an outside agent (Putnam, 1989). The hallucinations are usually perceived in the head rather than externally.

DID has now come to be accepted as a complex post-traumatic stress disorder (Spiegel, 1984), as these clients frequently have the three symptom clusters of PTSD, that is avoidance, re-experiencing and arousal symptoms. Much of the literature suggests that post-traumatic aspects of DID stem from childhood abuse and neglect (Coons, 1994; Martinez-Taboas, 1991; Swica, Lewis & Lewis, 1996). In another study, 88.5% of 236 DID clients reported sexual and physical child abuse (Ross, Norton & Wozney, 1989). Putnam et al. (1986) found that 97 out of 100 DID clients reported sexual or physical abuse or witnessing violent death in childhood. Abandonment, extreme poverty, long periods of solitary confinement were also reported. The abuse may be severe, chronic and of early onset (the lower threshold being up to 3½ years old, and the upper threshold about 8–10 years old).

Other important variables are a predisposition to dissociate under stress, a poor familial environment without much emotional support after the trauma, and an insecure attachment to the primary caregiver (Barach, 1991; Kluft, 1993; Tillman, Nash & Lerner, 1994). Borderline personality features are often present in DID, such as self-harm which is usually to relieve psychological pain or dissociative states, or to punish themselves. It is seldom that DID is recognised when the client first enters the mental health service as the client has so many symptoms overlapping with other conditions such as PTSD and BPD (borderline personality disorder). With so many different diagnoses and a history of failed treatments, it is not surprising that some clinicians and false memory advocates fail to recognise DID as a valid condition. In DID it is important to recognise pathological dissociation combined with severe childhood trauma. There is a failure of psychological somatic and sensory integration which cause all these different symptoms. In the early stages of therapy they display a considerable number of dissociative symptoms such as numbing, switching, depersonalisation and trance-like states. The basic cause of this extreme form of dissociation is the impact of the childhood trauma on their psychological development in terms of attachment, intimacy and trust.

Other dissociative disorder clients report severe and multifaceted childhood trauma (Nijenhuis, 2000). Both somatoform dissociation and psychological dissociation were present in a number of clients with dissociative disorders. They were related to early onset of severe, chronic and multiple traumatisation, and this apparently often occurred in an emotionally neglectful and abusive social context. Somatoform dissociation was associated with physical abuse and threat to life, but was also seen in survivors of sexual abuse and sexual harassment. Physical and sexual abuse are a threat to the body and therefore are more likely to cause somatoform dissociation, which Nijenhuis considers to be similar to animal defence reactions in the face of threat, namely freezing and anaesthesia. It is also interesting to note that disturbed eating patterns are among the most characteristic symptoms of dissociative disorders and are linked with somatoform dissociation and are also seen in animals. It is not uncommon for survivors of abuse, both sexual abuse and physical abuse, to present with eating disorders.

Sexually abused women often have medical, psychological and sexual problems later in life which seem to be related to the abuse. They also engage in self-destructive behaviours such as substance abuse, self-injury, indiscriminate sexual behaviour, and bingeing, purging or self-starvation. Research has shown that there is a positive relationship between CSA and eating disorders (Smolak & Murnen, 2002). It has been hypothesised that body image may have a role in the relationship between CSA and these psychopathological symptoms. Certainly Andrews (1995) found that experiences of body shame were associated with child sexual abuse in a study of 101 women. Wenninger and Heiman (1998) considered that in cases of CSA, behaviours which result in more damage or numb them, such as misusing food, drugs, or self-inflicted pain, may be attempts to cope with a history of pain, misuse and disrespect for the body and their right to take care of it.

There are several theories why there are relationships between CSA, body image and disordered eating. One theory is that CSA survivors in general feel bad about themselves and their bodies, and this may lead them to a desire to be thin which they see as related to both beauty and success, so they can enhance their self-worth. A second theory is that they blame themselves for the abuse of their bodies, and thus resort to self-harming as a form of self-punishment. The eating behaviours can also be seen as a form of self-abuse (Briere, 1992). Sexually abused women may blame the feminine qualities of their bodies for the abuse they received. This blame of the body can lead to body image distortion (Bolen 1993). They may starve to de-feminise the body. A recent study by Williams and Gleaves (2003) found that CSA did not appear to have direct influence on body image, but there was a direct effect of CSA on bulimic behaviour. In their study they also used measures of PTSD and found a fairly large correlation between PTSD and all the eating behaviours. This would suggest that survivors of CSA engage in eating behaviours as a form of self-harm relating to their trauma, rather than their concern over body image.

In a survey of young Asian women who self-harmed (Muntaha 2004), there was a range of self-harming behaviours including cutting, overdoses and eating disorders. They reported experiences of sexual abuse or rape, and physical and emotional abuse from their spouses. The reasons they gave for self-harming were a coping strategy when they had distressing feelings, and to give a sense of control and relief, or a coping strategy to deal with self-loathing, and to prevent them from 'exploding' or 'going crazy', or to punish themselves.

Schwartz and Cohn (1996) consider that eating disorders, which are so often seen in survivors of CSA can be categorised as secondary symptoms of PTSD. Young (1992) has emphasised the importance of a child's sense of body boundaries in the development of a personal identity. Child sexual abuse is a serious violation of body boundaries and body integrity. Purging in the form of self-induced vomiting or laxative abuse may be motivated by a need for self-punishment arising from guilt, shame and low self-esteem, and serve the same purposes as other self-harming acts. According to Rorty and Yager (1996), all boundaries have been violated in child sexual abuse, and a sense of separateness of self and integrity of the psychological and physical is lost. The child and later the adult struggles for boundaries and control. The body has to be under self-control, not invaded, exploited or overwhelmed. Lack of controllability is an essential ingredient of any traumatic experience. In the case of child sexual abuse, there is also the lack of control over one's own body boundaries, and self-starvation, as in anorexia, can facilitate dissociation in this kind of trauma. The child escapes from the pain of the body, which is being violated. In self-starvation the anorexic initially experiences a sense of euphoria due to the release of endorphins, and the pain lessens. Some anorexics have reported 'out of body' experiences, in which the anorexic self is looking down from above at the other 'normal weight' self.

Not only is there a link between eating disorders and dissociation, some researchers have found a correlation between compulsive eating and trauma (Everill & Waller 1995; Lightstone, 2004; Vanderlinden, Vandereycken & Probst, 1995). Hypnotisability is also related to attitudes towards food intake and fear of being overweight (Groth-Marnat & Schumacher, 1990). These authors considered that suggestibility may be a factor in the transmission of shared beliefs in family and culture regarding thinness and attractiveness; but the dissociation aspect of hypnotisability could relate to perceptual distortions of body image. Sanders (1986) studied dissociation in bulimics, and found that a high level of emotion, dissociation and hypnotisability correlated with each other in this particular population. Nijenhuis (1999) found a key correlation between dissociation and particularly somatoform dissociation and eating disorders. Lightstone (2004) considers that somatoform dissociation and eating disorders may be linked to unconscious and unspoken distress.

Compulsive eating and body image disturbances may be symbolic ways of expressing strong emotions. She believes that compulsive eating can also disguise dissociated, dismissed and denied experiences of trauma or abuse. The binge may be triggered by an event or thought that is related to an earlier shaming or traumatic experience. The food medicates the shame or trauma symptoms, and at the same time directs attention to the present eating behaviours helping the client to dismiss or dissociate from the feelings which were the initial triggers. Lightstone also considers that binge/purge/diet cycles can be viewed as traumatic re-enactments, so the shame (particularly in cases of CSA) which was originally triggered by the trauma, gets displaced onto the body and eating behaviour. It is important to uncover such traumatic re-enactments, but it may be a while in therapy before the client will even disclose such abuse. It is equally important to bear in mind that it is not always the cause of eating disorders. Where there is a history of trauma and dissociative symptoms, the therapist should be aware of the role of dissociation in eating disorders and particularly somatoform dissociation.

Most of the literature on child abuse relating to eating disorders has highlighted the prevalence of child sexual abuse among clients with eating disorders with little reference to other kinds of abuse. A recent study by Treuer et al. (2005) tested their hypothesis that physical abuse history was more common in eating disorders than sexual abuse history and that the body image distortions were also greater in those who suffered physical abuse.

This was initially based on the authors' clinical experience and also the fact that both survivors of sexual and physical abuse have poor health outcomes; the latter being the worst. There were 63 eating disordered clients in the study. Four subgroups consisted of (1) anorexia nervosa (restrictive); (2) anorexia nervosa (purging type); (3) bulimia nervosa; and (4) bulimia nervosa with a history of anorexia. No group had less than 10 clients. The prevalence of physical abuse far exceeded that of sexual abuse. Physical abuse cases were 92% of all the clients. These consisted of anorexics of the purging type. There were more severe body image distortions in those who had been physically abused. Laxative abuse was also most frequent in this group. It would seem that physical abuse, laxative abuse and binge/purge subtype of anorexia altogether will present the risk for severe distortion of body image. Whether this would also indicate more dissociation in this group is not known. There would probably be somatoform dissociation in both physical and sexual abuse cases in view of their poor health outcomes.

These attempts to 'escape' from the pain of the body and dissociate often fail badly. Their origins are in the nature of the trauma and can be conceptualised within the model of PTSD. Van der Kolk and Fisler (1994) have highlighted five main areas of disturbance in those suffering from interpersonal trauma in childhood: (1) alterations in regulating affective arousal; (2) dissociation and amnesia; (3) somatisation; (4) characterological changes in the areas of self-perception, perception of others and relationship with the perpetrator; (5) alterations in systems of meaning (p. 147). It is this last area of disturbance which is probably best addressed by models other than the PTSD model.

The trauma responses to child abuse are quite complex and the PTSD model is not totally adequate for understanding all the long-term psychological effects of child abuse. Christo (1997) has observed that PTSD ruminations cease in adult survivors when an experience has been assimilated into an early maladaptive schema. These might include self-denigratory beliefs. Mollon (1998) also comments that PTSD studies provide a good model for amnesia and memory disruption seen in survivors of CSA particularly, but they do not throw light on the coherent narratives which are apparent in some dissociated states. One would expect the memories to be fragmentary. Mollon poses the question whether these coherent memories may derive partly from actual experience and partly from internally generated imagery in the dissociative state. However, this would suggest that the disconnection of explicit or declarative memory and implicit memory of a somato-sensory kind, which is what happens in cases of trauma, may to some extent have been partially reduced by the person themselves transforming the fragmentary memories into a narrative declarative form. However, according to Horowitz (1986) fragmented traumatic memories repeatedly intrude into the ongoing stream of consciousness until the person is able to assimilate the memories and give meaning to them and modify the belief system accordingly.

In view of these anomalies, it is worth looking at some of the alternative models to PTSD, which throw light on other long-term sequelae of CSA, and other forms of defence, most of these models apply to survivors of CSA, but some also apply to other forms of abuse. According to Smith and Bentovim (1994), there are six main areas of long-term effects of CSA:

1. Sexualising effects, such as heightened sexual activity in both child and adult life, a sexually abusive orientation, and possibly confusion over sexual identity.
2. Emotional effects, such as guilt and a sense of responsibility for the abuse, and of powerlessness in relation to the opposite sex.
3. Depressed mood including feelings of helplessness, hopelessness, and low self-esteem.
4. Anxiety effects including intrusive mental activity, hyper-vigilance, phobias, poor mood regulation and relationship problems.
5. Behavioural effects such as conduct disorders, self-harm, eating disorders.
6. Specific effects of sex rings such as feelings of responsibility for being involved.

Some of the categories would be embraced, as primary or secondary symptoms, by the PTSD model of Carlson et al. (1998). However, some of the sexualising effects and some of the behavioural effects need further explanation and understanding which may be provided by other authors (Alexander, 1992; Finkelhor, 1987). Not all survivors suffer PTSD, nor indeed other severe forms of dissociation.

THE MAIN THEORETICAL MODELS OF THE LONG-TERM EFFECTS OF CSA

Terr (1991) has proposed two types of trauma:

- Type 1 trauma is the single traumatic event which occurs in an environment which is otherwise trauma free;
- Type II traumas are those which are ongoing in childhood and involve a variety of defences of denial, repression, dissociation, self-hypnosis, identification with the aggressor and aggression turned against the self, with character changes as a result.

Betrayal Theory (Freyd, 1996)

Freyd developed the betrayal-trauma theory. She postulates that dissociative amnesia or motivated forgetting arises not just from an external trauma but also from an internal mental conflict. In the kind of scenario in which a parent or caregiver is also the abuser, the child cannot afford to detect this betrayal of trust, since this would threaten the dependent relationship with the parent, and thereby also threaten the child's physical and psychological survival. Freyd argues that in this case the perception and memory of the abuse becomes blocked or dissociated in some way. In fact she found that sexual abuse by a trusted caregiver was the kind of abuse which was most likely to produce amnesia. In a more recent study Freyd et al. (2001) suggested the symptom clusters of PTSD could be understood in terms of two factors; life-threat and social betrayal. Life threat can lead to anxiety, hyperarousal and flashbacks. The symptoms of numbness and amnesia can arise from social betrayal, that is, the carer becomes the abuser. Freyd et al. (2001) found that significantly more memory loss was seen in cases of abuse perpetrated by a carer rather than an adult who was not a carer. Denial, forgetting and dissociation were related to both duration of abuse and degree of child's dependency on the abuser.

Finkelhor (1987) has argued for two models to explain the sequelae of child sexual abuse. First he believes that the PTSD model has contributed much to understanding child sexual abuse as a trauma, not totally unique, but sharing dynamics with other traumas. It has also provided a clear description of what many survivors of CSA are suffering from and provides a framework for treatment in a structured way. Lastly it has de-stigmatised victims and enabled them to see their problem as arising from outside and not self-inflicted. However, he considers the PTSD model is not adequate, mainly because its emphasis is on the affective realm, and many symptoms are of a cognitive nature, such as distorted beliefs about the self, sexual misinformation and sexual confusion.

Finkelhor considers the scenario of child sexual abuse occurring without the conditions of danger, threat and violence as described above, an issue also observed by Carlson et al. (1998). In this case, it may only be in retrospect that the survivor realises they were exploited. The abuse may be viewed as a 'relationship' or 'situation' rather than an 'event' or 'events'. He sees the problem as the child being entrapped in a situation rather than experiencing an overwhelming event. There may not be a failure to integrate the sexual abuse experience but an 'over-integration' of the experience, so what is learnt from the abuse is then applied to other situations inappropriately. Finkelhor has postulated four traumagenic dynamics, that is, four experiential events of a child's life of sexual abuse, as follows.

1. Traumatic sexualisation

Sexually abused children are often rewarded by abusers for sexual behaviour inappropriate to their stage of development and thus learn to use sexual behaviour as a way of getting their needs met, and as a way of expressing themselves. Because of the attention they receive, certain parts of the child's body become fetishised. The child may get confused and acquire misconceptions about sexual behaviour and morality because of what the abuser has told them. The child's sexuality may become traumatised because of frightening memories that became associated with sexual activity. Sex abuse is often presented to the child by the abuser as a way of showing love. This can create confusion, which is difficult to disentangle. For one such person, a sexually abused woman who had experienced sodomy and bestiality at the hands of her stepfather and experienced excruciating pain was unable to develop any loving, meaningful relationship because she believed love implied hurt. Betrayal and lack of trust learnt in the past also led her to search endlessly for some person she could depend on, who would not hurt her or 'let her down'. Her extreme dependency and misinterpretation about sex and love thus thwarted every attempt she made. She would endlessly 'test the water' with everyone she met, and always failed in developing trust. Another woman who suffered abuse, neglect and involvement in a pornographic ring believed that sex was dirty, and she dissociated from her sexual feelings. In therapy she slowly got in touch with her sexuality and was keen to develop a loving intimate relationship with her husband. She wanted as an adult to learn that love could also involve sexual intimacy (see Chapter 6). Dissociation and defence mechanisms are clearly intertwined with the learning and the development of the child as suggested by Courtois (1997).

2. Betrayal

The child discovers that the person on whom they were dependent caused harm or disregarded their needs, causing a deep sense of betrayal. This may happen after the early abusive experiences or later in retrospect when the child realises they were tricked into something bad. Feelings of betrayal may also extend towards the mother who is seen as unwilling to believe or protect the child. Anger, hostility, dependency and inability to judge, trust, or see worthiness in others may ensue and also become linked with sexual traumatisation.

3. Stigmatisation

This is another dynamic. Feelings of being evil, worthless or ashamed may stem from derogatory statements made by the abuser to the child, blaming the child for the seduction. On disclosure later in life the adult survivor may be viewed as 'spoiled goods'. Sometimes the child feels they are to blame, as they were targeted by the abuser. Therefore, they think there must be something wrong with them or something terribly different from other children. Low self-esteem, guilt and self-harm may follow from the sense of unworthiness.

4. Powerlessness

The fourth dynamic is the result of the child's wishes being overruled and the child experiencing threat of injury. One essential aspect of this power-lessness is the experience of one's body space being repeatedly invaded. There is a lack of a sense of efficacy and a strong need to gain control. This may result in an attempt to identify with the abuser. There are other ways in which the child may try to gain control and a sense of mastery, such as developing an eating disorder as already discussed.

Attachment Theory

This is probably the most important theory relating to the full understanding of the impact of abuse and neglect on the development of the child and later on the adult. The very early experiences of childhood impact on the development of the whole personality, the sense of self, emotional expression and behaviour. This development is dependent on the relationship between the baby or child and the primary caregiver. Attachment is this biologically based bond between the child and the caregiver. This should provide a safe and firm base for the child to begin to explore their immediate environment. It is a bond of emotional communication between the child and the caregiver in which the latter (usually the mother) gets attuned to the internal states of the child. The mother and child begin to learn by non-verbal cues, such as facial expressions, gestures etc., the moods and feelings of each other. The mother tunes into the child during periods of engagement and then may quickly withdraw, but wait for the child's cues to re-engage. The mother needs to understand the child's mood or state as well as her own, and to modulate the levels of stimulation in the child and herself. It is in this way that the child learns eventually to modulate their own feelings and emotions and also develop a secure attachment or bond with the mother. From this secure base the child is then able to explore the environment without fear.

Theories about abusive and/or neglectful care by the primary caregiver are especially relevant for understanding the consequences of the abuse and neglect of children when it is the primary caregiver or givers who are abusive or neglectful.

The first to research in this area of mother–child relationships was Ainsworth (1985) and Bowlby (1988) and this has been followed by Cole and Putnam (1992); Alexander (1992) and Schore (1994). Schore (2003) has researched the neurology and psychology of this process of the child's development, particularly in relation to the regulation of emotions and behaviour, both in normal development and in the case of child abuse and neglect where the development of the child has been disrupted.

First what happens in normal secure attachment relationships is that there is a dyadic regulation of emotion involving the child and the mother or primary caregiver. The child's developing autonomic nervous system (ANS) begins to be regulated and the child–mother communications imprint the maturing central nervous system and the limbic system which processes emotions, and the ANS which produces somatic effects of emotions. The attachment relationship directly affects the limbic-autonomic circuits in the right hemisphere, which develops before the left hemisphere, and also has a dominant role in the stress response. The primary caregiver's care plays a big part therefore in the child's stress response (Schore, 2003). The right orbitofrontal region is also involved in self-regulation (Schore, 1994). This region is not functional at birth, but as a result of attachment experiences, it begins to mature in the latter part of the first year. In the second year, the child develops further attachments to other carers, and this results in further development of the orbitofrontal region. As described in an earlier chapter, the amygdala processes sensory incoming stimuli and acts like a gateway to the limbic system, where more complex processing of emotions takes place. The orbitoprefrontal region in the right cortex is at the top of the hierarchy, in the social-emotional right brain. It is involved in 'the emotional modulation of experience', as expressed by Mesulam (1998). It is essential in the regulation of aggression.

With this secure attachment, the mother or primary caregiver mostly responds appropriately to the emotional expressions of the child, even when there are periods of separation, when she does not have access. In the case of an abusive or neglectful caregiver, there is no such consistency or predictability; instead the mother or primary caregiver does not interact appropriately with the child, and often induces traumatic states of negative hyperarousal in the child. The child's attachment is insecure and disorganised, and the primary caregiver provides little protection for the child. In fact, rather than assisting the child in modulating the emotions through her interaction, she creates negative emotions in the child which increase in intensity, frequency and duration. The sympathetic branch of the autonomic nervous system (ANS) of the child is then highly activated. Inevitably the stress hormones in the brain, adrenaline, noradrenaline and dopamine are elevated and the child is in a state of fear and terror.

As a result of this traumatic scenario, the child dissociates and disengages from the external world. This can be seen from the child's lack of postural control, withdrawal and absence of self-comfort. The facial expression becomes fixed as if frozen; there is avoidance of eye contact, and an absence of any relationship with others. Physiological correlates of this state of pain numbing are decreased blood pressure, metabolic activity and heart rate, indicating parasympathetic arousal as a survival mechanism (Schore, 2001). The outcome of this disorganised/disorientated insecure attachment is often hostile and aggressive behaviour in the child. As the child is alarmed by the parent, they cannot approach or flee or shift attention. They show apprehension and confusion as well as behavioural freezing. They are known to have very low stress tolerance and an inability to develop coping strategies to deal with interactive stress.

The mother's aggressive expressions and the changes in the child's bodily state, with dissociative defences related to it, are all retained in the child's limbic system. They are stored in implicit memory in the right hemisphere which is involved in autonomic conditioning of aggressive expressions, and the physiological and cognitive components of emotional processing (Schore, 2003). Not only does the child dissociate, but the mother may also become alarmed by the child and withdraw. Main and Solomon (1986) commented on the dissociated and trancelike behaviour in the parents of children with disorganised attachments. However, it is the dissociative state of the child which leads to the inability to process information from both the external world (such as the abusive caregiver) and also the internal world which is their chaotic bodily state. This persists into adulthood, and those who have disorganised attachments will show dissociative signs and symptoms later in life. According to Stuss and Alexander (1999), the learning mechanism of attachment is imprinted in the developing right prefrontal circuits, and is retained in long-term implicit memory.

Attachment Patterns and Dissociative Self-States (Ego-states) and Related Diagnoses

Attachment patterns are internal representations about the self and others named 'the working model of the self' and 'the working model of the world' (Bowlby, 1973). They are based on the individual's perception of events and act as a 'working blueprint' for interpreting the behaviour of others. The working models are complex schema consisting of emotional, defensive and cognitive components relating to the self, the attachment figure, and attachment interactions. The working model of others reflects the extent to which the child believes the attachment figure can be relied upon. The working model of the self reflects the extent to which the child believes they are acceptable to the attachment figure. These internalisations of others and the self determine the child's capacity to cope with distress. They have been shown to remain stable throughout the lifespan.

There are four basic attachment patterns: secure; insecure avoidant; insecure anxious/ambivalent; and insecure disorganised (Ainsworth et al., 1978, 1985; Holmes, 1993). With a secure attachment the child feels loved and protected and has had their needs met consistently by the caregiver. If the caregiver has been rejecting and consistently insensitive, the child feels unloved, and sees the caregiver as uncaring. This results in the child forming an avoidant attachment. If, however, the caregiver is unpredictable and may or may not be available for the child, then the latter feels very uncertain about themselves, and may sometimes become angry, or more often shows signs of distress and is pre-occupied with soothing the caregiver. In this case the child has an anxious/ambivalent attachment pattern. In both these insecure attachments, the child tries to avoid emotional pain and a negative view of self by adopting two defensive processes; deactivation and disconnection.

In the case of deactivation there is an attempt to exclude the information from consciousness either cognitively or behaviourally by turning away or by failing to recall it. In the case of disconnection, painful information is cognitively disconnected from awareness and the child focuses on soothing the caregiver. The child may then be unaware of the reason for their behaviour and feelings. Deactivation is seen more in avoidant attachment, as the child focuses on the environment and not the attachment figure. If the child has an anxious/ambivalent attachment pattern, they are more likely to disconnect the painful experiences of inconsistency and continue to follow the caregiver. If, however, the attachment system is continually activated in this way, and the child has no satisfaction and is rejected and punished for attachment seeking, then the child has to prevent cognitive, emotional and behavioural breakdown. This may result in the child setting up separate systems which enable them to exclude attachment information from consciousness, and form multiple representations of self and others which are incompatible and difficult to integrate. This becomes disorganised attachment. Disorganised attachment develops when the caregiver frightens the child, and the latter can neither flee nor approach the caregiver, nor shift attention onto the environment. The child then freezes, or alternates between approach and avoidance.

Disorganised representations of attachment prevent important aspects of the self and objects from being integrated, so the self structure becomes fragmented and dissociated. Interactions in the attachment relationships become contradictory and create double binds. This leads to the development of dissociated self-states or ego-states. Attachment theory plays an important part in understanding the development of such dissociative psychic structure in survivors of child abuse and maltreatment (Blizard, 2003). Blizard maintains that while it is accepted that trauma causes dissociation, it does not explain the variability of dissociation and the development of dissociated self-states which contain these contradictory models of attachments. Disorganised attachment (or D. attachment) patterns explain how these dissociated self-states emerged. The results of double bind and the D. attachment can be seen in alternating self-states in personality disorders, post-traumatic disorders and dissociative disorders. As stated earlier, in PTSD, which is simple and uncomplicated, two self-states emerge and alternate, the 'apparently normal personality' and the 'emotional personality', that is the 'survivor self' who deals with everyday present practicalities and the 'victim self' experiencing the post-traumatic event (Steele et al., 2001). These self-states will also have attachment patterns which developed (in early childhood) long before the trauma.

With such insecure attachments, dependency increases and becomes more intense. In the case of survivors of child abuse and neglect, their families did not provide support for them and they had insecure dependency as well as insecure attachment (Bowlby, 1988). This can lead to excessive dependency or excessive independency. Those who have anxious/ambivalent and preoccupied attachment patterns usually show excessive dependency, while those with avoidant attachment patterns will become overly independent. Most dissociative clients develop preoccupied or disorganised attachment patterns and exhibit dependency styles which are extreme and contradictory. Their alternating personalities oscillate between excessive dependency and counterdependency (Steel et al., 2001). The clients may be unaware or confused by their dependency needs and behaviours which are dissociated. The relationship between dissociation and variations in insecure dependency is important for the therapist to understand as it impacts on the therapeutic alliance and relationship. Dependency includes emotional, cognitive and behavioural strategies (both conscious and unconscious) to seek a secure attachment and care taken from another until security is attained. Dependency is necessary to maintain individual and social homeostasis.

Steele et al. (2001, 2005) have described the theory of structural dissociation and dependency needs in relation to complex post-traumatic stress and dissociative disorders, and the implications this has for therapy.

Dependency in a traumatised person is usually accompanied by a poor capacity for integration, and an inability to think critically and reflect. Such persons may use the support of a therapist to become more integrated, whereupon the perceived availability of a caregiver activates the attachment systems towards a caretaking person. In addition to this, chronically traumatised individuals have increased activation of a defensive system relating to their survival needs. This dampens the activation of systems relating to practical everyday life adaptation, so they have difficulty with independence and adult functioning, and at the same time need a secure attachment to reduce the feelings of helplessness and fear arising from the past trauma.

Steele et al. (2001, 2005) make it clear that structural dissociation which involves separate self-states namely the 'apparently normal personality' (ANP) and the 'emotional personality' (EP), does not only apply to DID (Dissociative Identity Disorder), but also other post-traumatic conditions, such as PTSD. The EP is the defensive emotional system which is fixated on the trauma, with somatosensory experiences of it, and the EP therefore disorientates to the present. The ANP is directed by an emotional system focused on daily life in the present, including attachment. Its aim is to function adequately as far as possible. In order to do this it is necessary to be detached from the trauma, and amnesic for it, so there is avoidance and emotional numbing. This dissociation of a single EP and a single ANP is termed *primary structural dissociation*, as seen in simple PTSD.

If trauma is prolonged and severe, more fragmentation may result, so there are more defensive subsystems. In this case there may be two or more EPs and one ANP. This is called *secondary structural dissociation* which is found in complex PTSD, or borderline personality disorder and dissociative disorder, not otherwise specified. *Tertiary structural dissociation* can be seen only in DID where there are more fragmented EPs and also fragmented ANPs. The increased dissociation of the ANPs is caused by the extra pressure to manage everyday life, and to avoid the trauma memories which become more and more overwhelming, and decrease the integrative capacity. Patients with DID may also have borderline personality disorder and complex PTSD. The neurological disconnection seen in simple PTSD (see Chapter 2) creating only two dissociative states, one EP and one ANP, would also explain the many dissociative self-states in more complex cases.

The ANP in all cases is related to the attachment pattern to maintain social contact and relationships. In insecure attachments, the ANP will become dependent in ways which would not be seen in secure attachments, namely in creating an intense dependency on the therapist for help in managing overwhelming emotions. This could provide a secure attachment with the therapist. This attachment and dependency would not be seen if the person were under extreme threat, in which case the EPs who are fixed in defensive positions such as fight, flight or freeze, would come out and not be concerned with dependency and attachment. However, if there was a threat of attachment loss and being totally alone, then the EPs might make an attempt to regain safety through caretaking, and make repeated attempts to contact the therapist. When a child is being abused or neglected by an attachment figure, the attachment and defensive systems have to compete. This will trigger structural dissociation, and both systems will involve EPs, while ANPs will only be involved with the attachment system. Most secondary and tertiary dissociative patients have experienced abuse, neglect and disrupted attachment as a very young child. Patterns of insecure attachment develop and particularly disorganised attachment. This latter attachment pattern involves the alternation of defence and attachment emotional systems, that is EPs from both systems and ANPs from the attachment system, and with this intense insecure dependency and a phobia of attachment.

In secondary and perhaps tertiary structural dissociation (Borderline Personality Disorder and Dissociative Identity Disorder), Cole and Putnam (1992) consider that the consequences of incestuous abuse particularly involve disruption in three main areas of self-development:

1. Self-integrity, i.e. disturbances in the sense of self (physical and psychological) which lead to identity confusion and dissociation of aspects of the self.
2. Self-regulation, i.e. poor impulse and mood control including self-destructive symptoms.
3. Social problems, i.e. insecurity in relationships, distrust, lack of intimacy and isolation.

These disruptions are manifest in borderline personality disorders in which there are identity problems, impulsivity, self-mutilation and unstable relationships with a deep-seated fear of abandonment. They have moods swings with alternating idealisation and devaluation in their relationships. All these features arise from a disorganised attachment pattern as described above.

The dissociated self-states are otherwise known as ego-states, as mentioned earlier. The ego-state theory developed by Watkins and Watkins (1997) was the result of research with traumatised patients. Claire Frederick (2005), a specialist in ego-state therapy confirms the fact that cumulative trauma produced by the failure of a caregiving parent to meet the developmental needs of a child, can cause this structural dissociation of several ego-states. She maintains that attachment styles or patterns may vary from one ego-state to another. This inevitably affects the transference and countertransference field in therapy, which reflects this variation, giving the impression of 'spiralling' or 'cycling'. The therapeutic alliance is essential in restoring or establishing secure attachments in ego-states. Developing secure attachments among the ego-states is one of the main aims of ego-state therapy, and is essential for integration (Frederick, 2005).

As mentioned earlier in the chapter, ego-states have boundaries between them, which vary in terms of the degree of dissociation or separateness.

According to Watkins and Watkins (1997), the relationship of one ego-state with another ego-state is on a continuum of separateness vs. closeness, which they called the Differentiation-Dissociation Continuum. When the boundaries become 'thicker than normal' or there is a greater separateness or dissociation, then clinical symptoms may emerge. There may be no control or conscious awareness of the shifting from one ego-state to another, and there is a partial or total amnesia barrier between them. The clinical symptoms may be PTSD, depression, obsessions, panic attacks, sexual identity problems, intractable pain and eating disorders or personality disorders. These ego-states are not differentiated, but dissociated.

Further along the continuum there will be Dissociative Disorders, Somatisation Disorder and Conversion Disorder. At the end of the continuum, where there is extreme separation and dissociation, Dissociative Identity Disorder manifests with 'alters'. Total amnesic barriers exist between all the 'alters', so they have no conscious awareness of each other or control over their emergence. The degree of amnesia and the clinical symptoms are clearly related to the degree of structural dissociation as suggested by Steele et al. (2001), namely primary structural dissociation (PTSD simple) with one EP and one ANP with some conscious awareness of each other; secondary structural dissociation with more than one EP, but only one ANP, seen in borderline personality disorder, eating disorders and complex PTSD, where there are partial amnesic barriers between the ego-states; and lastly, tertiary structural dissociation (DID) with more than one EP, and more than one ANP, where there are total amnesic barriers between the 'alters' or ego-states.

Some Examples of Dissociated Ego-States

The self-states or ego-states discussed so far are usually child states arising from developmental stages in child abuse and neglect and very much linked to the child attachment systems. Mollon (1996) identified four forms of dissociation which include ego-states which may have developed later:

1. Psychotic dissociation: giving up reality in the face of shattered self-esteem.
2. Child and adult parts of the personality.
3. The 'true' self and the 'false' self.
4. Different stages of life dissociated.

Mollon (1996) has described the observed dissociation between the child self and the adult self in those who have been severely traumatised. Sometimes in a session, a client may present as a calm, rational, well-adjusted adult, and later may slip into an emotionally disturbed state and become rather childlike and even disorientated for no apparent reason. In one such case, a client who had survived serious sexual abuse by her grandfather, but did not fulfil the criteria of DID, expressed concern when she recognised some of these shifts. She arrived for a session one day, having first returned from attending an interview for a job. She said she felt as though it was not her at the interview; she was calm, confident, finding all the appropriate answers. However, as she then sat in front of her therapist, she felt sad and helpless, not knowing what to do. This change was so dramatic for her, she wanted an explanation of what had happened. She said 'Which is the true me?' The relatively adult part of her is dissociated from the traumatised child part, and the contextual situation determines which part or ego-state will emerge.

Another client, who had been gang raped and tortured as a child, stated 'when I talk about the sexual abuse of my childhood, I feel as though it happened to someone else' (see case illustration Chapter 6). She knew it happened as she had continuous memory for it and there was corroborative evidence. Mollon maintains that the lack of communication between dissociated states becomes a 'structuring dynamic within the personality'.

Another extreme form of dissociation Mollon considers is psychotic dissociation, where the person has lost contact with reality and the external world, and hears inner voices, but interprets them as being external and real. This has also been seen in survivors of child sexual abuse in particular. Watkins and Watkins (1997) believe that in cases of severe childhood trauma the terrified child has three options: to die; to disintegrate into a psychosis; or to split off a part of the 'self' and turn it into a 'non-self' or object. The ego energies from the abusive experiences are then cathected with object energy and dissociated. In this latter case, Dissociative Identity Disorder manifests in the person. These different identities or 'non-selves' are ego-states which are a part of the person nonetheless. They are childlike and have different memories of past events.

One client who was 35 years old, divorced and with one son and had remarried, reported that she had begun to recover many early memories of childhood sexual abuse when her son reached the age of 12 years. This was the age she was when she first told her mother about an incident involving her uncle. The memories of her earlier abuse returned in a very fragmented way in the form of child ego-states. She reported there was a 4 year old, 6 year old and 12 year old in 'her head'. These 'children' had different emotions: the '12 year old' was very angry (at 12 she had confronted her uncle and disclosed the abuse to her mother); the '4 year old' was frightened; the 'adult', however, felt she was probably not aware of all the 'children' and their ages. While the '12 year old' knew of the '6 year old', the reverse did not hold. 'They' needed to talk about what happened to them, but the adult part of her was reluctant at first to let this happen (much as she felt the need to) for fear of losing control.

It is interesting to note the manner in which the '4 year old' first manifests. She (the adult patient) was in a therapy session and asked the therapist if there was a little girl sitting next to her. The therapist said no, this was not the case. The adult 'self' then expressed concern as she could see the child (about 4 years old) sitting there throughout the session; but there was something about the perception which she felt was not quite real and solid. When she went home after the session she began to wonder if she had hallucinated herself, and started to look up old photographs. She discovered one photo of herself at age 4 wearing the same dress she had hallucinated earlier in the day and which she had forgotten she once wore.

Following this realisation, the 4 year old 'child' was internalised and she only ever communicated with her 'in her own head'. These dissociated child ego-states emerged at inconvenient moments in her life following the recovery of memories of abuse. One example she gave: when she was getting into her car on some occasions, one of the 'children' would 'come out' and she would be quite unable to start the car as she did not know what any of the controls were for. She (the adult self) reported that part of her was aware that she should know what to do. She learnt a way of accessing the older part of herself, by taking a cigarette out of her handbag and smoking it – an action clearly associated more with her adult life. This way she could access the adult self and her memories of how to operate the car came back to her. This seems to be an example of dissociation between implicit memory and explicit memory. The 'child' who 'came out' (implicit memory) had her own agenda while the 'adult' was trying to engage in an everyday experience of a non-traumatic kind (explicit declarative memory). The memories seem different from one ego-state to another and are compartmentalised without communication between the two (see Chapter 6 for a full account). This particular client initially fulfilled the DSM-IV criteria of DID and borderline personality disorder (see Chapter 6).

SUMMARY AND CONCLUSIONS

Dissociation

Dissociation can be understood as a disruption in the normally occurring connection between feelings, thoughts and behaviours (Briere, 1992). Dissociation may result in experiences of detachment from oneself, or from the surroundings or a lack of integration between various mental processes, or various degrees of amnesia (total or partial). It is often a defence mechanism in the face of trauma (Cardena, 1994). There are degrees of dissociation and it may not be solely a response to trauma. Some authors, (Watkins and Watkins, 1997) consider there is a continuum of dissociation. At one end of the continuum one sees the normal development of the child in which he/she learns segregation and differentiation of experiences. This results in separate ego-states, that is, organised systems of behaviour and experience whose elements are bound together by some common principle and which are separated from other such states by a boundary which is more or less permeable (Watkins and Watkins, 1997). At the other end of the continuum one sees the pathological effects of trauma in DID in which ego-states develop which are separated and may not be permeable.

Various authors have considered different kinds of dissociation and different categories of dissociation. Van der Kolk, Pelcovitz et al. (1996) pointed out three categories of dissociation: primary dissociation (somatosensory fragments of trauma memories); secondary dissociation (a separation of the observing ego and the experiencing ego in depersonalisation and derealisation) and tertiary dissociation (as in ego-states). Nijenhuis highlighted the distinction between psychological dissociation and somatoform dissociation. Nijenhuis also supported the emergence of ego-states in the face of trauma and identified the 'apparently normal personality' and the 'emotional personality', and found there may be more than one of each in certain post-traumatic disorders.

More recent research (Holmes et al., 2005) shows that there may also be two distinct types of dissociation, namely 'detachment' and 'compartmentalisation', which are manifested in different symptoms and pathological conditions. Detachment is the label for depersonalisation and derealisation, while compartmentalisation refers to more dramatic phenomena such as dissociative amnesia, fugue states and DID. The conclusion is that dissociation is a 'multifaceted collection of distinct but overlapping dimensions as opposed to a unitary trait' (Briere et al., 2005, p. 228).

Origins of the concept of dissociation

The historical background of dissociation goes back to Pierre Janet, a contemporary of Freud. He recognised that his traumatised patients could only remember parts of the traumatic event, and that some parts of the memory were kept out of conscious awareness by dissociation which he understood to be a defence mechanism. These dissociated parts of memory for the event continued nonetheless to influence the patient's moods and behaviours, and he labelled them 'fixed ideas', since they were not 'lost'.

Repression and dissociation: from Freud and Janet to contemporary views

At the same time, Freud had developed the concept of repression, an unconscious process whereby conflicting impulses are suppressed and kept out of conscious awareness. The defence of repression is an unconscious response to inner threat, unlike dissociation, a response to external threat and danger. Dissociation can be seen as 'horizontal splitting of the mind', whereas repression can be seen as a 'vertical' split or a division of the mind into the conscious and unconscious. Later, however, Breuer and Freud (1893–95) who worked together, recognised a kind of 'detachment' in patients who had been traumatised, producing a kind of 'hypnotism'; a state of mind which seemed empty and vacant. Freud called this 'splitting'. Modern psychoanalysis recognises this splitting and considers it a major defence mechanism (Klein, 1952/1975). Repression is different, as it does not result in disintegration of the self, nor does it involve an alteration in consciousness (Mollon, 1998). Dissociation is also observable but repression is not – it can only be inferred. Repression gives rise to neurotic symptoms, but dissociation is a symptom in itself as well as a defence.

Some researchers believe that suppression and repression involve cognitive processes such as cognitive avoidance, selective attention and inhibition. By not thinking about an event can 'degrade' the memory, and it could be distorted too (Erdelyi, 1996). Pope and Brown (1996) also consider cognitive processes are involved in repression. The processes or factors that may be relevant in the memory disruption seen in survivors of trauma may include a failure to encode, dissociation, simple forgetting, repression, conditioned extinction (certain conditions can activate inhibition), state-dependent learning, long-term depression (International Society for Traumatic Stress Studies, 1998).

The main defences are denial, suppression, repression, splitting and dissociation. The advantages of dissociation are that it needs distance in order to enable the person to survive psychologically: it compartmentalises; it causes discontinuity in experience; it helps the person to maintain, gain or regain control. The body may then handle some of the worst responses.

Long-term Effects of Child Abuse:
Various Responses and Dissociation

Child abuse has been categorised into four main areas: physical abuse; child neglect; sexual abuse; emotional abuse (or psychological abuse) (Wolfe, 1999). Not all forms of abuse have the same consequences and in some cases there are several forms of abuse experienced by the same child. Dissociation is a common factor in the outcomes of various forms of abuse, while lack of adequate parental bonding is often a major contributing feature. The early primary caregiver and child bonding and attachment are crucial to the child's ability to regulate their emotions. The abused child is in emotional turmoil and often lacks a secure attachment whereby they can learn basic relationship skills and self-regulation. As a result, a child abused by a

primary caregiver from an early age is likely to have poor self-control, negative emotions and to find great difficulty in building up trust. Children who
have suffered physical abuse may become aggressive and might become
perpetrators of violence.

Psychological abuse is often a part of physical abuse; it may manifest as
rejecting, isolating, terrorising, ignoring, degrading, exploiting or corrupting the child. Research has shown that those who suffer combined forms of
abuse have more dissociative experiences later in adult life and receive more
psychiatric diagnoses. Child sexual abuse has been found to have a major
influence on psychological functioning too. In terms of the long-term effect
of child abuse, there is no one psychiatric condition that emerges, nor is there
such a label as 'abuse syndrome'. Most of the research on the long-term
effects of child abuse has been carried out on survivors of child sexual abuse,
in whom many psychological disorders are manifest, such as borderline
personality disorders, histrionic disorder and Dissociative Identity Disorder.
They may also have dual diagnoses such as eating disorders, clinical depression, anxiety disorders. Most of these disorders could come under the
heading of complex post-traumatic stress disorder.

There are many dissociative symptoms including self-mutilation and
behavioural re-enactments, and dissociative ego-states, depersonalisation,
trance-like states and numbing. Somatoform dissociation can also be seen,
particularly in survivors of child physical abuse, and/or child sexual abuse,
where there has been a threat to life or the body. Eating disorders where
there is concern over the body and low self-esteem are common in CSA.
Bulimia particularly is common and seems to be another form of self-
harming. CSA can be seen as a serious violation of body boundaries and
body integrity, so a sense of self and integrity of the physical and psychological is lost, and the child and later the adult strives for boundaries and control.
Eating disorders are high in hypnotisability and also in somatoform dissociation. It has recently been found that survivors of physical abuse are also
prone to develop an eating disorder, most commonly purging anorexia, and
have severe body image distortions (Treuer et al., 2005).

The main areas of disturbance in complex PTSD are: (1) alterations in
regulating affective arousal; (2) dissociation and amnesia; (3) somatisation;
(4) characterological changes in areas of self-perception of others and relationship with the perpetrator; (5) alterations in systems of meaning (Van der
Kolk & Fisler, 1994, p. 147).

The Main Theoretical Models of the Long-Term Effects of CSA

Most of the theories based on the consequences of child abuse refer mainly
to child sexual abuse, as this has been more researched than the other kinds

of abuse. These theories include the Betrayal Theory by Jennifer Freyd (1996). She maintains that the dissociation and amnesia is caused by the unbearable betrayal of trust by the caregiver and parent who should protect them, but has abused them. The symptom clusters of PTSD can be explained by two factors; life-threat and social betrayal (Freyd et al., 2001). Finkelhor (1987) considers that there can also be an 'over-integration' of experience in survivors of CSA rather than a failure to integrate the sexual abuse. They may learn aspects of the abuse which they apply to other situations inappropriately. Finkelhor postulated four traumagenic dynamics, namely: (1) traumatic sexualisation, which applies to the survivors' learned use of sexual behaviour to obtain what they need in areas of their life, and it may become a way of expressing themselves; (2) betrayal caused by the same situation mentioned by Freyd could generalise in the mind of the survivor to other people, so they felt they could not trust others; (3) stigmatisation, which can arise from the survivor blaming themselves for what happened and feeling they are 'spoiled goods'; (4) powerlessness is the feeling produced by the person's body being invaded (as in CSA) and thus losing a sense of control in one's life.

A very significant theory relating to survivors of all kinds of child abuse and neglect, and especially relevant to the abuse of a developing child by the child's primary caregiver or givers is Attachment Theory, based on the work of Bowlby (1988) and developed by Ainsworth et al. (1978), Alexander (1992), Main (1995) and Schore (1994). Attachment is the biologically based bond between a child and the caregivers, which should provide a safe and firm base for the child to explore its environment. This bond is also important in facilitating the child to regulate emotions and behaviour. This bond is obviously disrupted in the case of children abused by the caregiver. The abuse causes in the child negative emotions which increase in intensity, frequency and duration. The fear and terror created in the child cannot be modulated by the caregiver who is also the abuser. This scenario has serious implications for the neurological and physiological development of the child. The attachment relationship affects the limbic-autonomic circuits in the right hemisphere, which is the first to develop before the left hemisphere. Dissociative defences set in the somatosensory experiences of the abuse are retained in the limbic system as implicit memory.

Attachment Patterns and Dissociative Self-states (Ego-States) and Related Diagnoses

Attachment patterns are the internal representations about the self and others named 'the working model of the self' and 'the working model of the world' (Bowlby, 1973). These are complex schema with emotional defensive and cognitive components relating to the self, the attachment figure and attachment interactions. Where there is a good bonding with the attachment figure, then this leads to a secure attachment pattern in the child, that is the child feels loved and protected. In the case of child abuse, when the caregiver or attachment figure has been significantly rejecting, uncaring and inconsistent, then the child develops an insecure attachment. An insecure attachment may involve behaviour described as anxious/avoidant or anxious/ambivalent, or disorganised.

The two main insecure attachments, in which the child adopts two defensive processes to avoid emotional pain, are deactivation and disconnection. The former is seen in insecure avoidant patterns where the child turns away from the attachment figure and focuses on the environment. The latter (disconnection) is seen in the insecure anxious/ambivalent pattern where the child disconnects from the painful experiences and continues to follow the caregiver, only to be repeatedly rejected. In order to prevent emotional breakdown in this situation, the child may set up separate systems to exclude attachment information from consciousness. In this case the multiple representations of self and others are not integrated as they are incompatible. This is responsible for the creation of double binds which in turn lead to dissociated self-states or ego-states (Blizard, 2003). This is what is referred to as disorganised attachment pattern, which can be seen in personality disorders, post-traumatic disorders and dissociative disorders.

In the event of such insecure and disorganised attachments with lack of support from the caregiver, dependency increases. Insecure dependency can manifest as over-dependency or counter-dependency, or a dependency style which oscillates between the two extremes, revealing alternating 'personalities' with different attachment patterns.

Steele et al. (2001, 2005) have called these dissociative self-states 'structural dissociation', of which there are different degrees, and which are also related to the diagnoses and extent of the trauma. The authors also identify two types of dissociated self-states, the 'apparently normal personality', which is focused on the practical matters of the present daily life and the 'emotional personality', which is fixated on the trauma of the past and is a defensive system focusing on threat or danger. In simple PTSD, there are only two dissociated self-states, one ANP and one EP. This is labelled primary structural dissociation. In complex PTSD or borderline personality disorder or some dissociative disorders, there is one ANP, but more than one EP. This is secondary structural dissociation. In DID there are more than one ANP, and more than one EP. This is tertiary structural dissociation. The decrease in integrative capacity in DID, and the pressure, therefore, to deal with everyday life makes it necessary to have more dissociated self-states.

Ego-state theorists (Frederick, 2005; Watkins & Watkins, 1997) confirm that cumulative abuse in childhood accompanied by significant failure of the caregiver in meeting the developmental needs of the child can cause this structural dissociation with a number of ego-state or dissociate self-states. Frederick (2005) maintains that each ego-state has a different attachment pattern and that one of the aims of ego-state therapy is to help each ego-state to develop a secure attachment.

The continuum of Differentiation to Dissociation can be identified in the degree of separateness between the ego-states (Watkins & Watkins, 1997). The boundaries between some are 'thicker than normal' so there is a greater degree of separateness or dissociation. In this case there will be an amnesic barrier between them, so they will not know about each other, as is the case of the 'alters' of DID. There may be only partial amnesia between the ego-states of borderline personality disorders, where there are fewer ego-states, and better integrative capacity.

Dissociated ego-states can also be created in different stages of a person's life through adulthood, but perhaps as a result of childhood trauma. Mollon (1996) discusses dissociation: see pages 97–98.

Dissociation is a complex phenomenon, which clearly has great survival value in the face of trauma of all different kinds. The forms that it takes are very different too, which has inevitably generated many theories regarding its varied manifestations. Research continues to be carried out regarding the mechanisms involved, and its relation to repression, if any. Both concepts are important in understanding and treating survivors of trauma of all kinds.

4

HYPNOTIC INTERVENTIONS TO RESOLVE TRAUMA MEMORIES IN THE TREATMENT OF SURVIVORS OF CHILDHOOD ABUSE

This chapter covers some of the main hypnotic interventions which can be used at various stages in the therapy for survivors. It will be clearer in the next chapter how and when any one of these interventions should be introduced into the process of psychotherapy.

It is important to mention again that these hypnotic procedures should only be used by practitioners qualified to use hypnosis in their particular field of expertise. Although some of the scripts may seem simple and unsophisticated, they are very effective and can be quite powerful. The wording can also be adjusted to suit the individual.

SAFETY AND PERMISSION

Before embarking on work on past trauma there are two absolute prerequisites. One must ensure that the client is willing to work on the material and this should be ascertained in hypnosis as well as out, by obtaining 'Yes' to the question, 'Is it alright to work on this now?' A simple head nod while the client is in hypnosis may suffice or ideomotor finger signals may be set up and used (see later in chapter). A good safety anchor is also essential. If the client is dealing with traumatic material it is very important that the client has a way of taking themselves away from the negative affect when needed or of gaining support from the therapist. This can be done in various ways – using special calm place imagery previously set up with the client or by using a handclasp 'the stronger you clasp my fingers the calmer you can feel' or 'as you feel the pressure of my hand on your shoulder you can feel calmer and stronger and know that you are not alone here'.

It is important before using these techniques that not only the therapist is aware of the concept of false memories, but that this has been discussed with the client. Both must understand that material 'recovered' using any hypnotic technique is the 'working memory' of an event – i.e. what they think happened. It may bear very little resemblance to the historic truth. However, since it is what they feel happened, it is what must be accepted for those purposes, and worked on in order to achieve resolution of their emotional problems. It is common experience that two witnesses to the same event can have totally different memories of whatever happened. It can also be useful to talk about how the 'unconscious' works with symbol and metaphor so that whatever is 'remembered' may be a symbolic or metaphorical representation of the problem.

ESTABLISHING HYPNOSIS AND BUILDING RESOURCES

Hypnosis and the Special Place

A standard hypnosis procedure may be used as a basis for subsequent therapy sessions and for teaching the client self-hypnosis, which then may be carried out by the client on a daily basis if wished. A safe and special place thus becomes a positive anchor.

Before commencing hypnosis the client may have identified a Special Safe Place. This has to be the client's choice. It has many uses in the course of therapy which can be seen in the next chapter. Dolan (1991) has called it 'developing associational cues for the safe adult-self'. The following steps can be taken:

- Ask the client to select a peaceful, relaxing, safe place which they can remember from their experience, or which is a fantasy place also peaceful, safe and relaxing, or a mixture of fantasy and reality. As long as the place has positive associations for them, it is acceptable. The client may need a few days to think about it, or it may come to them spontaneously.
- Ask the client to write a full description of the place, using all their five senses; sights, sounds, smells, the texture of things they touch, the temperature, and even the taste of something they might like to eat or drink in their imagination.
- The client can then select a symbol of the special place, which can be a sensation (e.g. warmth of the sun), or an object or part of the landscape

(e.g. the hills). The client is then asked to write this on a pre-selected coloured piece of paper, cut into a shape such as a star or diamond etc. Then the same symbol has to be written on the reverse side of this piece of paper with the non-dominant hand. The rationale of this is that writing with the non-dominant hand requires more effort and concentration, and the words are therefore better remembered. The symbol of the special place can then be used as a trigger to bring good feelings of the special place at a later time when needed. The piece of paper is a reminder to be carried by the client in a pocket.

The initial hypnotic induction may be eye-closure followed by suggestions of muscular relaxation of the legs, shoulders, arms and neck; and then slow gentle breathing.

A deepening procedure can follow using the imagery of garden steps or a lift leading to the Safe and Special Place. If, however, the client has been unable to select a particular place (either fantasy or reality or a mixture of both), then another hypnotic image can be introduced called the Magic Carpet Script as follows (J.H. Owens, personal communication):

Magic Carpet Script

This is a transport means to the place of safety. After induction use the stair-case as a deepener, having the client see the carpet from about halfway down and stepping onto it as a natural progression or give the following suggestions, using the carpet as a deepening technique:

In your mind's eye look up and see hovering just above you a beautiful magic carpet. See its colours . . . Patterns . . . Perhaps a fringe around it . . . This carpet which is big enough for you to lie on lands gently beside you. (Ideomotor signal from client to ascertain they have a carpet – see next section regarding ideomotor signals.)

Bend down and touch the carpet . . . Smell it . . . Sit on it . . . Stretch out and feel its warm soft pile beneath your body . . . Feel this Magic Carpet cradling and supporting you . . . 'Now' feel it rise up gently and notice that as it does it carries you deeper and deeper . . . When it reaches the ceiling it hovers and you can look back into the room seeing all in it (ask client to describe the room you are in). *Look down into the room . . . See the furnishings* (ask client to expand and give suggestions of going deeper as the carpet rises). *Now feel the carpet rise higher still and float just above the building . . . Up here on your carpet you're safe and serene . . . Calm and confident . . . Look down at the roof tops . . . the streets around the building . . . the cars . . . the people . . . the noise . . .*

and then become aware that this magic carpet is taking you on a journey . . . Safe on your magic carpet you are travelling over the cities . . . towns . . . rivers . . . and coun-tryside . . . See beneath you all the hustle and bustle of life . . . down there . . . below you.

Your carpet will land somewhere special to you. It may land in a place you know well or somewhere you have never been before but wherever your carpet chooses to land it is for you a calming and relaxing place. (Therapist may give suggestions: *It may land in a garden . . . on a beach . . . or in a park . . . For some it may land on a cliff top . . . perhaps on a mountain side . . . or even beside a lake . . .*) *This place that your carpet has chosen to land is for you a calming and relaxing place.*

Look around this place your carpet has chosen to land and tell me (therapist can write these down and use in therapy):

Where are you?
What time of year is it?
What time of day is it?
Are you alone or with some one?
How does it feel to be here?

(If this really is a safe place for them then ask client to get off the carpet)

(Now ask for imagery, e.g. if on a beach) *What do you notice about the sky? What else do you notice about the sky? What else?* (Exhaust the sky imagery before moving on)

Bring your eyes downwards. What do you notice about the horizon?'

Continue in this vein exploring their safe place with them.
(If it is not really a safe place then get them to instruct the carpet to continue journeying.)

Once the Special Safe Place has been selected and the imagery incorporated into the hypnotic session, the client is encouraged to spend some time becoming absorbed in it and accessing all the good feelings it produces for them. The symbol chosen can always be used by the client to bring back the good feelings of their Special Place wherever they are and whenever they need. A post-hypnotic suggestion to this effect is then given to the client. The hypnotic session is then terminated by such as counting down. This correction may last 20 minutes or more. The client is then taught how to do this by themselves. It may take a shorter time.

The client is encouraged to practise the associated symbol and the positive feelings during their self-hypnosis sessions.

The self-hypnosis sessions empower the client and provide them with an important resource throughout the therapy and beyond.

The Calvert-Stein Clenched Fist Technique (Stein, 1963)

Anchors can also be established in hypnosis for negative emotions and feelings. This can provide the client with a way of releasing the feelings in hypnosis and also in managing them in everyday situations too. Stein's 'clenched fist' technique involves the effective use of both positive and negative anchors. The guidelines for this procedure are as follows.

Begin by asking the client to identify any situation that the client feels unnecessarily anxious about, and would like to handle in a calmer and more confident way (the client need not disclose the nature of the situation). Then ask them to identify a situation in which they experience feelings of calm and confidence. This may be a present-day situation or one from the past (again client need not disclose its nature). The Special Place can also be used as a source of positive feelings.

After hypnotic induction, ask the client to imagine being in the good situation, experiencing or imagining the positive feelings of calmness and confidence (or use the Special Place as a source of good feelings). Ask the client to make a fist with the preferred hand (note which it is) when they are in touch with those positive feelings, and to associate the clenching of the fist with these good feelings. Ask the client to imagine holding those good feelings and images now in that hand, so they are ready any time they need them.

Ask the client to relax the hand when they have made the connection, and say:

> From now on, each and every time you wish to remind yourself of those same thoughts and feelings of calmness and confidence, just make a fist with your preferred hand, and experience again those good feelings, ready to hand, to bring to bear in the situation you are in. Do this now. Make a fist with that hand ... good ... and experience again those feelings of calmness and confidence.

When the client has done this, ask them to relax the hand again. Then ask the client to go in imagination into the situation which they find difficult. Instruct the client to experience or imagine as vividly as possible the feelings of tension and anxiety. When the client is in touch with these feelings, instruct them to slowly make a fist with the non-preferred hand, while imagining all the tension leaving their body and streaming down into the fist as it gets tighter and tighter. (Ensure that the client keeps the rest of the body relaxed, and does not hold their breath.) Then when ready, the client releases the tension by opening the hand, imagining the tension drifting away leaving the body relaxed. (The client may then be asked to actively throw the tension away, take a deep breath, and relax the hand on exhaling or count 1–5 while relaxing the hand.) Then ask the client to remain in the imagined situation, clench the preferred hand, and imagine bringing back all the resources, strengths and feelings of calmness and confidence into the situation, and coping with the situation the way they want to. Ask the client to stay with this until they are satisfied, and then to relax the hand.

Give a post-hypnotic suggestion that each and every time the client is in an anxiety-provoking situation, inappropriate tension can be expelled using the (non-preferred) hand, and resources of calmness and confidence can be brought to bear, using the (preferred) hand.

This technique can be used, not just to control anxiety, but with modifications, to dispose of fear, anger, disgust etc., and to replace them with positive feelings.

Indirect Uncovering Techniques

Uncovering techniques are means of enabling the client to access material safely, which they are unable or unwilling to confront or to identify, and which is relevant to their current problems. Direct regression and abreaction techniques are not appropriate for the majority of survivors of childhood abuse.

The following techniques described are either indirect approaches, or direct approaches which have safeguards included in the procedures so that the client is not overwhelmed or re-traumatised. Most of these involve hypnotic questioning which is quite simple and requires a 'Yes', 'No', 'Do not know', 'Not prepared to say' or 'Not ready to know about' answers. These answers can be given by a specific motor signal from the client rather than verbally. This procedure is as follows.

1. Ideomotor responses (IMRs) (non-verbal, involuntary signals)

Verbal responses are often thought through first, and are conscious and voluntary responses. If it is suggested in hypnosis that a signal can be generated from the unconscious mind or 'back part of the mind', the response is later reported as involuntary. This is what is called an ideomotor signal. It is different from a conscious, voluntary signal which is usually smooth, well co-ordinated and occurs promptly after the question. The ideomotor involuntary signal is usually jerky, slow and delayed until long after the question is asked. This 'unconsciously' generated signalling can be a means of accessing material which may not be readily available to consciousness, and is often used as an uncovering technique.

A common way is to have the index finger of one hand as the 'Yes' finger, the little finger of the same hand as the 'No' finger, and the thumb as 'I am not ready to know about/talk about that.' It is not necessary to limit ideomotor signals to finger movements. Any observable set of responses can be used. Some examples of the use of ideomotor signals are as follows.

In the context of retrieving positive childhood memories the following can be suggested to the client:

Let your unconscious choose a long forgotten pleasant memory that will be a healing resource for you now and in the future. When your unconscious is ready to give you a long forgotten memory of a pleasant time in the past that will be helpful in your healing ... your finger will lift all by itself. When you have remembered what is appropriate about that resource, your finger will effortlessly drift back down to rest on your lap (Dolan, 1991, p. 149).

For more painful materials, more complex sets of unconscious signals may be necessary, as follows:

When the client has achieved a comfortable state of trance, ask the client to sit back and when ready, 'to notice which finger lifts first, knowing it will be a "Yes" finger, signalling readiness to do unconscious work, also a way to signal "Yes" in response to questions. The next finger to lift can be the "No" finger, and the third finger to lift can be the "I am not yet ready to know consciously finger"' (Dolan, 1991, p. 144).

Another way of implementing ideomotor signals for 'Yes', 'No', 'I do not know' or 'I do not want to tell you' is as follows.

These signals can be established in hypnosis by the suggestion that the client thinks very deeply and honestly about the word 'Yes', and while this is happening, the unconscious mind will choose one of the fingers on one of the hands to convey this message by slowly, and without conscious effort, lifting this finger. The other messages may be established in the same way via other fingers. When this is completed, the therapist proceeds by asking questions which demand an answer of 'Yes' or 'No'. It is assumed the client's responses are involuntary and 'unconscious', that is that they need not know the answer consciously. For example, a question might be 'Is your problem associated with an experience you have had in the past?' or 'Is there any important reason why you have the pain now?' (Heap & Aravind, 2002b, p. 217).

2. Hypnotic dream suggestion

This involves suggesting in the hypnotic state that the client will have a dream, which will throw light on their problem. This can be in the form of a post-hypnotic suggestion that the client will have this significant dream at a later time during the day or night. Alternatively a suggestion is given that they will have a dream in the hypnotic session, if this is preferred by the client (Degun & Degun, 1988).

Hypnotic dreams might be particularly useful in therapy when the client is uncertain or unclear about a problem, or if there are many factors contributing to the problem, and it is not clear which one to address first.

The main advantages of hypnotic dreams are that the procedure is non-directive and client-orientated, facilitates focus on important elements and also on recall. Through the disguised language of dreams the client can slowly confront painful material and at their own pace face the reality of the problem. The client therefore has more perceived control in the therapeutic process.

Studies on hypnotic dream suggestion (Stoyva, 1967) have shown that post-hypnotically suggested dreams have an effect on the sleep cycle, particularly REM cycle. The context of the subjects' reports elicited from REM and non-REM awakenings were influenced by the post-hypnotic suggestion. The following procedures for this hypnotic intervention have been based on these studies (Degun & Degun, 1988).

Preparation of the client

- It is necessary to explain the nature of hypnosis and its value in accessing material which they may not be consciously aware of.

It is also important to explain something of the nature of dreams. For example, sometimes we are worried about something, but we may push it to the back of our mind while we continue with our daily routine. Our worry may then surface later in a night dream. These dreams may not always be logical and seem to make no sense. This is because in dreams we use symbols and other methods of disguise, so our worry is lessened and we continue to sleep.

The client may say that they do not dream. Everyone dreams but some do not remember their dreams. It is necessary to elicit dreams by giving a post-hypnotic suggestion to have a night dream, which can be very similar to any other dream during sleep. Alternatively, if the client wishes, a suggestion can be given to have a dream in hypnosis. Either way, hypnosis is a useful tool to elicit dreams which will reflect aspects of the problem which are important to them. Furthermore, even if the client does not understand the dream it is possible to learn how to interpret the dream by hypnotic dream elaboration. This method can then be explained to them.

The above preparation is essential before commencing the hypnosis as follows:

- *The first hypnotic session*
  This consists of a hypnotic induction and deepening and the Special Place with an anchor. The purpose of this is only to familiarise the client with the experience of hypnosis and to learn self-hypnosis.
- *The second hypnotic session*
  The client has a choice of having a dream in the hypnotic session or of having a post-hypnotic suggestion to have a dream during the night,

and to awaken and write it down before going back to sleep. Then either of the two following procedures can be selected, according to the client's choice:

(a) *Suggestion to dream in the hypnotic session*

First induce hypnosis with deepening and implement IMR. Then proceed with *either* of the following scripts:

> *You may find a thought coming into your mind or you may have a dream which will throw light on your problem. You will remember it and relate it to me now or afterwards, as you wish. As soon as you have had the thought or finished dreaming, let me know with your 'Yes' finger. Remember, once you have perceived the problem, you will be able to find a solution with help from me.*

Or:

The client may prefer to project the dream on to a screen or an imaginary theatre stage. Then the following script can be used:

> *Imagine you are entering a theatre with me and walking into the stalls. We are the only ones in the audience. We go to sit in the front stalls. Before us is the stage and curtain drop. Slowly the curtain rises and reveals the full stage. Here in your own time, you can begin to watch a play or drama about your problem. You can begin to describe to me what is happening in your own time. You can stop the play or pause, or have an interval as and when you like, or tell me what it means to you when you like. Remember, once you have perceived the problem you will be able to find a solution with help.*

(b) *Post-hypnotic suggestion to have a night dream*

First induce hypnosis with deepening. In this intervention, there is no need to implement IMR. The following script can then be used:

> *You may find in the next day or so, a thought comes into your mind, or you may have a day dream or a night dream, which will throw light on your problem. You will remember it and write it down so you can tell me. Remember, once you have perceived the problem, you will be able to find a solution with help from me.*

After this suggestion, the client is brought out of hypnosis and given instructions to have a paper and pencil by their bedside at night, so that when they awaken from a dream, they can roughly write it down before either going back to sleep or getting up. They are also advised to keep paper and pencil in their pocket or handbag during the day, in case they have a thought in the day or day dream.

The 'out of the blue' nature of the involuntary post-hypnotic response can easily be forgotten or dismissed. They should be encouraged also to write down anything and everything they recall of their dreams even if it seems nonsense to them at the time. Even if the client says they never dream or never remember their dreams, reassure them that with a post-hypnotic suggestion they could well remember the dreams. If they are hypnotisable and motivated it should work.

The therapist, should not be deterred by the fact that they do not understand the dream. However, if the therapist feels they do understand it, they should not be tempted to interpret it. The meaning could be quite different from what they anticipated.

- *The third hypnotic session (if the client does not understand the dream)*
  If the client brings in a report of a dream written on paper, then the following script for dream elaboration can be used in hypnosis:

> Dream elaboration script
>
> *You will now be able to recall the whole dream and understand the meaning. Imagine you are in a room looking at a blank screen (either TV or cinema screen). You have the remote control of the video screen or controls of the projector. In your own time you can turn on the controls to start the film of the dream. You will be able to see it unfold on the screen in all its important detail, and relate it to me. Where you can, you will be able to tell me what you think it means to you. Remember you have the controls and you can stop the film, pause, or freeze the frame when you want, or you can switch it off completely when you want.*

There may be several dreams the client has reported. Each dream must be addressed in separate sessions of hypnotic dream elaborations. Often the client sees more meaning in all the dreams once the first dream has been elaborated, and it may not be necessary to elaborate them all in hypnosis. The client may also talk more about the dream after they have finished the hypnotic session. The hypnotic session in itself seems to open several 'doors'.

- *The fourth hypnotic session*
  The purpose of the hypnotic dreams is to open the way to making appropriate and adaptive changes in the client's behaviour, thinking, feeling and maybe lifestyle. This needs to be discussed in the fourth session and maybe other sessions.

  If the client has completely failed to understand a dream, it is possible to repeat the post-hypnotic suggestion to dream the same dream with different symbols until the inner meaning becomes obvious. This is not usually necessary.

- *Other advantages and uses of hypnotic dreams*
  When there are disturbing flashbacks, which the client cannot relate to and is unable to understand (this occurs particularly when there are recovered memories which are partial and not complete), hypnotic dreams can throw light on the triggers. When problems arise, solutions can emerge in a dream. When there is another dissociated self-state of

which the client is not aware (nor the therapist), it can emerge in a dream. Sometimes in Dream Elaboration, resolutions may be needed at the end, but this is not usually the case. For resolutions see later in this chapter.

Techniques for Safe Recall and Resolution of Traumatic Memories

The hypnotic procedures for uncovering and re-experiencing earlier traumatic events in a safe and protected way incorporate dissociative techniques. This enables the client to stay in control of the degree of contact and involvement with the events. It also enables them to distance themselves and to adopt eventually a more objective view of what happened.

In order to enable traumatic memories to be processed, regression to the past may be necessary. Eliciting dissociated information and integrating it with the whole content of the experience is essential to processing it and to making adjustments in thinking, behaving and feeling.

It is important to explain to the client these reasons for talking through a traumatic event, and for using safe hypnotic procedures to do this. Reassurance that it will not lead to re-traumatisation is also necessary. The client needs to remember that it is only a memory they are recalling and not present reality. This time they are not alone and the therapist is always with them. Whatever bad feelings the client may have will not last, and they will be helped to resolve them. Furthermore, they will see what is happening in a dissociated way, that is to say they will be distanced from it, and they will see it 'out there' as an observer. They can also stop at any time to return to the Special Place, which they have already visited in hypnosis.

It is also important to convey to the client that hypnosis gives them more control; they are not surrendering to the will of another person. This has particular relevance for those who have been victimised and feel helpless. Because of the overwhelming emotions when traumatised, they dissociated from the event and blocked off their feelings. They have already experienced dissociation, which is also a component of the hypnotic state. Hypnosis is therefore not unfamiliar to them. This hypnotic talent can also help them to re-associate with their feelings at their own pace.

The first technique to be discussed may or may not include dissociative imagery.

1. The affect bridge

This is an age regression technique introduced by J. Watkins (1971). It can be used as an uncovering method when the client experiences sensations or feelings which have a somatic component without any apparent connection to a situation or particular context. The affect or emotion is used as a bridge to take the client back in time to its origin. The emotions are a link or bridge to take the client from an event with an unpleasant emotion attached in the present (or recent past) to a previous event whose emotion is driving the fear or has sensitised the client in some way, so it can be resolved.

Throughout life, events occur where the client, for one reason or another, does not express, deal with, or come to terms with some negative emotion or affect.

In this model negative emotion from past events is 'trapped' under successive memories that are laid down like layers in an onion. An event in the present can have a link back to somehow related events in the past, so that the person experiences not just the affect from the present but also that from the past.

This may help to explain for instance why someone who has not been able to grieve for a parent when they die may have a seemingly inappropriate display of grief when their dog dies.

This also explains the effect of negative (and positive) anchors and spontaneous abreaction.

An *affect bridge* can allow the client to regress, often in stages, to the sensitising experience and open it up to psychotherapeutic intervention.

The way to use the affect bridge is first to get the client to experience some of the negative emotion (affect) of a particular event in the present. Then they use that affect to back track (bridge) to a previous time when they felt the same affect. By resolving the earlier time when they experienced that negative emotion, the emotional problem in the present may be lessened or resolved.

On some occasions there may be a chain of events which one travels along, using the affect bridge, resolving the difficulties at each event.

It is important to trust your client and rather than thinking that you know what is relevant for a particular client to explore in relation to a problem, it is much better to allow the client's 'unconscious' mind to go back to whatever comes up as relevant and deal with that. Do not give direction, simply 'go with that feeling and notice where it takes you'.

Case example:

Zoe, thirty-six, was terrified at the thought of having to have an MRI scan because she was claustrophobic. She had a memory of her brother bullying her and pretending to smother her with a pillow. Inducing hypnosis and, suggesting that she 'Go with that feeling of fear at the idea of going in the scanner and just see where it takes you', she went back to an incident that she had forgotten. When she was six or seven she had climbed up to look at a present that had been hidden on top of her wardrobe and she had fallen with the wardrobe on top of her. She had struggled to get out and her father had been very angry with her. By resolving that incident her fear lessened markedly and she was able to cope with only 'normal' amounts of apprehension and anxiety.

If you are using affect bridge in this way:

1. Always establish a *positive anchor*, after an initial hypnotic induction.
2. Check for agreement and safety before continuing.
3. Use the affect bridge to regress to earlier events. 'Go with that feeling' . . . 'where does it take you?' Hop back in stages to the primary experience.
4. Give no suggestion of earlier events. Give no suggestion of content or events. Such suggestions could lead to false memories.
5. Perform the appropriate therapeutic intervention. This will usually be some form of dissociative imagery, as described in the next section on dissociative techniques.
6. Suggest that the client signal 'yes' when they have completed whatever they need to do.
7. Selective amnesia – 'You will remember from this session only what you are ready to deal with in the here and now.'
8. Take them to their special place and ego strengthen them after thanking their unconscious mind for the wonderful work it has just done.
9. Reverse trance and check that all is well – 'How are you feeling now?'
10. Allow the client to talk but don't remind them if they don't remember what happened or what they said in trance.

Another procedure for the affect bridge (Heap & Aravind, 2002b; Watkins, 1971) is as follows:

1. After hypnotic induction and deepening and implementing IMR the client is asked to recall and re-experience a recent situation in which they had this particular feeling or emotion. The client is then requested to re-live this event in their imagination.
2. It is then suggested to the client that they increase the intensity of the feeling by twice as much, then three times as much, until it is as strong as it can get.
3. The client then has to hold on to that feeling, while detaching themselves from the situation in which it occurred.
4. The client is then asked to hold on to the feeling while they travel back in time to the first time they experienced this feeling. They can do this by leaving it to the 'unconscious mind' to locate the relevant experience. This can be a straightforward regression with the end point being identified by the affect or emotion.

Alternatively, appropriate imagery can be suggested such as travelling over a bridge, a road or corridor accompanied by the intense feelings, to reach the time when the feelings were first experienced.

Some therapists would not want to use this second method for fear of flooding the client. However, although this tends not to happen in practice, the first method is advisable for those who have this reservation about method two.

5. Once the client has reached this point, ask the client to lift their 'Yes' finger. Then ask them to describe the event. At this point the client may need help to resolve the issues which arise. Procedures for resolution can be seen in the next section.

6. The client can then return along the same road or bridge to the recent memory. The therapist needs to be sure that the client now feels better about it in an important way, such as being able to cope with it.

Regression and abreaction has been used extensively in the past where the client is regressed back into the past experience and relives it. Emotions are worked through and integrated into the client's 'current narrative'. This, when done properly with the therapist keeping the client firmly anchored in the present, can bring catharsis and re-interpretation. However, it is easy to re-traumatise the client without bringing resolution, and is often distressing both to the patient and the therapist. The use of dissociative techniques and dissociative imagery both protects the client from unnecessary distress and is just as effective.

Spontaneous regression and abreaction can occur both inside and outside the therapeutic arena. It is important that if this occurs the client is given support, and the suggestion that they are dealing with, and therefore resolving the problem. The client can also be encouraged to dissociate and to access the resources needed to help resolve the problem.

Dissociative Techniques

Using a dissociative approach in treatment means that the event can be dealt with, and any necessary learning or understanding made, and the negative emotion released without the client having to experience the full impact of the negative emotion.

There are several ways of doing this, but they all involve dissociating the client from the event that is being dealt with:

1. Imagine watching a video, TV or cinema screen.
2. Imagine being in a protective bubble (or a spaceship) through which you can see and hear, but not feel emotion.

3. Imagine looking down from a hot air balloon or magic carpet.
4. Simply see it 'over there', while you remain feeling comfortable 'here'.

Ways to help resolve the trauma may be any one of the following:

- Identify resources from adult experiences, or from the unconscious, which would help the younger self (the part of them being traumatised 'out there').
- Finding a 'resourceful you' or contact with the 'higher self' that can comfort and heal.
- Giving advice/resources to the younger self and/or significant others in the event.
- Replaying the event differently.
- Using symbols or metaphors to allow the client to take control.

Dealing with the traumatic incident from the past

Before starting explain to the client what you intend to do and how it will enable them to deal with the problem. Back in the past, they have experienced a trauma which still causes them anxiety and negative feelings. When they know what they need for their protection they no longer need the feeling of fear and anxiety.

The client cannot change *what* happened but they can change the *emotional impact* that it has in the present.

Whatever the trauma, the client felt helpless and impotent to do anything at the time . . . but that was then, and they now know that however awful the event, they managed to survive it, and this can be the most important part of the treatment.

They also need to take back control and this can be done in many ways using imagery.

Case example:

Peter was seven years old and had suffered an attempted assault by a man in a local park. He had had his videoed interview with the police and was suffering from marked anxiety, not wanting to go away from his mother, becoming withdrawn and refusing to go to bed on his own at night. He was asked to imagine a television screen and to play on it a film of himself playing football (a favourite activity) which he clearly enjoyed – saying that he had scored all the goals! He was then asked to play a film of the event in the park and to talk with that little boy and decide what would be a good thing to do to help the little boy in the film feel better. They decided to climb a tree with a large container of bright orange gloop and when the man appeared again they tipped it up over him and ran home laughing at him. That simple use of the young boy's imagination completely resolved his anxiety and within days he was back to his normal self.

Explain that one of the things they might want to do is float down as their confident, resourceful adult self to comfort and reassure their younger self; they know best what that younger part of themselves needs to feel better because they are from their future . . . they survived that time. Alternatively some other person – real or imaginary – can come into the event to support the client.

Floating up high above the incident means that the client does not need to experience the full impact of the emotion as they learn what they need and let the feeling go. If they start to feel distressed then they can float higher and higher up.

The following hypnotic techniques are some examples of dissociative imagery to facilitate resolution of trauma.

1. The Video Booth

Following the hypnotic induction, the client is asked to imagine they enter a room which is set up specifically for viewing videos. There is a screen, controls and video-playing equipment. The client has full control of the apparatus and can start, stop, fast forward, freeze frame, and zoom in and out of the images. The room also contains cassettes which contain scenes from the client's life. The client is then invited to select a video scene to play which is relevant to the problems they have, and which is important for them to recall now to gain understanding, to move on in their life, and to achieve what they would like to achieve. The client can make this selection themselves, or allow the 'unconscious mind' to do so for them. Once the client is comfortable controlling and viewing the scene on the video, a suggestion can be given that when they feel ready to do so, they can take advantage of the 'virtual reality' facilities of the video booth, and enter the scene and become their younger self. Alternatively, the client can enter the scene as one of the other characters in the scene or as her older and wiser self. The client can also 'take a break' from the scene they have entered, by simply moving back out of it again and viewing it on the screen. If watching the video is too much for the client, they can stop the video, and play a scene of the Special Place, or even leave the booth completely.

2. The Screen (Spiegel, 1993)

This is another hypnotic intervention using the dissociative technique of a screen for visiting the past. The script may be as follows:

On the count of one, look up, on two slowly close your eyes, and take a deep breath. Then, on three, breathe out, eyes relaxed but keep them closed and let your body float. Then imagine one hand or the other floating up into the air like a balloon, and that is a signal to yourself and to me that you are ready to concentrate. Now feel your body floating somewhere safe and comfortable. It might be a bath, a lake, or just imagine floating somewhere in space, each breath deeper and easier. Enjoy this pleasant sense of floating.

Notice how you can use your store of memories and fantasies to help yourself and your body to feel better. Now picture in your mind an imaginary screen. It could be a movie screen, a TV screen or a piece of clear, blue sky. Picture on the screen a pleasant scene, somewhere you enjoy being. Again notice how you can use your store of memories and fantasies to help yourself and your body to feel better. Now we are going to try something different. We are going to picture some memories on the imaginary screen, but with this rule: Do your thinking and feeling out there on the screen, and leave your body out of it. Keep your body floating here safe and comfortable, while you picture the memories on the screen.

It is then possible to split the screen, and have the traumatic situation on the left screen, and a view of a recent memory as a survivor on the right screen.

Resolution of the trauma can be carried out in very similar ways as mentioned previously. For example, the survivor self can enter the left-hand screen from the right-hand screen to offer comfort. Changes in imagery can also be introduced into the left-hand screen. This opens the way for integration of the two sides. A further advantage of the screen technique is that the client can fast forward, freeze or rewind the film, if they need.

Another method of double dissociation is often used with the screen. In this case, the client watches themselves viewing themselves on a video, and introduces a third person into the scene to provide reassurance.

The following technique is another example of double dissociation.

3. The Cinema Technique (G. Ibbotson, personal communication, 2005)

This is a dissociative technique that is extremely effective in resolution of past trauma. Even extremely distressing past events can be resolved and handled in a comfortable and sensitive way. The process can be done content-free.

No formal induction need be undertaken. The client is asked to close their eyes and then imagine a cinema, which can be one they remember or one that they make up. They enter the cinema and feel safe and secure. There is no one else in the cinema and they go and sit on the second row of the cinema and look up at the blank screen. Ask them to tell you the colour of the seats and their response confirms that they are succeeding with the imagery. They then imagine leaving their body comfortably sitting there and float back to the projection room and look through the glass to see the back of their head as they sit on the second row watching the empty screen.

Hence they are doubly dissociated from the activities on the screen.

They allow an image to form on the screen of a good event that involved them. They play this through over a period of approximately a couple of minutes. They then play it through again and this time they float down into the image and really enjoy experiencing the good feelings. Then ask them to float back to the projection booth and designate a button on the equipment that, if pressed, will float them down into the good event. Ask what colour it is. Check on the client's visualisation and ask them to test the button and enjoy their happy event for a few moments. They are told that if you ever ask them to press that button they are to do so, and find themselves enjoying the good event. If they themselves need to press the button at any stage they can do so – but they must tell you that they have pressed the button.

This is a visual image used as a safety anchor.

Ask them if they are prepared to work on some significant past event in order to feel different about it. A head nod can be used as an ideomotor response but some prefer to set up a finger signal.

Their head nod is permission at an unconscious level to work on the material.

They then allow their mind to project a still image of themselves, just before the significant event on which they wish to work, onto the screen. They may make it an old black and white film in sepia colours with odd scratches on the film or it may be in full colour. They play the film of the event from start to finish over approximately two minutes and nod when it has finished. When they nod ask them to score the emotional response of watching that film on a 0–10 scale with 0 being not distressing at all and 10 being the worst experience they could imagine.

Ask them in a few moments to rewind the film and remind them that as it is rewound the sounds will go backwards (demonstrated by tonality) and the actions will go backwards and look and feel totally different. Anyone who had said anything is made to eat their words. They rewind the film quickly. Ask them in their own time to play the film backwards and forwards about three times and then give you a nod when they have finished. They then tell you what number the score has fallen to.

Suggestion and presupposition

They go back to the image of 'the younger you' as a still picture before the event. That person will need comfort, reassurance and insight. Who can give that? Would it be another person or could the 'older you' now help? Whoever is going to offer the assistance steps into the picture and they see them whisper something but may not be aware of what was said. They may see a change in the expression of the 'younger you' as they receive the advice and comfort. The action is played through with the supporter present and at any time the action may be stopped for the person to offer comfort or support. When the action is completed they are to signify with a nod. As the still picture at the end of the action is still visible then they are to imagine an infinite source of love and comfort being poured out upon the 'younger you'. An alternative approach is that someone may enter the event and speak to the other parties involved in the action.

The separation of the 'younger you' and 'older you' aids the dissociation of the present self from the younger self who suffered the trauma.

They are now the director of the film and have total power over the film. They are to try out a change and play it through. If it improves things the change is kept but if not then another change is made. They are told to go on their own to make these changes and rewind between each change. Suggest that they may want to use their sense of mischief or the absurd. When they are satisfied with the result they are to nod. When during the process there are changes of expression showing improvement then simple tonality or 'that's right' is fed back to them. One final run through is made and they are asked to score the film on a 0–10 scale. If the score has lowered ask them if this is a low enough score. If so, that's fine.

If it is not low enough then bind them with the suggestion that they now know how to alter the film and they are to do whatever is necessary to get it down to that score, and give a nod when it is at that score.

If it is not possible to lower the score sufficiently then there is probably an earlier event that also needs resolution. Ask them to store the present film safe for a while and to look at the empty screen and allow an image to form of an earlier event that is connected with this event. Give a nod when it is there. Use the same process to sort out that event and then put the film back on again. Play the film and check the score of the original film. It may have already dropped to the desired score or can easily be lowered using the interventions already described.

After the final run-through of the film ask them to press the happy scene button just as they start to rewind the film. This means that they rewind back past the start and go into the happy scene and really enjoy it. This may be seen as collapsing anchors.

When the process is completed reintegrate them back to the second row and then they leave the cinema 'all parts working together, leaving behind what they want to leave behind and bringing back what they want to bring back'.

Sometimes individuals give an initial score that is quite low. This may mean that they are, consciously or unconsciously, trying the process out on a fairly safe procedure. If this seems to be the case then after resolution ask them to look at the blank screen and see if another image comes up that needs working on.

Summarised process

- sit in the stalls facing an empty screen
- float to projection booth . . . seeing yourself in the stalls
- see a calm, happy scene on the screen – this acts as a visual anchor – link to safety button
- picture a younger you before the event
- run a film of the event, i.e. dissociated
- score the film
- rewind film
- give advice, resources and comfort to younger self/significant others in film
- re-run film incorporating above
- score the film again
- when the score has lowered to an acceptable level – run right back into visual anchor
- reintegrate

4. Vehicles, Capsules and Bubbles

As an alternative to the video booth or cinema screen, some clients might prefer the idea of travelling through time and space inside some vehicle or enclosure, such as a capsule or bubble from which they can view important scenes from the past, and at the same time be protected and at a distance from the events. It is usual to suggest they can let their 'unconscious mind' select a scene to visit, which is important for them to understand in order to recover. It is also suggested to them that they will only encounter as much as they are able to deal with at present.

The client is again able to stay within the safe enclosure or leave it and become part of the scene and to return to safety at will.

Capsules and bubbles have less constraints of reality than the video booth or screen, and the client may find it easier to understand telepathically the thoughts of others in the scene.

The capsule or bubble has strong walls and while allowing the client to see through, can prevent others from seeing in. It can in fact be invisible to others. The client selects their own means of transport and also specifies its features, contents and colour. In one particular instance a client who had been sexually abused chose a helicopter. She had already selected a safe, special place in hypnosis which was a rock fortress with a roof garden. The roof garden acquired a helipad and she was able to try out her helicopter. She flew it herself 'over the years back to a happy occasion as a child'. This was a trial run. As she flew, she felt herself becoming smaller and younger, and she was able to alight at the end of her flight as a six year old wearing 'a pretty dress' with blue and yellow flowers and white sandals. She was in a barn with her younger cousin for whom she was making a salad out of china eggs and dock leaves. The client later said she had not recalled this occasion in such detail or with such powerful positive affect since her childhood. She commented in particular on the smell of the grass and the sounds of the horses on the next farm. She did not, however, comment on the incongruity of a six-year-old child landing a helicopter in a barn. The helicopter proved to be a great asset to the client in exploring and resolving her childhood trauma – it could land and take off quickly and could hover at a distance – it represented safety and control (Oakley et al., 1996).

5. The Bubble Induction

This particular hypnotic intervention has proved very popular with many clients. The script (see below) was first introduced by Daniel Brown and later published by Phyllis Alden (1995) with his permission. Certain safeguards have been introduced at the beginning of the script in the following way as suggested by Dolan (1991):

- Hypnotic induction and deepening procedures are carried out; then the IMR (ideo motor response) is implemented.
- The following suggestions are then given:
  - (a) You will only learn information from the past which is necessary and helpful.
  - (b) Whatever is best left unconscious will remain unconscious.
  - (c) You can recall only what you can cope with at this moment in time.
  - (d) Whenever you need to stop, you can do so and return to your Special Place or remain safe in your Bubble.
- Hypnotic questions requiring an ideomotor response are then asked:
  - (a) Do you feel ready at this moment in time to go into the past, and revisit an event, which is necessary for healing, and you feel you can cope with now?

(b) Would you like to choose the event, which you can cope with and which is important for you now? (If the answer is 'Yes' then proceed to the Bubble script. If the answer is 'No' then suggest that later, when they are ready, the 'unconscious mind' will let them know. Then terminate the hypnosis).

• The Bubble script which follows is only intended as a guide:

Settle yourself comfortably into the chair. When you feel ready, close your eyes . . . and just imagine that around you . . . all around you . . . there is a safe protective bubble. It is just the right size . . . not too small and not too large . . . Just the right size to give you that sense of space and yet . . . a safe sense of containment and protection.

I'd like you to imagine yourself inside this bubble . . . safely comfortable . . . comfortably safe and you can just float there comfortably . . . and I'd like you to notice the walls of the bubble . . . just notice how thick they are . . . just as thick as they need to be to help you to feel safe . . . and comfortable . . . to have that comfortable sense of containment, but not so thick that you can't be in touch, in contact with the world outside.

Now ask your client to describe exactly what the bubble is like, the texture of the walls, the colour, and everything about it. This of course will help deepen the trance. And you can repeat, and reinforce appropriate comments from your patient, e.g.

C   *It's all soft, like silk.*
T   *That's right. It's so soft, just like soft silk.*

Then continue . . .

Now just imagine yourself there more and more clearly . . . feel it . . . feel yourself really floating comfortably around that bubble . . . and enjoy that comfortable . . . floating sensation as you're there inside . . . protected . . . and whatever thoughts you have, can just be put aside while you float in comfort . . . so comfortably around . . . float carefree . . . away . . . enjoying that security . . .

And as you breathe naturally and easily . . . you can just float comfortably . . . notice how you can relax more with every breath you take . . . notice the warmth of the bubble, how you move as you breathe . . . and how you can be more and more secure . . . deeper and deeper . . . and relax . . . deeper and deeper into trance . . . as you float comfortably. And as you can enjoy that carefree sense . . . feeling calm and secure . . . deeper and deeper . . . and when you feel that you're as deep as you comfortably need to be right now in this trance . . . and though only a short time of clock time may pass you have all the time you need to find that trance level . . . to go as deeply as you need . . . and then you can let me know that you are there by allowing a finger to lift.

Wait for IMR before continuing.

> *And you might be curious to know just how deep your trance might be. The number 0 is alert wide awake and the number 10 is the deepest trance that you can have and when I say the word 'state' to you, you'll find a number just floating into your mind spontaneously and you can give voice to that number to tell me.*

After a pause say the word 'state' and get a measure of trance depth and you can then check out if your client wishes to go deeper or stay the same, whichever they want to do you can carry on as follows:

> *Now imagine that your bubble, you and your bubble can float . . . float anywhere you like . . . you can float inside your bubble, around a room or go anywhere you choose . . . and really enjoy that wonderful free sensation . . . and I'd like you to allow yourself to float until you find just the right place to settle . . . to have just the right space between where you are and where I'm talking to you . . . and just as soon as you and your bubble have settled exactly where you want to be then you can let me know by allowing that finger to lift.*

Again wait for IMR.

Then ask your client to show you where they are. Then you can elicit from them a description of what the trance is like and reinforce whatever makes that person feel more comfortable and secure.

It is worth checking out perceived trance depth again by the previously mentioned method, then you can symbolically move your client out of the bubble into a beach scene, a comfortable chair, anything, and then suggest as they do that they can keep that wonderfully safe, secure comfortable feeling.

> *Now I wonder if you would enjoy floating in your bubble to a safe . . . comfortable . . . relaxing place. A place where you can feel just as safe and secure as you need to . . . where you can safely come out of that bubble and rest . . .*

Ask for IMR, and again wait.

> *Good . . . so whenever you are ready . . . just let yourself come out of the bubble and just settle yourself . . . walk around . . . do anything you want to do there . . . and when you are ready . . . find a place to rest . . . and just let me know when you are there . . . resting comfortably . . .*

Again, elicit descriptive information on the place which will not only enhance absorption but facilitate increased trance depth. Now the client is ready to work with the problem. It is important to remember clients suffering from PTSD or the effects of any abuse are prone to flashbacks and other intrusions. Safety, comfort and the ability to control exposure to traumatic memories are a priority.

Establishing anchors for comfort should be carried out prior to any exploratory or screen work. Make use of the bubble as an anchor. Give a suggestion that:

> *Anytime you need to, you can just imagine that safe, secure, floating sensation and find yourself right back in the bubble.*

- Then it is suggested to the client that they can travel backward in time in the Bubble until they arrive at the event they need to address. Then they can let the bubble settle on the ground at a comfortable distance from the event, which they can now view through the thick but transparent walls of the Bubble.
- The client is asked to tell the therapist what is happening as they view their younger self through the walls of the Bubble.
- If they need to stop at any time they can travel in the Bubble back to their Special Place and then they can either terminate the hypnosis or they can return to the traumatic event.
- When the client has finished all they need or want to say, the therapist asks them about the feelings of the younger self and what is really needed to comfort, rescue or make the younger self feel better. The client may well come up with some idea spontaneously. If not then one of the following choices of Resolutions can be offered by the therapist.

Resolutions to the trauma

- Introduce the adult self to rescue, comfort, reassure, or promise future protection.
- Introduce another protective adult, and change the imagery with rescue or mastery of the situation.
- Facilitate escape through any means, including entry of the police.
- Telescoping trauma into 'too late comfort' (having the mother enter the scene to comfort the client).
- Step-by-step progression to the present: the past memory becomes absorbed in the present context.
- The therapist reassures the client, and may suggest forgetting 'what you cannot cope with now – it will emerge when you can cope with it'.
- Suggest to the client that they can access an 'inner advisor' for further help.

- Change the imagery so that the client is imagining a third person sitting in a chair opposite to them and telling them his or her problem, which is the same as the client's. The client then has to give advice to this person. This will be the same advice they can give to their younger traumatised self. By introducing a third person in this way, it is far easier for the client to realise what is needed in the way of comfort and advice.
- It is important to ask if the younger self needs anything further, and provide it. Once this is completed, the younger self and the older, wiser self can come together into the Bubble and return to the Special Place. If necessary the older self can leave the Bubble to meet the younger self and bring them back into the Bubble away from the scene. A post-hypnotic suggestion can be given that the older self will be able to comfort the younger self or child self whenever it is needed.
- Once the Bubble has returned to the Special Safe Place, the hypnosis can be terminated. It is suggested to the client that in a few seconds of clock time, but they can have more than enough time to float all the way back to where they first started; to where they first found themselves getting comfortable with that safe, secure bubble. When they are ready to come out of the Bubble into the present, then they can take a satisfying breath and open their eyes, becoming alert etc.

This technique is very useful for traumatised clients whom one wishes to protect from re-living negative experiences. The floating bubble is so reinforced that it anchors back to safety whenever they think of floating.

Guidelines for using the Bubble induction

Once the therapist has established that the client can float around in the Bubble and get back into it whenever they wish, then in preparation for therapeutic work, it is advisable to have some practice runs to pleasant past events first. It is also advisable to have the client floating away from the event, and getting in and out of the Bubble. The client should feel very much 'in charge' of the Bubble, and also feel safe and comfortable in it. It is also important to remember the following points:

- *Reviewing a traumatic event:*
  Ask the client to float back to an event, and view it from the safety of the Bubble. It brings them closer to it, than when watching it on a screen or in a film. However, the Bubble provides a 'safe boundary', keeping the event at a distance.
- *Regression to an earlier time in the client's life, such as childhood:*
  The Bubble becomes a time machine in which the client as an adult can

revisit and meet 'their younger self'. They can either decide where they are going or they can allow the Bubble to take them to 'a time relevant to their present problem'.

- The therapist should encourage the client to 'mind read' the characters they meet, and have conversations with the 'younger self' to discover and elicit cognitions and beliefs.
- The client should also be encouraged to engage in cognitive restructuring of an event before moving on. Otherwise re-living a trauma even from a distance will not be therapeutic.
- Before trance termination, it is helpful to the client to take themselves to a really pleasant place and to spend time there in comfort before 'floating back' completely to the present in the consulting room.

6. The Time Road Metaphor (A. Williamson, personal communication, 2005)

(a) First install a calmness anchor – a safe place that the patient can access immediately if asked to do so.
(b) Obtain permission (in trance) to work on the problem – do not rely on the conscious permission alone.
(c) Set up dissociation by imagining floating up over a time road:

> I would like you to imagine that in one direction there is a path, a road, or a line leading into the past; last week, last month, last year and all the way back to your beginnings; and in another direction is a path, a road, or a line leading into the future; next week, next month, next year and all the way off into the distance. And I would like you to imagine that as you sit comfortably here in the present, you can in some way float up, way above your time road and look down on it way down there. Give me a nod when you have done this.

If you don't get a nod you cannot proceed with this method – you need the dissociation. (Notice also the language: 'beginnings' rather than 'birth' as people have varying belief systems.)
(d) Ask their unconscious mind to float them back in time until they are over the time relevant to the development of the problem or that they wish to work on, way up high and seeing it down below them. It is worth pointing out to the client that they may not get visual images but may just have an 'awareness' that they are where they need to be. They may not have any conscious knowledge of what they are looking down on but it really doesn't matter – ask them to stop when they get the internal feeling that they are over the correct time.
(e) Ask them to allow their unconscious mind to look down on what was happening and to learn and understand what they need to do, and let

the negative feeling go, and to tell you if they get stuck or give you a nod when they have done this.

(As they are doing this you can suggest that they might want to float down as their confident, resourceful adult self to comfort and reassure the younger them or have someone else come in to help them, maybe the older wiser them from the future; they know best what that younger part of themselves needs to feel better because they are from their future . . . they survived that time etc. They can speak to people or help the younger them to do whatever they feel is necessary to help themselves feel better. You can also suggest that they can draw strength and comfort from a universal source or their 'higher self' if they want to do so.)

If the client is having problems resolving the event then you may need to use the cinema technique as described earlier (or VK Dissociation as it is called).

(f) It is a good idea to check when the client indicates that they have finished:

> *I would like you to float back up, if you are not already there and just look down and check – is there anything else you need to do?*

If you get a nod at this time then the client needs to continue to work further on the event.

(g) *Come back to present, dealing in the same way with any related events between then and now and give me a nod when you are in the present or tell me if you get stuck.*

If they get stuck then remind them of their adult resources that they can draw on and include a universal source or higher self. In other words repeat (e) as necessary.

(h) *I would like you now to see yourself a little way into the future, when in the past you would have felt those old feelings and just check out how it is.*

If they say that it feels alright then ask them to float down into that new them and enjoy it. From that position in the future ask them to turn to face the present and ask their unconscious mind to notice what internal adjustments and changes they needed to make to be like this and 'when their unconscious mind knows what it needs to know, then they can float easily back to the present and the here and now' (a double bind).

If they say that it is not alright then you need to ask if it is alright to resolve it, if 'yes' – ask the client to use the negative feeling still there to enable their unconscious mind to float back in time until it is above the relevant event and then repeat steps (e) to (h). If you get a 'no' you can ask if it would be alright for their unconscious mind to work on it in their own time, maybe in a dream, without any conscious distress and congratulate them on the work they have already done.

The value of hypnosis in safe remembering

- Hypnosis is an excellent tool for accessing traumatic memories, which are not in narrative form, and have been acquired in a heightened emotional state. Hypnosis can access state dependent memory, that is to say the client can access the same thoughts and feelings they had at the time of the trauma, at their own pace and in their own time. The dissociative hypnotic techniques allow the client to have this degree of control. The client can then slowly retrieve more information regarding their thoughts, feelings, behaviours and the context of the events too. Emotional and informational processing then takes place. The client re-associates with that from which they were dissociated.
- The whole approach is client-orientated and permissive. The therapist is guided by the answers to the initial hypnotic questioning of the client.
- Furthermore, safeguards are introduced into the hypnotic imagery so that the client can leave the scene and return to a safe place, whenever they need. These 'breaks' are client-led completely. This prevents any re-traumatisation.
- There are many ways of helping the client to resolve the trauma by re-appraising the event, by creating hypnotic scenarios of escape and/or comfort etc., which have a very effective and powerful impact on the client. The fact that this imagery does not represent what really happened in reality does not detract from the successful resolution and the emotional processing – rather it assists it. The client knows this ending is not veridical truth, but they can feel calmer, more empowered and in control of themselves. It releases the pathological tie with the past. Their cognitive appraisal of what really happened is far more realistic from this contained perspective.

7. Ego-state therapy with hypnosis (Watkins & Watkins, 1997)

In some survivors of childhood trauma, abuse and/or neglect, dissociation may have resulted in more than two ego-states, the survivor self and the victim self as in PTSD. If they are borderline personality disorders, there are likely to be three dissociated ego-states or even more (see Chapter 3 on structural dissociation). Partial amnesic barriers exist between the ego-states, so they are not in control or even not aware of the shifts from one ego-state to another. They often feel there is confusion in their minds or an inner battle between the ego-states, which they cannot control.

Ego-state therapy with hypnosis is a method for accessing these ego-states in order to facilitate communication between them. In this way the therapist and the client understand their separate purposes in the client's life and can begin a negotiation process, whereby the ego-states can satisfy the needs of the client in a more adaptive way, and work together in harmony. The 'inner battle' then subsides, and confusion disappears and is replaced by under-standing, and a sense of mastery for the client, and a decreased tendency to dissociate. Different issues arising from the childhood trauma, which caused this degree of dissociation then become resolved. Although the resolution of trauma using other hypnotic techniques also involves ego-states, namely the child self and the adult self, the procedure used with ego-state therapy for those with more than two ego-states is somewhat different.

In the case of child abuse with a number of overwhelming traumatic events to cope with, the development of ego-states may become very pro-nounced and the boundaries between them become less permeable. For example, it is important for the child to 'forget' the abuse last night ever happened in order to focus on work and play at school. A different ego-state has to block out this abuse for the child to function properly in other situations. When the child grows up then the way the ego-states operate may not be so appropriate to the changed conditions, and hence the 'inner battle'.

One of the procedures for ego-state therapy is as follows:

- *After hypnotic induction and implementing IMR:*
  When the therapist presumes on the basis of the description of the behav-iour by the client that a dissociated ego-state is present, permission is sought from the client's unconscious mind to explore the hidden ego-state that provokes particular behaviour.
- The client is asked to imagine carrying out the behaviour, and to concen-trate on the part inside. The therapist then asks the part to make itself known.
- As soon as that part has made itself known, the therapist thanks it for its appearance and asks for its name.
- The therapist will then try to find out when the part first manifested itself, and what its intention was. One often finds it pursued a specific goal: for example, to protect or to comfort the client, or to punish the client for feelings of guilt.
- At this stage the therapist reformulates in a positive way the purpose of the part, but asks the part if it wants to co-operate to find new and more effective ways to achieve this goal (such as comforting or protecting in a different way). A negotiation process then arises between the client and the part to agree on a more constructive and effective approach (e.g. to comfort the client).
- The part is then asked to try out this new method during the following week, and is thanked for its co-operation. It is important that the client

learns that the part is not an enemy that will have to be conquered time and again, but that the part may become an ally, signalling that the client must reflect on his/her life and plan some concrete change.

Principles of ego-state therapy

- Do not do what the client's abusive parents did.
- Build up trust – one is dealing with child states.
- Do not favour one state over another. Treat all with respect. (A malevolent state may have a protective purpose.)
- Imagine you are talking to all of them.
- Do not get rid of alter egos unless agreed by other fragmented egos.
- Look for something positive and constructive in the family.
- Some create the therapist as an ego-state within themselves.
- Part of the therapist is with the client and can resonate with the client and part is in reality.

Important points in ego-state therapy

- Convince the ego-state that his/her needs can be satisfied by new behaviours which are more adaptive and age-appropriate.
- Skill is needed to convince the ego-state that change is worthwhile.
- Suggest that change is for the sake of the whole (integration). Ego-states must take account of other ego-states.
- When the ego-state agrees to make the change, practical homework must be given.

Ego-state theory and therapy is consistent with the theory of structural dissociation mentioned in the previous chapter. The hypno-analytic technique of ego-state therapy is an obvious choice for many cases of complex post-traumatic stress in addition to the Safe-Remembering technique with the Bubble. Either or both can be used at different times depending on the needs of the client. Other methods of ego-state therapy will be discussed in the next chapter. These could be carried out without hypnosis and incorporated into the different stages of therapy.

MOVING ON

Hypnosis can be very effective in helping the client to make new changes in their life and put the past into the past. Techniques of age progression are often used to enable the client to get a positive image of themselves in the future.

Age Progression

Age progression can be applied in several ways. The client can be asked in hypnosis to imagine themselves at a future point in time which can be specified, or the suggestion can be made that they can see themselves in the future when they no longer have the problem or when they have reached their goal. It is necessary for the client to set the scene so they know how old they will be, where they are likely to be, and also how they are likely to feel and behave. It is important the client has a vivid image, as though they are really there already, and that the therapist asks questions in the present tense, and encourages the client to speak in the present tense too, describing how they feel.

Another method can be to ask the client in hypnosis to imagine a crystal ball, and to suggest that as they look into it they will gradually get a picture of themselves in a few months or a few years' time (whichever is appropriate) and they will see the changes in their image in the crystal ball. The screen technique can be an alternative, and the client can then imagine themselves stepping into the screen and becoming the 'future' person.

Another hypnotic technique for age progression involves the client imagining standing between two full-length mirrors. One mirror is behind them, and the other mirror is in front of them. The client first looks into the mirror behind them and sees an image of themselves as they are now. Slowly this image fades and becomes less clear. The client then looks into the mirror in front of them, and sees themselves in the future with all the changes in appearance, feelings and posture. This image becomes brighter and clearer and vivid. The client can then walk into the mirror of the future and become that person in the mirror. Any one of these approaches can help the client become future-orientated, and put the past into the past. It may also help the client to gain insight into the extent to which they have been living in the past. Using these images in a daily practice of self hypnosis can also reinforce the need to move on and clarify their goals. There may be difficulties at first for the client to get a clear image of themselves in the future but it can be worked on in a gradual way with all these techniques.

Back from the Future

Torem (1992) has described an age progression technique called 'Back from the Future'. First he discusses with the client a future image with which they would feel comfortable. Then hypnotic 'time travel' to the future specified time is facilitated. The future reality is enhanced by suggestions involving all the five senses, and using ego-strengthening suggestions too. Further suggestions can be given of positive thinking, pride in reaching a solution to a problem, and a sense of strength and inner resourcefulness. The client is then asked to store these positive feelings, images and sense of accomplishment and to internalise them, as they are guided back in hypnosis from the future to the present. The client is told that these feelings are a special gift they take with them on their trip 'back from the future' into the present, and that these gifts will guide them in their journey of healing and recovery. Afterwards the client is required as a homework assignment to write down the experience and describe what it was like to have a journey into the future. Torem found that the symptoms of futurelessness, helplessness and hopelessness were significantly reduced. They were replaced by new hope, self mastery and belief in one's recovery.

More techniques of age progression are described by Phillips and Frederick (1992).

Dealing with Anger and Payback

Most hold fairness and responsibility for our actions as core values. Hence if they are 'wronged' in some way then it is important for there to be an apology and compensation in order to redress the balance.

In the case of those who have been abused the abuser will often threaten dire consequences if the person tells anyone and makes the person feel unworthy of an opinion. The effect of this control situation is to make those who have been abused feel that they in some way deserved it and that they must be very bad. In the initial stages of therapy it is vital to build rapport and validate the client. Then during therapeutic interventions 'payback' can be utilised.

The use of the criminal justice system a long time after an event or series of events is often not helpful. Obtaining a successful prosecution long after events such as CSA is very difficult. Often the offender is found not guilty or given a sentence that the person who was abused feels is totally inadequate. The effect of this is a double insult in that children are often not believed at the time of declaration of abuse. If an attempt is made for criminal justice when they are an adult then they have to undergo giving evidence in open court only to find that the outcome of the case in no way satisfies their needs.

Imagery in order to allow payback is a very effective and safe process. While it is vital that the payback is imagery developed by the client it is, in my opinion, very important to set ground-rules prior to undertaking such an approach. If the client was to imagine something that could be possible in real life such as stabbing or running over the perpetrator then it is possible that such imagery might increase the likelihood of such behaviour. The more the imagery is clearly fantasy the better it is. It is important to emphasise that imagining carrying out a harmful action is acceptable, but this is very different from actually behaving with intention to harm, which is unlawful and criminal.

Clients who have post-traumatic memories often feel anger towards the perpetrator or others involved in the trauma. This may be acknowledged or suppressed depending on the client's personality. It is often inadvisable for the client to express these feelings to the parties concerned, but it is some-times useful before embarking on resolving the trauma 'to lower the level' of anger. On the other hand, clients may have managed to resolve issues of fear, self-blame or pain, but are left with considerable anger. In both instances, the anger can be released by using imagery for 'payback' as in the hypnotic technique called 'silent abreaction'. Silent abreaction is a useful tool to teach clients so they can use it for themselves whenever they have the need.

Silent abreaction

This technique was developed by Helen Watkins (1980). It is most helpful for clients who hold back their anger towards their abusers or perpetrators, as well as those who cannot contain it. They also may have guilt over the anger, believing it is unacceptable, and therefore minimising it. This hyp-notic method, described below, enables the client to release this anger and any other feelings of frustration, disgust etc. without getting out of control or experiencing guilt. Ego-strengthening is also included, so that the client is left with very positive feelings about themselves, and a sense of freedom to move on.

There are two methods of silent abreaction:

- *Method 1*
  Phases in silent abreaction (after hypnotic induction and deepening)

  Phase 1
  Describe a scene walking along a path in the woods. They come to a boulder waist high covered in dirt and moss. There is a stick lying nearby and the client can pick it up and give the boulder a whack. Suggest the boulder represents a specific person, traumatic experience etc. The boulder is a symbol of all the frustrations ever experienced – all wrapped up in this mass of stone.

  Script:

In a moment I want you to start beating the boulder, hitting it harder and harder until you are exhausted and when you are worn out and too tired to go on, signal me by lifting a finger. Even though you won't be heard in this office, you can yell and scream and do and say whatever you wish in this place of ours beside the boulder. I will make sure no one will intrude on our scene in the woods.

You can egg the client on: 'Come on! Harder and harder – don't give up.'

Phase 2
Ask the client to picture walking with the therapist up a small rise to a meadow with wild flowers, the sun shining and a slight breeze. The scene is filled with positive feelings of warmth and happiness. There is a clump of trees where the grass is green, tell the client they can sit on the grass and you the therapist can sit on a stump nearby.

Script:

Before we go to the third phase I need to hear something positive you are willing to tell me about yourself.

Phase 3
Script:

Pay close attention to your toes. In a moment you will note a warm glowing tingling sensation in your toes. When you feel it, indicate with a finger.

Then suggest it goes to foot and ankle, and ask them to signal again. Do the same for knees, thighs, trunk, shoulders, arms, head. Then state it comes from the client's own positive feelings about themselves, from inner resources.

Then suggest warm, tingling feelings getting stronger. Then they can signal when they feel stronger again. Then suggest this comes from another well-spring – from the therapist and your belief in the client. It is a reward for letting go of the anger.

- *Method 2*
  This procedure can be modified with some changes in the imagery to suit the client as follows (Ann Williamson, personal communication, 2005):
  (a) Settle yourself down comfortably and spend a minute or two using self-hypnosis.
  (b) Imagine going far, far away from anywhere to a rocky place, maybe a quarry or a cliff face. Scattered around are various rocks and boulders.

(c) Select a rock to represent the anger that you want to get rid of and project that anger into it. Mark the rock in some way so that you know what it represents.

(d) Then look around and find some way of smashing up that rock into tiny pieces, using whatever your imagination comes up with, maybe a sledgehammer, a drill or a hammer and chisel – and enjoy doing it.

(e) Do whatever feels appropriate with the dust etc. left, once the rock has been smashed.

(f) Go to some place, maybe by a stream or lake, where you can get in touch with calm feelings once again before returning to the here and now.

Alternatively the imagery of a dead tree in a clearing in a wood can be used. The anger is then attached to the tree in some way and the tree felled and maybe made into a bonfire.

Another popular method of venting anger and frustration safely is to suggest that the client writes a letter to the person concerned but then to destroy it. No one needs to see what has been written but the act of writing it out onto paper allows some dissociation and externalisation of the feeling.

If the client does not feel comfortable writing then they could use some coloured felt tips or pencils and allow themselves to draw out onto a blank sheet of paper whatever their anger feels like. They need to be instructed not to try and draw a beautiful picture but rather to doodle and draw whatever comes into their mind. If the client finds it difficult not to evaluate their drawing then suggesting that they hold the pen in the 'wrong' hand may allow freer expression. On a second piece of paper they then doodle or draw whatever comes to mind as they focus on how they want to feel as the anger leaves them.

Sometimes people find it useful to 'act out' a silent abreaction such as by pummelling bread dough into which they have projected their anger or smashing up old plates (previously marked appropriately with a felt tip).

Advantages of silent abreaction

- It is more easily initiated than the behavioural abreaction.
- It allows the client to yell and scream without being heard. So it becomes safe and easy for the client to feel less afraid.
- It offers the opportunity to unlearn messages such as 'it is not nice to be angry'. Then they can think it is alright to rid oneself of anger.
- Although comparative studies have not been done, it seems to be as effective as behavioural abreactions.

- It can be used in an office without disruption.
- It can facilitate behavioural abreactions later if emotional release is partial.
- Clinical abreactions do not lead to more expression of anger later, contrary to laboratory studies.
- It can be used as self-hypnosis at home or a tape made of it for the client.

In all these hypnotic procedures there are important aspects of hypnosis which contribute to the recovery as follows:

- The client can become deeply relaxed.
- There is enhanced vividness of imagery.
- The retrieval of information and recalling of events is facilitated.
- The re-association of affect and emotions is produced at the right pace for the client.
- Reframing and cognitive restructuring is more easily achieved.

Also, in all these procedures, it is important to remember the following steps or requirements:

- Always install a positive anchor first such as the Special Place.
- Obtain permission from the client.
- Introduce dissociatve imagery if resolving trauma or wherever it is needed.
- Then use the therapeutic interventions.
- Future pacing (taking one step at a time to move on).
- Reintegrate and reorientate.

5

THE TREATMENT OF SURVIVORS OF CHILDHOOD ABUSE

AIMS OF THERAPY

1. Providing stabilisation and relief from symptoms related to the childhood abuse.
2. Enabling the client to grasp the full impact of the trauma or abuse, and to find a satisfactory meaning for themselves and thus incorporate this into the memories of their whole life experience.
3. Helping the client to have a complete narrative memory for the abuse.
4. Developing a positive and healthy future orientation to a satisfying life.

One of the main aims of therapy for any survivor of child abuse is to re-associate with whatever is dissociated, so the person achieves 'wholeness'. This means memory integration. Whether patients have partial memory or continuous memory for the abuse, they still suffer from dissociated memory problems (Brown et al., 1998). It may not be necessary to have complete memory for *all* events but to be able to recall those events which contain important issues for them. The result of integration is that the person grasps the full impact of the trauma and finds a satisfactory meaning for themselves of the event or events and thus incorporates it into the memories of their whole life. Remembering a trauma also does not necessarily imply that the trauma has been integrated into the conscious self-representation and belief system (Brown et al., 1998); this integration is an important treatment goal at an appropriate phase in treatment. Helping the person to have a complete narrative memory for the trauma and process all the information about it has been found necessary to resolve PTSD symptoms (Horowitz, 1976).

Therapy involves facilitation of recall for those for whom there is clinical evidence of partial amnesia so that they can integrate their memories (Brown et al., 1998). This is not the same as memory recovery, when suggestions are given by the therapist, and false memories implanted. Brown et al. (1998) emphasise the importance of this distinction, since this confusion has arisen in the False Memory debate. The use of hypnosis in the task of memory integration has also been a contentious issue due to misunderstandings mentioned earlier in Chapter 1. Although memory integration is a main goal of treatment of traumatic memories, it is unwise to commence with this before a thorough assessment of the history, other life events, personal characteristics (strengths and weaknesses) and social influence and risk factors that might lead to false memories, have been carried out (Courtois, 1997).

Other important primary steps for the therapist according to Courtois (1997) are monitoring one's own beliefs and counter-transference which might influence certain therapeutic techniques, and also consideration of issues concerning ethics, boundaries and self-care (Ennis et al., 1995). It is also possible and likely that as therapy continues those with partial amnesia may disclose more memories due to various triggers and cues, and it is the therapist's task to work with the client to reconstruct, understand and resolve the memories and symptoms, as and when they arise. Where uncertainty exists about the veridicality of a memory (sometimes clients are not sure if certain events actually happened or not) it is important to help the client to tolerate this uncertainty. Therapy should not be driven by memory retrieval (Courtois, 1997). This could pressurise and overwhelm the client before he/she has adequate stability and ego-strength to handle emotions. Pressure could also produce uncertainties and false memories. Furthermore while a narrative memory of the trauma is a vital goal this does not imply that everything has to be recalled, but rather that the memories are transformed into a narrative and have meaning and are thus resolved.

In addition there are other treatment goals which also need to be addressed. These hold for all clients with complex post-traumatic diagnoses. Trauma experts are agreed on the general format and phases of treatment for all post-traumatic conditions, which can present difficult and complex problems in many areas of the lives of survivors as seen in the previous chapter.

ASSESSMENT AND PHASE-ORIENTED THERAPY

Assessment

It is important to take a detailed history, and carry out a psychological assessment using questionnaires and checklists. There are a number of measures of traumatic experiences, and also structured interviews for post-traumatic and dissociative disorders, which can be found in the literature (Carlson, 1997).

The value of a diagnostic assessment is that it provides information on the nature and severity of the trauma responses. It is also necessary to establish a differential diagnosis of post-traumatic stress disorder and the co-morbid conditions of anxiety and depression.

In taking a history, the therapist should explore the various stressors the client has experienced, and at the same time be aware of defences such as denial, avoidance, forgetting and maybe mistrust of others. Clients need to feel safe and should not be pressurised. Leading questions should be avoided. The interview should be conducted with empathy and concern. Any disclosure from the client should be done at their own pace. Validation of the client's information, and reassurances that it is the abusive and traumatic events which are abnormal and not themselves, are what the client needs to hear. The therapist should also remember that this is the beginning of setting up a therapeutic alliance and conveying understanding and trust. The memory of events is not necessarily accurate, and the focus of therapy is on what the client felt happened.

The therapy has three main phases which should be carried out largely in this particular order, although clients may need to move back and forth according to the needs of the moment, perhaps returning to issues of a previous phase in more depth.

The phases are:

Phase 1   Stabilisation and psycho-education.
Phase 2   Return to the experience of the trauma, and memory integration.
Phase 3   Further integration of all aspects of the trauma with survivors' view of self and full rehabilitation.

Brende (1985) has identified four important ways in which hypnosis can be used therapeutically for post-traumatic stress disorder as follows:

1. As a supportive technique to control anxiety (including flashbacks and dissociative symptoms).
2. Facilitating recall where there is partial amnesia for trauma.
3. As an abreactive technique to ventilate feelings.
4. As an integrative technique to heal the splits in the psyche.

These four uses will be seen in the following account of the phase-oriented treatment.

Phase 1: Stabilisation and Psycho-Education

The first stage of stabilisation involves setting up treatment goals, and giving information and education about the consequences of trauma including PTSD, the nature of memory and the part played by dissociation in order to survive.

The initial therapeutic sub-goals of this phase are concerned with self-protection and self-care, developing coping skills and generally trying to help the client develop a positive identity (Brown et al., 1998; Chu, 1998). Stabilising the mood and controlling behavioural symptoms of self-harming, eating problems and addictions are important at this stage to increase ego-strength and confidence and because the safety of the client is a priority. Stress management and dealing with flashbacks would also be part of the therapeutic programme. The client should also be helped to deal with relationship issues, building trust and trying to set up a support system. This may seem an ambitious list of tasks, and understandably it is often necessary to return to them from time to time throughout therapy; what James Chu (1998) calls 'riding the therapeutic roller coaster'. The following approaches and interventions have been found helpful in the stabilisation phase.

Initial approaches for psycho-education and stabilisation

The solution oriented/focused therapists, Bill O'Hanlon and Bob Bertolino (1998) and Yvonne Dolan (1991) have presented very simple but effective introductions for treating adult survivors of child abuse. A therapist may or may not continue with solution-based therapies. Incorporating multimodal therapy and working in collaboration with the client is perhaps most important. O'Hanlon and Bertolino (1998) start with acknowledging and validating the client's experience and points of view. By so doing they show respect for the client, their experiences and expectations.

Care is taken to value the client and their experience and points of view, while at the same time standing against any harmful actions they or others might undertake. Permission to feel, together with accountability for actions is emphasised. The client's experiences may be understood in terms of the '3 Ds'; those aspects of themselves which they have *dissociated*, then *disowned* and *devalued*.

The process of therapy is explained as revaluing the disowned and dissociated aspects of the self. Additionally, the client usually wants to find more workable patterns of behaving and viewing their problems. The basic philosophy is to be present-oriented and future-oriented and to make use of readily available resources especially those already shown by the client, even if only a glimpse has so far been apparent. There is a need to look at ways forward and future possibilities. The authors make a valid point that it is the client's choice to talk or not to talk about the past traumas, and the choice may vary at different times in therapy. It is not always the best thing to go over and over past events. To learn from the past is one thing but to 'wallow' in it is another (O'Hanlon & Bertolino, 1998). When the client needs to review their past in therapy, it is important they do so at their own pace.

With regard to the issue of the choice of the client, it is worth taking note of the warnings of James Chu (1998) that the therapist should not be persuaded by the over-enthusiastic client to address past traumas too early in therapy.

It is not uncommon to have clients who present with PTSD and who believe they are going mad. This only serves to raise the anxiety and exacerbate the symptoms. To explain something of post-traumatic stress disorder to a client who has a clear diagnosis of the condition can have a normalising effect (Dolan, 1991). Similarly a simple explanation of dissociation and why it occurs and how it has helped them to survive also de-stigmatises the client. Understanding, normalising and validating the client are essential first steps. Giving the client hope and a sense of a future is equally important (O'Hanlon & Bertolino, 1998). Dolan also recommends as a starting point the First Session Formula Task (de Shazer, 1985; Dolan, 1991) which was developed by Milwaukee Brief Family Therapy Centre. The aim is to help the client focus on the present and future with some sense of hope. This is essential but is frequently difficult to achieve, especially with severely depressed clients. Anti-depressants may be needed to facilitate therapy. The task involves the client listing the things in their present life which they would like to continue in the future. This gives the client something to 'hold on to', rather than being overwhelmed by bad memories of the past. It also makes a future with positive aspects into a possible reality.

'Constructive Individual questions' focus on thinking of the first smallest sign which would indicate they were getting better; what they would be doing differently; what changes there would be in their life (Dolan, 1991, pp. 37–8). There is also the letter from the future, i.e. the client imagining themselves writing a letter as a wise old person to the present younger self and giving advice on what is necessary to heal; or as an option, the present young self writing to the older wiser self about the struggle they are going through at present, and subsequently the older wiser self replying in another letter (Dolan, 1991, p. 132). This exercise Dolan calls 'accessing unconscious resources and creating a positive future orientation'. The psychological splitting of the self in this way is an interesting exercise in hypnotic dissociation, which one might initially think could be counterproductive, since survivors are too well practised in dissociation and this might encourage it. Here lies the paradox of utilising the hypnotic talent which brought about the dissociative disorder, for healing purposes. That which created the splits can heal the splits (Brende, 1985).

Where there is a partner or close significant other, the next step is for the therapist to spend at least one session seeing the client with the partner if the client agrees. This can help the two of them to understand the impact of the past trauma and validate the responses to it. This further helps consolidate an important relationship in the present which can be a source of future happiness too. This intervention sows the seeds for moving on right at the beginning of therapy (Dolan, 1991). At this stage, the client can also identify what the partner is doing which is helpful, and the partner can focus on signs of healthy feelings and behaviours. The client's strengths become an important focus of therapeutic change. It further enables the survivor to keep 'one foot in the present' as well as 'one foot in the past', the latter perhaps becoming a later focus for change.

If at this stage the client has a need to disclose the trauma, but perhaps does not realise how much of this emotional material they can cope with, three letters (*not for posting*) can be very helpful (Dolan, 1991). The first letter is written by the client to a person they would like to disclose the past to, the effect it has had and what they would like to hear from the disclosee. The second letter the client writes is an imaginary reply from this person reflecting all their worst fears, such as being blamed, not believed and rejected. The purpose of this is to provide innoculation for the client. The third letter is one of resolution; the client writes an imaginary reply from the person reflecting all the hopes and needs such as love and support. Writing can feel like a hypnotic state to the survivor (e.g. like automatic writing) but it is also in their control and they will only go as far as they are able at that moment. However, the main therapeutic emphasis at this initial stage should concern the 'foot in the present'.

Stabilisation through control of dissociative symptoms

This phase of treatment also involves a number of cognitive behavioural techniques to modulate out-of-control behaviours. It addresses flashbacks, repetitive self-harming, addictive behaviours such as substance abuse and eating disorders, and other trauma-related difficulties which may endanger the client's life. These self-damaging behaviours are often attempts to reduce inner states of tension or uncontrollable emotions such as anger; or paradoxically to put an end to numbness or painful dissociative states, and flashbacks (Chu, 1998). Characteristically survivors of child abuse are very poor at seeking support from others because in the past such attempts to seek help have been frustrated and followed by more abuse, and as a consequence they may have great difficulty in communicating these feelings or in gaining support from others (Chu, 1998). They often report feeling very alone. Self-harming may be the only way they have of communicating distress.

Dealing with self-harm is an important part of stabilisation. It is often seen by others as attention seeking or manipulating others or attempting suicide. Others may also consider that the depth of injury indicates the depth of distress. This is not necessarily so. The causes of self-harm can be various. It may just be an expression of hurt or distress, a cry for help, an act of self-punishment, an act of anger, or revenge, an attempt to deal with lows of depression, or an attempt to dissociate from the body. The client may insert objects into the body, which they hate and despise. The body may represent hated aspects of the self. There is a split in the person, who feels cut off from the body; they are dissociated. An infected cut could be a concrete representation of the client's infected internal world.

At this point, it is necessary for the therapist to have empathy, warmth and genuineness, but to explore the reason and motive for this particular client, and disclose ways of dealing with it. Self-harm is a powerful body enactment of inner pain. It is compulsive and gives a short sense of release and euphoria, which can then be followed by depression. In helping the client to deal with the pain which often stems from the abuse, the therapist should not deal with the abuse memories at this stage as they may increase the self-harm. The client may not see the seriousness of their behaviour immediately, but they must learn to take responsibility for their actions, and be encouraged to talk through their difficulties in a non-abusive and thoughtful setting. The therapies which work well would include Dialectic Behaviour Therapy and Cognitive Analytic Therapy. There can be many coping strategies also to assist the client in gaining control. Much depends on the choice of the client, together with the therapist's full understanding of the purpose of the self-harm. It is necessary to discuss triggers with the client, not only to clarify motivations, but also to be able to distinguish between truly suicidal impulses and attempts at self-control (Chu, 1998). If suicide is a motive, this has to be addressed, and a safety contract established with the client, maintaining outside support, and helping the client to accept responsibility in the therapeutic relationship.

In the event of there being other psychological reasons for the self-harming which the client may not be aware of, then they can be encouraged to keep a diary and to write down when and where they hurt themselves and what the emotion was just before they did it and also just afterwards (Bell, 2003). This can be followed by other exercises, such as describing the consequences of self-harm to the family, friends or healthcare staff, as well as describing what function self-harming served for the client. Lorraine Bell (2003) then follows this with a request to the client to write a list of alternatives to self-harming. She then encourages the client to see the painful feelings as coming from the 'hurt inner child' (an ego-state) to whom the client, as an adult, can comfort and say positive things. This is self-soothing. If the client still needs to hurt herself, alternatives to self-harming are suggested, such as cut something else, crush an egg in the hand, hold an ice cube, bite on something hard or write in red ink (washable ink) on themselves (Bell, 2003, pp. 137–43). There are many other approaches Bell uses in this self-help manual, which is equally useful for therapists as well as clients. Learning self-regulatory methods is an essential part of this stage in therapy.

Bessel van der Kolk (2000a) has conceptualised the stabilisation phase as helping the frontal lobe by learning to observe and attend, which then reduces trauma-related sensations and emotions. The client has a need to observe and describe their feelings, and to distinguish between internal sensations and external events or stimuli which precipitated them. Many sights, sounds and smells in the environment act as reminders of abuse. When triggers are identified and the client can attach words to their emotions, the terror reduces. A calming and comforting influence in the first place is essential to reach this stage. Grounding techniques are vital in the stabilisation phase.

A grounding technique is a way of maintaining contact with present reality. One of the first strategies for grounding (Chu, 1998) is for the client to use adequate lighting wherever they happen to be and not to seek refuge in a dark or dimly lit room which only serves to facilitate dissociation from whatever painful inner experience they are having. It is important for the person to maintain visual contact with the environment to retain a sense of the present reality. Van der Kolk (2000a) suggests that a good grounding technique for a client who is hyper-aroused or dissociated is for them to change the body posture and to focus on different sensations of a tactile, visual or auditory nature, such as seeing familiar objects in the room or smelling coffee. Van der Kolk also emphasises the importance for the client of being able to communicate experiences and emotions. Repetitive self-harming is a sign of failure to communicate. Creative activities and daily diaries can also facilitate communication of feelings.

A good starting point for such control is to help the client access positive and good feelings which she might not be in touch with. This can be achieved by using the hypnotic interventions described in Chapter 4 in the section on establishing hypnosis and building resources (see above, pp. 106–34).

Hypnosis can be introduced at this point and explained fully to the client, with particular emphasis on the fact that it is their own inner talent which is involved and their own inner control is developed this way; that this is going to be an effective and adaptive way of dissociating which they can learn and which will enable them to make voluntary choices of actions, and control their mood; that the current habits of dissociating have been out of control and have often led to misery and self-disgust. If hypnosis is understood by the client as a talent they already have but are not using for their benefit in their present life, they are happy to try learning a different way with it.

However, there are some cautionary warnings; firstly, survivors of child sexual abuse may find that a reclining position is a reminder of early abuse; usually an ordinary armchair is the best choice. Secondly, a permissive induction procedure, whether of a so-called 'direct' or 'indirect' approach is obviously indicated. The hypnotic approaches of O'Hanlon and Bertolini (1998) and Dolan (1991, 1998) which are Ericksonian are very effective and mostly acceptable to the clients. The third point concerns the choice of imagery if using the Special Place. It has to be the client's choice; nonetheless care must be taken to ensure that it does not contain any potentially bad associational cues. Chu (1998) gives the example of a client who chose an ocean scene which had good associations for him but later he spontaneously developed his own peaceful scene into crashing waves which took away his control (Chu, 1998, p. 115). Another client chose a mountain scene with a statue of the Virgin Mary at the top (a place she had actually visited on a holiday abroad). After one session she realised that it made her very sad rather than peaceful, because she learned when she returned home from that holiday that her mother had died.

Associations can be mixed, and one does not always cue into the different aspects of a memory. It is worth spending time with the client to discover the context and associations of the particular image they choose. An obvious bad choice of some survivors is to select a place from the past where they felt safe away from the abuser, (such as 'grandma's cottage') only to realise that this is also a trigger to unsafe painful memories. However, providing these issues are addressed and an appropriate choice of a peaceful place is made for them to return to, this approach is very helpful. Dolan calls it 'developing associational cues for the safe adult self' (Dolan, 1991, p. 124).

The powerful effect of an incorporated post-hypnotic suggestion in the hypnotic state has been demonstrated in other clinical contexts (Degun & Degun, 1983). The state of heightened suggestibility of the hypnotised client enables them to make an immediate switch in thought and mood without any protracted efforts. In the control of addictive behaviours and dissociative behaviours this is what is needed. The client is encouraged to practise self-hypnosis using this same imagery and suggestions. It may not act as a 'magic wand' nor be the sole solution to habit-change, but it can be effective as a first experience of gaining some control and providing positive experiences. Some clients have found it sufficient to help them gain control of flashbacks, giving them a sense of calm such that they are then able to take appropriate action. The use of the Safe Place or Special Place has also been highlighted by Kennerley (1996) as an effective grounding technique in dissociative symptoms.

Some clients may have difficulty finding a safe place for themselves if they have been severely traumatised. An effective hypnotic intervention is to suggest in hypnosis that they have a magic carpet which can take them to a very safe place (see Chapter 4). The therapist can build up this imagery of a strong and comfortable carpet which can magically transport them to this place. In the hypnotic state they can find the place, which they would have had great difficulty in imagining out of hypnosis.

Kennerley (1996) suggests 'distraction' and 'refocusing'. Distraction is focusing on something in the present, which is non-traumatic and can prevent full dissociation from occurring. Re-focusing means concentrating on some stimulus in the immediate environment, such as the texture of curtains or the feel of a chair. Other strategies she suggests are using a grounding word, object, image or phrase. An example of a grounding word would be the current date or place of work; a grounding object might be a small toy or stress balls which could be portable. One client combined a grounding object with the symbol of her Special Place. Her safe place was the woods and her symbol was a pine cone. She also carried a pine cone in her pocket to touch when she needed. Kennerley's grounding image is very similar to the hypnotic Special Place. The grounding phrase can also be a useful addition to the Special Place. Statements that abusers have made to the survivor in the past can 'stick', such as, 'you are a tart'; 'you deserve nothing' etc. An alternative statement such as 'I am a human being and deserve acceptance and affection'; 'I am not to blame' etc. can be agreed with the survivor and rehearsed. This can negate some of the bad feelings.

Kennerley also suggests cognitive restructuring. This is helpful if the client can identify specific situations which are so distressing that they pre-cipitate dissociation. Challenging the negative cognitions regarding the situations can reduce the intensity of the feelings and thus prevent dissociation. Sometimes this exercise is too difficult at first for very dissociative and disturbed clients, and they do not seem to be aware of the triggers or situations which precipitate dissociation and/or addictive behaviours. However, persistence with self-calming methods such as self-hypnosis can facilitate better monitoring of triggers to addictive behaviours. Flashbacks and numbing are often precipitants of dissociative behaviours, and self-harming. It is therefore important to establish the exact antecedent to the self-harming. Control of flashbacks needs addressing early in therapy whether or not self-harming is involved.

Managing flashbacks

Flashbacks are sensory fragments from past experiences which suddenly intrude into the ongoing present experiences. They thus disrupt the present stream of consciousness and psychologically take the person back to the past. Some authors with a cognitive behavioural approach have suggested exposure (Foa & Kozack, 1986) followed by image modification (Layden et al., 1993). This can give the person a sense of mastery over traumatic memories. However, Kennerley (1996) has noted that this can elicit considerable affect associated with the memory and could lead to depersonalisation and dissociation in those who are prone to respond in this way; this could include most survivors of child abuse. Some authors (Chu, 1998; O'Hanlon & Bertolino, 1998) emphasise the importance of getting the client to focus on the present experience; such as the feel of the desk they are touching and the colours of different objects around them, or connecting with the ground they are walking on.

Dolan's (1991) four-step approach to deal with flashbacks is an excellent way of connecting the past with the present, as well as grounding the client to the present reality. When a flashback occurs, the client has to start describing silently what they are experiencing now and to ask themselves when they felt this way before, and what was the situation they were in.

Having done this, the second step is to examine in what ways this present situation is similar to the past situation, e.g. the setting, sights, sounds, similar persons involved etc.

The third step requires the client to examine the differences between the present and the past situation, e.g. current life circumstances, setting, personal resources and differences in the persons involved.

Fourthly, the client needs to ask themselves what is needed to feel better, e.g. is any self-protective action necessary to alter the situation at present? If the flashback is only an old memory triggered by something inconsequential such as a smell etc., then the client can engage in self-comforting and using the symbol of the special place. This exercise not only reduces the intensity of the flashback which ultimately disappears, but it trains the client to cue into the environment and to be discriminative about the cues that are noticed. If, for example, the environment contained an element of potential danger, the client would most likely have begun to be aware of it and to take appropriate action.

It has been well documented that survivors of child abuse often experience re-victimisation such as multiple rapes or physical assaults (Briere & Runtz, 1987; Chu & Dill, 1990). It was originally hypothesised by Freud, and later commented on by Chu (1998) that this may reflect a need to repeat a scenario of potential abuse like a replay in order to achieve mastery over the traumatic experience. In some instances, re-victimisation would appear to be a failure on the part of the client to perceive the environmental cues due to the habit of dissociating. Dissociation prevents the normal anticipatory anxiety response. In either case the four-step dealing with flashbacks could go some way to preventing re-victimisation. Therapists need to be aware of the risks of possible re-victimisation, and help the client to become aware of them. After the successful use of this strategy, it can be an appropriate moment to follow with any other grounding method such as cognitive restructuring or a ground phrase.

All grounding techniques and methods of dealing with flashbacks require constant and frequent practising inside the office and outside. Traumatised people feel out of control of what is happening to them and they perceive the symptoms often as controlling them. It is therefore often difficult to persuade them that by concerted effort in applying these techniques regularly they will bit by bit be able to gain control. To bring regularity and self-discipline into their lives is a major task for both therapist and client. Furthermore, the trust in the therapist only develops slowly throughout therapy. Small steps are all that is required from the client. From the therapist is required the skill to assess accurately the nature and purpose of their behaviour and to be guided by the client in selecting the most appropriate intervention.

The emergence of very painful feelings can often be overwhelming and hard to modulate or control. Some clients can learn to use imagery to cope with this. One client spontaneously used the imagery of a door which she could open or close as she wished. She could also partially open it if she so desired. Behind this imaginary door she could put her painful feelings and close the door on them. Unlike her usual habit of dissociating, this way she felt she could partially open the door when she felt it was safe to do so. This way she did not lose touch with her feelings but also felt she could be in control of them. Imagery does not come naturally to all clients. Nevertheless, Chu (1998) mentions similar images for clients, such as putting feelings and painful memories into a box or in a room, to help pace the therapy. An elevator to control the depth of dissociative experiences is another image Chu suggests. Kennerley (1996) describes a client who had painful sensory flashbacks which he perceived as the colour orange. He practised turning this into a scarlet cricket ball which was lifting out of his body and taking the pain away. All such imagery changes and innovations are hypnotic in nature and if necessary could be rehearsed in self-hypnosis.

O'Hanlon and Bertolino (1998) and Dolan (1991, 1998) recommend the use of rituals as well as imagery. We are all creatures of habit and have set rituals in our daily lives. These rituals are often lost in traumatised people whose lives are disrupted by intrusive flashbacks and dissociative symptoms. To reinstate some of the regular daily or weekly or seasonal rituals can give continuity and stability (e.g. going out to dinner once a week etc.) 'Connecting rituals' (O'Hanlon & Bertolino, 1998) are invaluable activities for clients who are very dissociative and disconnected. These authors describe a client who kept a daily diary to remind herself what had happened to her that day. She would also burn incense, play soft music and hold a cuddly toy. This built up an association of these auditory, tactile and olfactory stimuli with self-connection. Thus whenever she felt disconnected, she could put on the music or light the incense. This kind of ritual also lends itself to mental rehearsal in self-hypnosis when sensations can be vividly elicited. Such mental rehearsal linked with a post-hypnotic suggestion enables the positive associations to generalise appropriately outside the house.

Where images can be linked to actions and thoughts, the strategy can become even more powerful. The development of alternative actions to self-harming can in itself lead to change in thought and feelings, and sometimes best orient the client to the present. Dolan (1991, 1998) suggests a 'Rainy Day Comfort Box' which contains keepsakes which are reminders of good memories. These contents may be special letters, cards or photographs or herbal teas or perfumes. This box is to be opened on occasions when the client feels bad or overwhelmed by negative feelings. Accompanying this can be a 'Rainy Day letter'. This is a letter composed by the client to the client. The exercise starts by setting time aside when they feel calm and serene. The client is required to list the activities which are comforting and also the names and phone numbers of supportive friends and/or family members. The next things to list are reminders of the client's strengths, positive assets, talents and interests, and dreams and hopes for the future. These are all included in the letter together with any useful advice and any other helpful reminders. This letter can be put away in a safe place so that the client can easily access it at bad moments in time.

It is very easy to forget positive aspects of oneself and one's life during negative moments or days, but particularly so if one tends to be dissociative. It can also be useful to have a 'crisis plan' (Chu, 1998) which consists of a list of activities which are simple but which turn the client away from very negative feelings, such as playing music, taking a bath, phoning a friend, playing with pets or animals, toys etc. or playing a self-hypnosis tape. A large envelope of handouts and lists of this kind, kept in one particular place in the home is a good way for the client to build up the positive habits and maintain the homework assignments. Small steps can lead to big changes. It is also important for the therapist to remember that developing these skills and habits can strengthen and prepare the client well for addressing the traumatic memories of the past which can be the next stage in therapy.

Managing eating disorders

Relatively high proportions of clients with eating disorders have been reported to have histories of child sexual or physical abuse (Hall et al., 1989; Root & Fallon, 1988). Sometimes the diagnosis of PTSD or Borderline Personality Disorder has been favoured without giving equal emphasis and importance to the co-morbidity of an eating disorder, which then becomes minimised or overlooked.

Other behaviours such as self-mutilation, and antisocial or aggressive tendencies and alcohol abuse become the focus of therapy to the exclusion of the bingeing, purging and/or starvation. Vanderlinden and Vandereycken (1997) also stress the importance of co-morbidity in the eating disorders which are seen generally as disturbed self-control. All these self-destructive and/or aggressive behaviours need to be addressed simultaneously, as one behaviour often compensates for another in differing situations and the motives for the behaviours overlap and reflect overall impulse dyscontrol. Furthermore, the principle of phase-oriented trauma treatment still holds with the eating disorders. Vanderlinden and Vandereycken, (1997) have re-iterated that it is only when a client has gained sufficient control over the eating pattern and other symptoms, that the therapist should begin to explore traumatic memories. Nonetheless, full control of eating behaviours may not be achieved until after the trauma memories have been resolved.

I have found that group therapy employing cognitive/behavioural methods with hypnosis (Degun-Mather, 1997, 2003) has been effective for bulimics, anorexics and binge eating disorders. Although the clients who have been traumatised will not gain full recovery at this point, and benefits may be limited within this therapy, nonetheless including them within the group stabilises their eating habits and facilitates social interactions and connections which they often lack. They are then better prepared and ready to go on to address the traumas of the past in individual sessions. For further guidelines on treating eating disorders with impulse dyscontrol and trauma histories, the reader is referred to Vanderlinden and Vandereycken (1997), *Trauma, Dissociation and Impulse Dyscontrol in Eating Disorders.*

Hypnosis is an excellent adjunct to cognitive/behavioural techniques in the management of impulse dyscontrol in relation to substance abuse and food abuse in eating disorders. Cognitive rehearsal of coping strategies in the hypnotic trance enables clients to implement them in their lives far more rapidly. Firstly by mood enhancement in hypnosis a client can recreate the urge to binge/vomit and then reduce the tension by suggestion and rehearse an alternative pleasurable activity, feeling all the comfort and sense of achievement in a vivid way. The added advantage of post-hypnotic sugges-tion and the daily practice of self-hypnosis have excellent results in moti-vated clients. Rehearsal of problem-solving in difficult situations can also be effective in hypnosis. The reader is also referred to Vanderlinden and Vandereycken (1997) for other hypnotic innovations with eating disorders, and impulse dyscontrol. Most eating disorders are also highly hypnotisable, which makes them very amenable to these interventions.

Vanderlinden and Vandereycken (1997) also highlight the very low self-esteem in eating disorders particularly in those who have been traumatised.

This of course holds true for other trauma-related conditions, particularly childhood trauma. Survivors of sexual abuse in particular often blame themselves for what has happened (Jehu, 1988). They experience guilt, shame and worthlessness. Low self-esteem in eating disorders also seems to be related to the way clients perceive their bodies. Vanderlinden, Vandereycken and Probst (1995) found that negative perceptions and cognitions about the client's own body were the best predictors of dissociative symptoms in eating disorders. This would suggest that addressing low self-esteem and negative self-image at an earlier stage in therapy could facilitate control of dissociative symptoms. Yellowlees (1997) has introduced a cognitive approach specially devised for low self-esteem and body-image distortion as seen in subjects with eating disorders.

Challenging the cognitive distortions in the way he outlines in his manual and within a group situation has proved a useful way of facilitating change, particularly when also introduced into hypnotic cognitive rehearsal. Once the self-esteem improves and the eating patterns begin to change within a supportive therapeutic group, the survivors of trauma become ready to talk about their past. They may or may not talk about it in the group but they are ready for further individual therapy. The group contacts are often maintained after the group therapy is over and it has become a supportive network for survivors. Low self-esteem in survivors of child abuse (whether or not they have an eating disorder), can lead to self-harm. When cognitions about self are so denigratory, it often amounts to self-hate and a desire to punish the self for being so bad or wicked. In a number of survivors who are very dissociative and disturbed, it can require patience, sensitivity and skill to access positive feelings or positive resources to enable them to cease the self-harming. These methods and strategies work equally well for those with complex borderline personality disorder, as for those with a single diagnosis of post-traumatic stress disorder.

Steele et al. (2001) emphasise the importance of developing a secure attachment with the client at this stage. There is an unmet need in the chronically traumatised client to seek a secure attachment, and this can manifest at times in their intense dependency wishes and behaviours. The therapist has to provide a secure attachment with understanding, empathy, and consistency. At the same time the therapist has to ensure that boundaries are not violated in this therapeutic alliance. The therapeutic work can then promote integration, adaptation and a good balance between autonomy and interdependence. Steele et al. (2001) summarise the agenda of the stabilisation phase as: containment of traumatic re-experiencing, alleviation of severe symptoms, establishment of relative safety, building a therapeutic alliance with both Emotional Personalities (EPs) and Apparently Normal Personalities (ANPs), affect management, impulse control and developing social support.

The therapeutic relationship is considered by Van der Kolk, McFarlane & Weisaeth (1996) to be of prime importance, and they have expressed concern that re-enactment of traumatic relationships can occur within therapy. They stress the need to help the client to attach new meanings to old sensations.

Phase 2: Memory Integration

The question may now arise of creating false memories with the use of hypnosis in memory integration, even though it is acknowledged that hypnotic techniques can be very useful in stabilisation and management of moods and behaviours. It is necessary at this point to explain the use of hypnotic safe-remembering methods, which include safeguards, so they only address what they need to address and can stop when they want to. They also need to know that memory integration involves translating trauma-related symptoms, such as flashbacks and behavioural re-enactments of the trauma (which are part of implicit memory) into a coherent narrative memory with meaning. By this process, the client makes meaning of the trauma, and realises that it is part of the personal history of themselves. It is true to say that most trauma survivors enter therapy with fragmented or partial memories which have no narrative and/or have no meaning for them. Where there is a clinical problem, there is a case for recall of memories, or therapists fail in their clinical responsibility (Brown et al., 1998). These authors further make the point that the crucial issue is the method of recall used.

The therapist has a responsibility to explain to the client about memory processes, the reconstructive nature of memory, developmental issues and the difference between narrative and historical accuracy. The client needs to know the therapist cannot either confirm or disconfirm the accuracy of what is recalled. The therapist must keep an open mind on what is forthcoming in therapy, and must follow the guidelines in Chapter 1.

Safe recall and resolutions of traumatic memories (see also Chapter 4)

It should be explained to the client that dissociative hypnotic techniques as described in Chapter 4 are a good choice for them to address the past trauma. First, they do not have to relive it and re-experience all the overwhelming emotions, as a dissociative technique enables them to see it all happening 'out there', either on a screen, or through a Bubble or 'down there' on the road below. They will see their younger self as though they were someone else. That may be similar to the dissociation they used in the trauma, that is thinking it is happening to someone else. This time it will be for healing purposes with the aid of a therapist. Furthermore, they will this time come out of it, be rescued and survive with the use of any of the hypnotic images of resolution.

It is far better for the client to select the appropriate modes of comfort and statements at the point of resolution of the trauma. Many clients are happy to select their own dialogue. One client selected her husband to enter the Bubble with her 'younger self' to comfort her, although she had not met her husband in reality at that stage in her life. The soothing and comforting effect is what is needed for resolution and facilitates the process of moving on. This imaginary ending is not a false memory. Both the client and the therapist know this is not reality, but the client needs to understand that the trauma can be resolved by creating an imaginary scenario of comfort, and awareness of survival. One survivor of child sexual abuse did not want to go through this procedure when she complained of flashbacks to the rape by her ex-husband (see Chapter 6). She commented, 'This won't do for me, because I know the end of that event was terrible for me.' After some explanation of how it could help if she changed the ending, she agreed to try the procedure though she had serious doubts. She was surprised when she felt so much better afterwards and weeks later said that she was never 'haunted' by that event again. The 'older wiser self' had been introduced into the hypnosis to resolve the trauma.

It should be mentioned that the psychological reality of an inner child self in traumatised adults has been recognised and discussed by some authors (Watkins & Watkins, 1997). It also exists in every adult, as something that existed in the past, but also a system functioning in the present.

Resolution of trauma comes from 'closure', that is, ventilating feelings and re-appraising or re-evaluating the event from a more mature, wiser and rational perspective. The return to the Special Place in hypnosis after this procedure is always necessary since it ensures that positive resources are reinforced at the end before terminating the hypnotic session. Schmucker et al. (1995) have used imagery re-scripting for resolving childhood trauma, which seems to be very similar. Although they do not call their method hypnosis, and do not introduce the safeguards mentioned above, they do utilise the concept of the inner child in the same way.

Once a hypnotic age regression has been carried out in one session, it is always advisable to spend the next session checking out the reactions during the last few days and addressing matters of the present. Keeping the client stabilised and not allowing the client to be overwhelmed by painful past memories is of paramount importance. To have continual sessions of hypnotic age regressions is not wise; helping the client to face present difficulties as they gain strength from resolving past traumas at their own pace is the best policy. At subsequent sessions which may involve addressing the past, the same hypnotic intervention for safe remembering can be used. After implementing the ideomotor signalling in hypnosis the therapist might also ask the following two questions:

1. Is there anything else in the past you need to address for the purpose of healing? If there is a signal 'yes', ask the next question:
2. Do you feel ready to go back to this now and feel able to cope with help?

The order of events becomes the client's choice and not everything has to be recalled. In this way the therapist prevents re-traumatisation of the client through being flooded with painful memories or what Dolan (1991) calls 'the rape of the unconscious'. Knowing when to stop age-regressions is as vital as knowing when to start them. Blume (1990) who employs hypnosis in treating survivors, also cautions against both imposing premature remembering on the survivor, and 'unblocking' *all* memories that have been 'blocked'. Spiegel (1993) who has used hypnosis extensively for resolving traumatic memories well justifies its use for trauma victims with his eight-step approach. He claims that while survivors might fear they will drown in the memories if they (the memories) enter consciousness, this need never happen. He argues that since hypnosis is a narrowly focused state of concentration which enables clients to turn on the memories, it also enables them to turn them off when the therapeutic work is completed. He also emphasises the importance of giving the client a sense of control over their memories with hypnotic exploration by allowing them to remember only what they care to remember.

The resolution of the traumatic memories, whether using hypnosis or not, may often involve releasing emotion associated with the trauma, cognitive restructuring and re-evaluation of the event and thereby being able to translate the memories into a narrative that has meaning; (the dissociation-integration model of treatment according to Van der Hart and Brown, 1992). The expression of feelings as well as the relating of happenings of the event has been found to be a most beneficial aspect of the therapy (Pennebaker & Beall, 1986). Hypnosis can be a most effective tool in achieving emotional release again at the client's own pace. It can also enable the affect to be integrated with the memories.

Van der Kolk (2000a) has warned of the danger of flooding the client with traumatic memories and strengthening their fear and anxiety. This can happen if exposure techniques are used. This method of hypnotic recall safeguards against this happening. The client is given a choice of what to address from the past, and they are able to pace it, returning to their safe place when they need to. This method is client-oriented in this way, and the client remains in control. Furthermore, with the imaginary means of transport to the past, such as the Bubble, they are initially able to distance themselves from the trauma and re-engage at their own pace. Van der Kolk (2000c) suggests saying to the client 'stay with it – I am with you while you face it'. This also prevents the client from freezing. He also believes the client needs to learn mastery instead of feeling helpless as they did at the time of the trauma. The above hypnotic interventions prevent freezing and also provide inner self-calming and reassurance which is the first step to self-mastery.

Lastly the 'black hole of trauma' which is discussed by Van der Kolk (1996) refers to the inability of the client to move on psychologically because of the continual repetitions of the fragmented memories and behavioural re-enactments. They are stuck in the middle of the trauma and cannot appreciate they have survived. Talking through the trauma is not enough in itself. The client needs to have a narrative with a beginning, a middle and an end. This enables them to re-evaluate the experience. In hypnosis the client is able to re-associate with feelings and bodily sensations, and connect them with the events of the past, and finally experience the relief of having survived with strength and resources.

Middle and later memory integration

Further therapeutic work on memory integration is usually needed. Although the client may have a number of narratives concerning specific traumatic episodes, some organisation of the trauma narratives is required (Brown et al., 1998). There may still be some amnesic gaps or the client may still have a fear of being overwhelmed or reluctant to report something still for fear of the consequences, such as the response of the therapist, or loyalties from the past (e.g. the abuser). As a consequence of continued free recall, the client spontaneously may begin to organise a whole trauma narrative and this may be a shift to a more complex level of cognitive organisation (Brown et al., 1998).

Brown et al. (1998) and Davies and Frawley (1994) have also stressed the necessity to integrate dissociated trauma-related self-representations into the conscious self-representational system. So-called 'introjects' such as the abuser self (the part of the self which has identified with the abuser) or the failed protector self need to be accessed and integrated. Brown et al. (1998) criticise some trauma therapists who omit this later therapeutic work. Steele et al. (2001) have also referred to the importance of a narrative which includes all the personalities (EPs and ANPs). When there are dissociated self-states, it is important to go through the stabilisation phase first. However, the next two phases may be modified or changed in order to communicate with the dissociated ego-states and set up a therapeutic alliance with all of them. Phase 2 of memory integration already described may not be suitable for this purpose, although it may have been used with the client following phase one stabilisation. However, if there are ego-states that have not been addressed, it will be necessary to follow some of the following procedures in order to bring further integration. This would be needed in some border-line personality disorders, dissociative disorders and certainly in Dissociative Identity Disorder.

Further integration of dissociated self-states (ego-state)

Effective therapy depends on the therapist's recognition and acceptance of the subjective reality of the client's separate ego-states, and the therapist's ability to help the client to break down the amnesic barriers between these ego-states (Fraser, 2003). There may be conflict between the ego-states, and the client may experience chaotic and uncontrolled switching of the ego-states. It is necessary for the therapist to communicate with all the ego-states and initially set up a therapeutic alliance with each of them before any degree of integration is possible.

In Chapter 4, one procedure of ego-state therapy was described, which the present author has found very helpful for a number of eating disorder clients. However, other methods and procedures would be more appropriate for some of the dissociative disorders, and particularly DID. One such procedure called the Dissociative Table Technique was devised by G.A. Fraser (1991) and has since been used by therapists at various stages of therapy. The technique allows the therapist to engage with the ego-states in negotiations so that there is resolution of any conflicts and reduced dissociation. Fraser (2003) makes the point that this is not a therapy in itself, it is a strategy to facilitate therapy, whatever orientation the therapist has. The table technique is a way to access and enter into dialogue with the ego-states. It also does not require a hypnotic induction, and although it is not a hypnotic intervention, it may produce some hypnotic phenomena since it is being used with highly hypnotisable clients who are already dissociative. However, Fraser (2003) stresses the need for the therapist to have training in hypnosis before using this technique.

Before commencing the therapy it is important to explain to the client that the ego-states have special needs and that they all have a role to play which must be understood. In order to set up a therapeutic alliance, it is also necessary for the therapist to accept initially that the ego-states are separate entities. This is also a procedure which should be part of Phase 2, so that the client is stabilised and has learned to control self-harming behaviour and eating disorder problems and to contain any other florid symptoms. The main aim of the table technique is to engage all the ego-states in a therapeutic process so that they form a new team which is harmonious and *not* to try and eliminate any of them. This also has to be conveyed to the client.

The Dissociative Table is an imagery strategy which is facilitated by the client's hypnotic skills. The procedure starts with the therapist asking the client to close their eyes and imagine themselves in a safe relaxing place (similar to the hypnotic special place procedure). This is followed by a suggested change of imagery to a safe room with a table in it, and chairs placed around it. It is explained to the client that the chairs are for them, and others who play a role in their internal life. The client is then asked to look towards the door and invite the others into the room and to take a seat. There may be only two or three ego-states at first, and more may come in later. It is left to the client to go at their own pace, as Fraser calls it 'inner directed imagery'. The various ego-states may represent different ages, depending on when they were formed, or they may be symbolic of their roles, such as being tough-looking or seductive. Further imagery is then employed to introduce a communication strategy. This is called the spotlight or microphone technique. The therapist suggested that the ego-states can speak to each other or can speak to the therapist directly or through the 'presenting personality', the client. A spotlight or a microphone (in imagery) can be used for whoever wishes to speak and then passed to the others in turn. For a full account of the whole procedure, the reader is recommended to look at Fraser's revised version of this technique (Fraser, 2003) in which he produces the full script and also methods of fusion of the ego-states if so desired and accepted by the client.

Claire Frederick (2005), who is an experienced ego-state therapist, has produced a monologue on ego-state therapy and recent developments. She maintains that ego-states can be seen in many diagnoses including PTSD, eating disorders, conversion disorders, amnesias, somatisation disorder and DID. Using hypnosis, she asks the client to create accommodation for a group meeting of the ego-states. She mentions that Helen Watkins created imaginary rooms for her hypnotised clients. It is this idea that Fraser used to develop his Dissociative Table Technique (Fraser, 1991, 1993). Frederick (2005) provides a list of methods and techniques to access ego-states including 'externalisation' techniques such as drawing, painting, playdo sculpture, automatic writing, doodling and the Gestalt chair technique (Watkins & Watkins, 1997), all of which do not require any formal hypnosis. Frederick also highlights the necessity for phase-oriented treatment when employing ego-state therapy as follows (Frederick, 2005, p. 381).

Stage I: *Establishing safety and stability*
             Building alliances with emerging ego-states and promoting co-operation and internal harmony. Ego-strengthening work with ego-states is presented in detail in Frederick and McNeal (1999).

Stage II: *Accessing trauma material*
           Each ego-state must be helped to address memory material,
           and have some cognitive coherence and sense of wholeness.
           Emotional abreaction is not advised. Stage II work might often
           be followed by more Stage I work to re-stabilise the internal
           system.
Stage III: *Re-association, re-working*
           This involves controlled affective release, re-association, devel-
           opmental work, correction of cognitive errors, and the develop-
           ment of new external resources. The ego-states achieve a greater
           sense of cohesion, developing stronger and sometimes new
           internal connections.
Stage IV: *Integration*
           Dissociated material is integrated into the personality, and the
           ego-states move into a seamless state of internal harmony and
           co-operation and enjoy co-consciousness (Beahrs, 1982).

Frederick considers that the issues involved in the stabilising phase, such as
suicide attempts, self-harming, substance abuse and other endangering
behaviours, have to be dealt with first before this treatment can begin. The
most important and vital element of ego-state therapy is, in her view, the
therapeutic alliance which has to be established with every ego-state. This
has to be maintained throughout the therapy. She has provided a road map
for forming therapeutic alliances with ego-states (Frederick, 2005, pp. 393–4)
which covers essential steps and issues for the therapist to follow:

1. *Communication*
   As the ego-states are immature and childlike, repetition is often necessary. The therapist's voice and presence, the consistence and repeated
   engagements provide a holding environment and constancy.
2. *Resonance with the ego-state*
   The intensified and comprehensive participation with the emotional life
   of the ego-states is validating. Intense emotional involvement with the
   ego-states may result in a high emotional price for the therapist, who
   should consider their own need for self-care.
3. *Interactive trance*
   This allows the therapist to tune into their own unconscious participation
   in the transference and counter-transference field, as well as resonating
   with the client's ego-states.
4. *Alliances with ego-states*
   The therapist's alliance with the ego-states provides the latter with a
   model for learning to create alliances with one another. It is necessary to
   help the ego-states to develop alliances with each other. They need help

in communicating and being empathic, and to be aware of the primary importance of the 'Internal Family'. Ego-states could become powerful therapists.

5. *Therapeutic alliances among ego-states*

   The strengthening of the therapeutic alliance among ego-states always moves the Internal Family towards integration. The therapist can encourage this with direct or indirect suggestion.

6. *Aspects of the therapeutic alliance*

   Many aspects of the therapeutic alliance are unconscious, non-cognitive and non-verbal. This includes a holding environment, providing transitional experiences, re-nurturing, engaging in spontaneous interactions that strengthen boundaries, and entering into fusional alliances.

Steele et al. (2001) who categorise the ego-states into ANPs and EPs, which have different attachment patterns, consider specific agendas have to be addressed within the three phases of phase-oriented treatment. The plan of therapy would be as follows:

Phase 1 – symptom reduction and stabilisation should include alleviation of several phobias; the phobia of attachment issues particularly related to the therapist; the phobia of mental contents (feelings, thoughts, wishes, fantasies etc.) and the phobia of dissociative personalities (EPs and ANPs).

Phase 2 – treatment of traumatic memories. There is the need to address the phobia of traumatic memories; phobia of attachment, particularly related to insecure attachment to the abuser.

Phase 3 – personality integration and rehabilitation directed to the phobia of normal life and phobia of healthy risk taking and change.

It may be necessary to go backward and forward in these three phases according to the needs of the client and their integrative capacity. Steele et al. (2001) focus on the problems of dependency and boundaries. Some clinicians believe in maintaining boundaries, while others believe it should be negotiated. However, these authors believe in an empathic understanding of the intense and painful nature of the client's dependency or their disavowal of dependency. Then there is more hope of developing a secure attachment. This dependent experience should be directed to motivate the client to engage in therapeutic work which promotes integration. Eventually the therapist can normalise the secure dependency and help the client identify insecure dependency behaviours. The therapeutic relationship can be discussed and the therapist can see how the ANPs and EPs experience it.

Phase 1 would address symptom alleviation, establishing safety and the other issues already discussed including building a therapeutic alliance with the ANPs and EPs who probably need impulse control and social support. This is a good basis for the management of dependency in secondary and tertiary dissociation. The phobia of attachment to the therapist can be addressed. Alliance with the ANPs and engaging them in problem solving in daily life, and also helping them to change their negative cognitions about dependency are all an appropriate beginning.

ANPs and EPs can be phobic of each other. Some of them may be excessively independent and avoidant of attachment. Conflict can arise between the dissociated ego-states regarding the issues of dependency. It is a gradual process to facilitate impulse regulation so that ANPs and EPs accept each other. For those who have intense dependency, it is necessary to establish clear boundaries in the therapy, and to have safe and empathic containment. For those with a counter-phobic response to dependency, they need to learn to normalise dependency.

Phase 2 involves the treatment of traumatic memories, when the client is sufficiently stabilised to attempt integration. This is when the portions of memories are synthesised or brought together to make a narrative. It is also important to include the ANPs who are concerned with everyday life, as well as the traumatic memories of the EPs. The ANPs must be aware of the trauma experienced and expressed by EPs at this stage. The therapist's role at this stage is to offer support and guidance to EPs, when profound dependency needs may arise, and to help them also appreciate the present in which there is secure attachment and help to prevent any more avoidance or dissociation. This therapeutic work must be paced so the client can tolerate it.

Phase 3 involves personality integration and rehabilitation in which the client can sustain integration, lessen dependency and focus on normal life with new coping skills and relationships. At times it may be necessary to revert back to Phase 2 if there are still unresolved trauma memories. There may also be a phobia for normal life due to the avoidance engendered by the traumatic memories. However, at this stage the defensive system of the EPs should be less activated and it will be easier for the therapist to support the client when needed since a secure attachment with the therapist has been set up. The role of the therapist here is to support the client through healthy risk taking and change. The phobia of intimacy is last to be dealt with as it requires a high level of integrative capacity. Dependency should be really secure in a healthy intimate relationship. The secure attachment developed during therapy will help the client to extend this to others in their daily life although it may hold more risks.

Blizard (2001, 2003) takes a very similar approach to Steele et al. (2001) in dealing with dissociated self-states and disorganised attachment patterns. She maintains the therapeutic relationship offers the first opportunity to the client to balance attachment and autonomy, and to experience a secure attachment without loss of boundaries. The role of the therapist is to be clear, consistent and predictable, without replacing the parent or being too protective. Steele et al. (2001) refer to these self-states as ANPs or EPs, whereas Blizard identifies them by their particular attachment patterns, that is preoccupied and dismissing self-states. The therapist's initial function is to function as a 'relational bridge' between the self-states in order to start facilitating integration. She maintains that the dissociated self-states have incompatible internal working models based on their opposing attempts to protect the client from attack or abandonment. The intensity of the emotions involved prevents the client from focusing on the discrepancy between these internal models, since the purpose of these models is to preserve the relationship with the caregiver in spite of rejection or abuse.

The development of a secure attachment with the therapist must be a slow process, as confrontation too early would increase resistance and therefore increase the dissociation. If the therapist is equally accepting of both hostile and helpless self-states, then a single enactive model of interaction is provided for the client. This is what Blizard terms the relational bridge. The client then has an internal working model which encompasses the therapist and self-states, and connection between the self-states can begin. The success of this internal working model of the therapeutic relationship depends on the predominant attachment style, the degree of dissociation, the frequency of alternation of the self-states, and the nature of the abuse (that is violent or coercive or sadistic). It also depends on the skill of the therapist in validating the needs of the self-states and the working model they have adopted. Listening to the client non-judgementally is vital as it enables the client eventually to understand the double-blind characteristics of the abusive relationships which cause disorganised attachment, and the development of dissociated self-states. This can then be the beginning of integration, that is both states begin to integrate their incompatible attachment patterns into a more adaptive working model.

Blizard (2001) provides steps for interpreting the defences and understanding the attachment pattern in therapy, and also understanding the ego-state shifts that can occur in therapy. For example, the maladaptive aspects of a masochistic defence may trigger a sudden shift into a sadistic ego-state which may unnerve the therapist. When interpreting shifts from one ego-state to another, it is important to know whether the dissociation between the ego-states segregates the working models of interpersonal relationships as in BPD, or whether it relates to a separate sense of identity and a separate history such as particular memories of the client, as in DID. In both instances there may be amnesia for traumatic memories. Blizard gives an appropriate warning that dissociative barriers should be broached gradually or there may be flashbacks, decompensation or suicidal impulses. In BPD, the behaviour of the alternate ego-state may be denied, or the client may say 'I was out of control, as if I wasn't myself.' In DID, communication between states may cause intense reactions, particularly masochistic and sadistic ego-states which reflect the child and abuser relationship. The therapist needs to help the client to slowly accept the roles of these states within the historical context of their origin, so that they gain the insight that all these states contributed to their survival. This is the basis for integration.

There are many ways in which a therapist can access the dissociated self-states in the cases of complex post-traumatic conditions including borderline personality disorder, eating disorders, dissociative disorders and Dissociative Identity Disorder. The approaches described above and the ego-state therapy in Chapter 4, are the ones that seem to be adopted mostly. Ego-state therapy is the approach which involves hypnosis, and possibly the Dissociative Table Techniques (Fraser, 1991). The approaches of Steele et al. (2001) and Blizard (2001, 2003) do not require the use of hypnosis, nor training in it. All the authors emphasise the important role of a good therapeutic alliance with the client. The issues to address are similar and the three-phase-oriented treatment for treating dissociated states covers very similar ground as the phases outlined by Frederick (2005) for ego-state therapy, and by Steele et al. (2001) for structural dissociation with the ANPs and EPs. All authors recognise that the ego-states have different attachment patterns which are insecure. It seems to be only Steele et al. who have categorised the ego-states into ANPs and EPs according to structural dissociation theory. The issues which are targeted relate to the Apparently Normal Personalities, who are concerned with functioning in the present and the Emotional Personalities, who are defence systems for survival. Those using ego-state therapy with or without hypnosis, Fraser (1991, 2003) and Frederick (2005), appear to be more client-led and wait for the client to allow the ego-states to emerge at their own pace; and predetermined agendas prepared by the therapist are not carried out at all, as happens in the therapy of Steele et al. (2001). It would be interesting and helpful to have some comparison of the outcomes of these different approaches. It should be noted, however, that some modifications should be introduced for DID which will be addressed later.

Regarding the decision whether or not to pursue any one of these approaches to deal with dissociated self-states, much depends on the progress of the client in therapy and if the dissociated states emerge. The resolutions of the trauma memories with the other hypnotic interventions of safe-remembering (see Chapter 4) do contain communications of ego-states. In less severe cases of survivors, this may be sufficient. It remains for the therapist to be vigilant. Certainly borderline personality disorders and cases of dual diagnoses, are most likely to need one or other of these dissociated self-state therapies. The present author has found that eating disorders with personality disorder respond well to ego-state therapy which seems to break through many of their so-called 'resistances'.

Another approach to access dissociated self-states in dissociative disorders and eating disorders is art therapy as suggested by Frederick. Art in the form of drawing or painting or even sculpture can enable the client to externalise their inner confusion. It also enables self-expression not through verbal language but through symbols, colours, shapes and forms. This can also be used with DID clients.

Phase 3: Rehabilitation

This phase involves consolidation of the changes that have taken place already, and perhaps learning skills in interpersonal relationships, and generally relating to the outside world. There may also be new situations that the client encounters which might necessitate new skills, or present triggers from the past which highlight more unresolved trauma (Chu, 1998).

It is also at this later stage that the client may express the wish to confront the perpetrator though this does not seem to be an issue for many clients. Some of them have already done so; others have decided not to bother to make contact. Dolan (1991) suggests three 'healing letters' (not to post). In the first the survivor writes to the perpetrator, stating what abuse occurred; the effects it has had on their life; what they feel about it now; what they did feel about it then; and finally what they need from the perpetrator now. This letter is not for posting. The second letter the survivor writes is an imaginary response from the perpetrator reflecting the worst fears of the survivor, e.g. blame, denial and threats. This can prevent the client from internalising the fears. The third letter written by the survivor is an imaginary response from the abuser expressing remorse, taking responsibility and offering restitution. This letter provides some degree of psychological resolution.

Some clients have expressed the wish to confront the abuser in reality. In such cases it is best if they agree (a) to be accompanied by the partner, (b) to prepare beforehand by doing the three-letter exercise above and (c) to consider what the best response would be to any of the worst scenarios in the second letter. In the case of one client, who confronted her father (her abuser) she felt he cut such a pathetic figure that she decided he was not worth bothering with. It also made her feel that her past was truly in the past. In another case, the client returned to the locality of her early environment and saw her sister still in the victim role and still influenced by her abusive mother. Her abusive father had died. This experience made her feel she did not need to re-enter her 'old world'. She decided she would never look back again (see Chapter 6).

In facilitating closure and resolution in Phase 3, there is an important place for rituals, letters and metaphors or story-telling. Low self-esteem or anger often seem to persist and prevent the client from moving on. Dolan (1991, 1998) has suggested a number of interventions.

Write, Read and Burn (Dolan, 1991) is a useful intervention to deal with anger or a negative memory. The client is required to write down any negative memory that still bothers them and the associated feelings, and to include thoughts and images and any statements they wish to make to a person involved in that memory. Then the client reads out loud what has been written. Then they burn the pages. The purpose of this exercise is to resolve any negative memories that are still constricting the client's life.

A modification of this exercise is to write this as an 'angry letter' to the perpetrator (not to be posted) which can also be very helpful. It can ventilate the anger and prevent the internalising of this emotion producing depression and reinforcing low self-esteem. Hypnotic interventions relevant to this stage of moving on for the client can be seen in Chapter 4 (Moving On). The Silent Abreaction techniques can be helpful to release anger or frustration or any other negative emotion.

Rituals of mourning can be very helpful. One client had been unable to mourn the loss of the baby she bore by her father. At the age of 15, she had hoped to keep this baby and leave the family home. Instead the baby was taken away and the incestuous abuse continued. The police and social services whom she went to at the time, did not believe her story, so she was further traumatised. Later in therapy as a 50-year old woman, recalling and resolving some of her traumatic memories, she had problems of unresolved bereavement. She decided she wanted to take some flowers to the grave of her mother-in-law who was like a mother to her, and to place them on the grave for her baby. Thus the grave for mother-in-law would become the grave for her baby too. The therapist accompanied her to the grave to ensure her safety but stood back to allow the client to go through her own mourning process at the grave. The client continued to make periodic visits alone afterwards, and said this really helped her.

To improve self-esteem, Dolan (1991) suggested a metaphor which consists of telling a story which evokes negative affect of a mild degree, and which has relevance to the client's problem. This is then followed by another story which evokes positive feelings of confidence. The purpose of this dual storytelling is to enable the client to build a bridge unconsciously.

This process is probably most effective if the details of how the storytelling might help are not discussed until after the storytelling, should the client be interested to know.

Many other metaphors and rituals can be applied (Dolan, 1991, 1998; O'Hanlon & Bertolino, 1998). Those that work best are those that are tailored to the client's needs and often prepared with the collaboration of the client.

Other therapeutic approaches sometimes needed

Hypnotic interventions for age progression are often needed to help the client move on (see Chapter 4). There may also be the need to address issues related to interpersonal relationships such as assertiveness or social skills training or couple therapy. Sex therapy, if required, would be appropriate in Phase 3. It is unlikely to be beneficial at the beginning of therapy. Psychosexual issues may well be closely linked with the problem of unresolved traumatic memories of child sexual abuse. Clients may present to the GP or other referring agency, with complaints of vaginismus or anorgasmia. Without a thorough history-taking and assessment, the therapist might overlook the relevance of early childhood abuse, particularly if the relationship between the partners in the present has been seriously affected by a psychosexual dysfunction. If child abuse has played a major role in this dysfunction, the more traditional approaches of sex therapy of either a cognitive/behavioural or psychodynamic orientation (Degun & Degun, 1991; Hooper & Dryden, 1994; Jehu, 1979; Kaplan, 1974; Spence 1991) may not be totally appropriate for these survivors of CSA.

Wendy Maltz (1988) provides excellent steps in sex therapy for these clients and their partners. The pacing of the therapy is more gradual and sensitive to the client's individual needs. Her approach is highly recommended. Dolan (1991) also has some interesting exercises, some of them hypnotic, which can easily be incorporated, such as the client in a dialogue with her own body parts, giving messages of comfort and healing; dancing and exercise as a way of re-connecting with the body; and noticing pleasant sensuous experiences of a non-sexual kind at first, and focusing on them and enjoying them. The survivor needs to learn that she owes it to herself to get in touch with her own sensuality and sexuality.

In concluding this final phase of therapy, the therapist may have a sense that it may not be final, and that the client may return to address other issues. It would appear sometimes that once the survivor begins to move on in their life, new challenges and/or new avenues open up, which is very positive, but they may require a booster session or further help along the way. It is important not to create dependency and to remember always the goal of autonomy even in long-term therapy. In this respect, group therapy for survivors of child sexual abuse following the above phase-oriented individual therapy can be invaluable. It encourages independence and problem-solving; reinforces the helpful coping strategies that have already been learnt and facilitates learning to establish healthy equal relationships. I have used a cognitive-behavioural group format based on the approach of Kennerley (1996); Kennerley et al. (personal communication). In a group situation the clients start relating to each other as well as the therapist, so they maintain the therapeutic alliance but also start to gain a greater degree of independence by sharing their experiences with other survivors.

Throughout this programme of therapy, the most difficult task of the therapist is to walk the tightrope of maintaining boundaries within the therapeutic relationship without conveying rejection, mistrust and/or insensitivity. When the client breaks boundaries, professional firmness combined with understanding has to be shown by the therapist. This all requires considerable skill as well as caring, and self-insight. Peer or individual supervision, or consultation is an essential part of the programme for those in the field of trauma, particularly childhood trauma.

Therapy for Dissociative Identity Disorder

This is the most extreme form of dissociation. There are amnesic barriers between the ego-states or 'alters'. It is the result of severe childhood trauma or serious double-bind communications in childhood. Great care and understanding is needed from the therapist. It is therefore worthwhile to highlight some of the important aims of therapy, to give some initial cautionary guidelines, and to refer to the uses and misuse of hypnosis in this condition.

The 'alters' or dissociated self-states were created when a series of highly traumatic, abusive experiences elicited a common affective state and began to have a life of their own. Each alter comprises memories, affect, cognitions and behaviours peculiar to itself (Mollon, 1996; Sinason, 2002).

Most authors (Chu, 1998; ISSD Guidelines, 1994; Kennerley, 1996; Mollon, 1996) are agreed that the main aim of therapy is to increase communication between the parts and thus facilitate more connectedness between the parts. Thus there is less fragmentation and more integrated functioning.

Full diagnostic assessment is necessary; for example, through the use of the Structured Clinical Interview for Dissociative Disorders (ISSD Guidelines, 1994). A mental state examination and specific questions concerning dissociative symptoms should be included. It is possible that it is only once therapy has begun that the therapist becomes aware of multiple 'alters' and assessment for DID is necessary. There may not be a dramatic presentation of different alters. The client may not be aware of them either, due to the amnesic barriers between the alters (Mollon, 1996).

A comprehensive treatment plan should include goals and coping skills already outlined earlier in this chapter, i.e. symptom stabilisation, control of dysfunctional behaviour and improvement in relationships. Initial stabilisation is important (Mollon, 1996). Premature discussion about integrating the alters and exploration of the trauma is contraindicated. It could frighten and destabilise the client. Mapping out the internal system of alters and indeed communicating with them should be done at the client's own pace. It is equally important not to create new alters or to give the existing alters names which they do not have (ISSD Guidelines, 1994; Kennerley, 1996). These highly dissociative clients are very vulnerable. The therapist needs to listen carefully to the alters and be empathic. The therapist's experience in family and group therapy can be a great advantage in facilitating communication. Solutions to problems should not be imposed, nor should the therapist have 'favourites'. One has to remember these are parts of the person; 'the family within', as it were, and each member with a different purpose for survival in the past. Trying to get rid of an alter by hypnotic elimination is also bad practice for the same reason. With these cautionary notes in mind, the reader is recommended to view the guidelines for treating DID, set out by the International Society for the Study of Dissociation (1994) and the guidelines produced by Kluft (1992) and Therapeutic Considerations (Mollon, 1996, pp. 140–59).

The role of hypnosis in Dissociative Identity Disorder

It is apparent that the DID client is frequently in and out of hypnotic states most of the time. As the alters, which are inherently child states, come out, the client is spontaneously age-regressing. The child ego-state originated during the past trauma and is virtually behaving and feeling as though the trauma is still present. Therefore the therapist, when communicating with alters, is inevitably working with the age-regressed hypnotic state of the client; as Mollon (1996) points out, it would be difficult to work *without* hypnosis. Mollon supports the therapist's utilisation of these hypnotic states as they appear spontaneously, rather than using a formal induction of hypnosis. He rightly cautions against the use of formally induced hypnosis for penetrative exploration of the client's mind, in order to uncover repressed or dissociated material. This is similar to Dolan's caution not to re-traumatise the client by 'the rape of the unconscious'. Mollon also believes formal hypnosis could lead to the creation of false memories in these circumstances. If the therapist delves too much into the subconscious, when the client is already in a hypnotic state, this could force them into creating more memories, some of which could be false.

Most therapists of DID (ISSD Guidelines, 1994; Putnam & Loewenstein, 1993) employ hypnosis in the treatment of DID for the purpose of stabilisation, that is, calming and relaxing the client, ego-strengthening, and supporting the client during a crisis as well as controlling flashbacks. It can bring back a sense of safety and containment.

One DID client used her 'Special Place' in hypnosis, which was a garden, to contain her child 'alters', and she, the adult, closed the gate to the garden for safety. This enabled her to contain them temporarily. It helped her gain control and the alters did not interrupt her daily essential duties (see Chapter 6).

Hypnosis is also invaluable for the ventilation of feelings in a safe environment of the consulting room. The 'silent abreaction' (Watkins, 1980) can facilitate the expression of anger. Challenging of the alters' cognitive distortions, and subsequent cognitive rehearsal can be carried out in the hypnotic state. This is an essential part of the therapeutic work with DID clients.

At the appropriate time and at the client's own pace, integration of the alters may take place quite naturally and spontaneously, when dissociation is no longer needed for the client. Sometimes fusion rituals can be helpful which can be carried out with the aid of hypnosis. Sometimes it seems appropriate for the therapist to ask certain alters if they are ready to join with each other. If they agree, and this happens, it can be a very joyful moment for the client, and very satisfying for the therapist. It is hard then not to realise the psychological reality of the trance state and dissociation (Mollon, 1996). The therapist can also enter the 'trance scene' when a child alter is relating abuse, for the purpose of reassurance, comfort etc. In the same way a non-DID survivor of abuse may begin to address their 'inner child' during the memory integration phase and re-construe the events or change the imagery by bringing a comforter into the trance scene.

Iatrogenesis

There is a school of thought that believes Dissociative Identity Disorder is produced by therapy. To date, there is no evidence that DID can be created in an adult who does not already have a significantly high degree of dissociation and a history of trauma or severe neglect (Chu, 1998). However, some therapists may be misled into believing that memories of abuse must be 'recovered' in certain clients who do not already have such memories, and then separate ego-states could be encouraged in the client. This bad practice can also lead to false memories. If, however, the client refers to experiences of identity confusion and internal voices (*not* externalised as in the case of schizophrenia), then the therapist might ask if it is alright to talk to one or other of these voices. This can often occur in EDs and BPD as well. There is no evidence that asking simple, non-leading questions of this kind leads to DID or false memories (Mollon, 1996). However, since DID clients are highly hypnotisable (Mollon, 1996), they will often display a number of features of the hypnotic state, such as source amnesia (not knowing where a narrative comes from) and comply too readily with suggestions and other's expectations. Their internal fantasies may get mixed with reality to a far greater extent than other less hypnotisable clients. This is further confirmation of the point that great care must be taken with DID clients, and that safeguards and guidelines must be adhered to, when using hypnosis in therapy with all survivors of severe child abuse.

SUMMARY AND CONCLUSIONS

The aims of therapy are outlined. The main aim is for the therapist to work with the client to reconstruct and understand the traumatic memories and find some meaning for themselves. In so doing, the client can have complete narrative memory of the past trauma and incorporate it into the memories of their whole life experience. This integration enables the client to put the past into the past, and develop a sense of self which will lead to more meaning and purpose in their present and future life.

In order to achieve this, a three-phase-oriented therapy is essential, after a full assessment and history of the client has been carried out.

Phase 1: Stabilisation

Stabilising the client involves teaching them how to control their symptoms and psycho-education, which includes explaining dissociation in respect of trauma, which is responsible for many of their symptoms. Validation of their experiences is important. However, it is also equally important to focus the client on the present and the future, rather than engage too much at this stage on the past traumas. Understanding, normalising and validating the client are the first steps. Ways of helping the client focus on the possibility of a future happy life are suggested.

Control of dissociative symptoms

Self-care and self-protection should be emphasised to the client. Many of the dissociative symptoms are self-harming addictive behaviours, which are damaging, such as substance abuse, eating disorders and other trauma related problems. It is essential for the therapist to identify the triggers to self-harming behaviours in order to provide appropriate coping strategies and/or alternative behaviours to deal with the painful causes which may be painful feelings, flashbacks, numbness, feelings of unworthiness etc. A number of strategies are suggested, including hypnosis with the Special Place and an anchor word to access good feelings and calmness. Much depends on a good therapeutic alliance with the client, and talking through all the elements of distress. Imagery, diaries, activities and 'crisis plans' can be used with benefit at this stage in the therapy.

The anchor of the Special Place can be useful as a grounding technique, which is a way of maintaining contact with present reality rather than past traumas. Methods of refocusing on the present and also dealing with flash-backs are discussed. Traumatised people often feel out of control and feel their symptoms are controlling them. If they practice frequently the methods suggested, they will gain some control and be more stabilised. Connecting rituals of everyday life, such as a daily diary, daily rituals, and listening to favourite music can all contribute to the client feeling in control of their life. Eating disorders also need to be addressed in Phase 1. Hypnosis can be used to help them gain control over their eating habits, and also to improve their confidence and self-esteem.

Phase 2: Memory integration

Following the stabilisation in Phase 1, the client is more prepared to address the issues of the past and attempt memory integration. The use of hypnosis in this phase needs to be explained to the client, as well as the whole process of memory integration and resolution of the trauma. The importance of putting the events of the past into a coherent narrative will enable the client to move on, and they need to understand this. The reconstructive nature of memory, the difference between narrative and historical accuracy should also be addressed.

The methods of Safe Recall using hypnosis with safeguards, such as hyp-notic questioning and employing dissociated imagery such as the Screen or the Bubble, should also be discussed with the client so they know they will not be overwhelmed and will only disclose what they feel ready to cope with. The methods of resolution which involve changes in the hypnotic imagery must also not be confused with creating false memories. Having a dialogue between the inner child and the adult self, for example, involves re-evaluation of the memory of the event and thus resolves the trauma. At this stage, it is important the therapist follows the guidelines in Chapter 1. Caution is also given against doing too many sessions of Safe Recall, as the client may be flooded with traumatic memories. Through the safeguard of hypnotic ques-tioning and ideomotor responses, the client and the therapist can discover if another regression is needed or not, and if the client is prepared for it.

At this stage in the therapy, it may also be necessary to return to some of the procedures in Phase 1 and then return again to Phase 2.

Middle and later memory integration

There are two reasons for this part of Phase 2. Firstly, as a consequence of continued free recall, the client may need to begin to organise a whole

trauma narrative, so there may be a more complex level of cognitive organisation (Brown et al., 1998). Secondly, in complex post-traumatic stress conditions, there are dissociated self-states who need to be integrated. They are
part of the trauma-related self-representational system. Therefore, following
the stabilisation phase, it may be necessary to add some more procedures to
those already discussed in Phase 2, in order to ensure the dissociated self-
states also become integrated.

Four therapeutic approaches to facilitate integration of the dissociated
self-states are discussed. The Dissociative Table Technique (Fraser, 1991,
2003) is similar to ego-state therapy but does not involve hypnosis, although
Fraser warns against using this without training in hypnosis. The ego-states
or self-states are accessed by the therapists asking the client to imagine a
table with chairs around it so that the 'others', who are part of their internal
life, can be invited round the table to communicate with each other. Fraser
goes into detail regarding the method of approaching these self-states.

Claire Frederick (2005) describes a similar approach based on ego-state
theory and therapy of John and Helen Watkins (1997). Her approach can be
used with or without hypnosis, but again it involves the client in creating
an imaginary room in which to invite ego-states for communication with
them. Frederick also modifies the three phases of treatment by making it
into four phases: (1) stabilisation; (2) accessing trauma material (each ego-
state addressing the trauma material); (3) re-association, reworking (emotional release, developmental work); (4) integration (the dissociated states
are in harmony, and enjoy co-consciousness). Frederick also produces a
Road Map for therapy, in which the emphasis is very much on communication with the ego-states and building a therapeutic alliance with each of
them.

The third approach for addressing the dissociated self-states is that of
Steele et al. (2001). These authors differentiate between the ego-states in
terms of ANPs and EPs which have different attachment patterns and also
different fears or phobias. Their plan of therapy remains three-phase-
oriented, but each phase addresses different phobias of both ANPs and EPs.
The authors focus on issues of dependency related to the insecure attachment patterns of these self-states, and endeavour to develop a secure attachment, which will lead inevitably to better integration of the self-states.

Ruth Blizard (2001, 2003) takes a very similar approach as Steele et al.
(2001). Her emphasis is on the therapeutic relationship, which she states is
the first opportunity the client has to balance attachment and autonomy, and
to have a secure attachment without loss of boundaries. Blizard also stresses
the importance of the therapist being equally accepting of hostile and helpless self-states, similar to the ego-state therapy of Frederick and Fraser
already mentioned. According to Blizard, this total acceptance of ego-states
enables the client to have a single enactive model of interaction. This is what

she calls the 'relational bridge', which then is the beginning of integration of the self-states.

Phase 3: Rehabilitation

This phase is mainly for the purpose of consolidation of the changes which have been made. This may involve skills in interpersonal relationships, or bringing closure to the abuse by confronting the abuser. Issues relating to this are addressed. There may be remaining feelings of anger, or low self-esteem. Ego-strengthening, and hypnotic procedures such as Silent Abreaction and Age Progressions (see Chapter 4) are helpful at this stage in therapy. With survivors of child sexual abuse, there may still be issues relating to sex; couple therapy and sex therapy may be necessary.

The most difficult part of this therapeutic journey for the therapist is to maintain boundaries in the relationship with the client without conveying rejection or mistrust. When the client breaks boundaries, the therapist has to be understanding but firm in dealing with it.

Dissociative Identity Disorder

Therapy for DID requires some modification in approach, aims, and also in the role of hypnosis. The main aim of therapy in this case is to bring about communication between the 'alters', and possibly ultimate integration.

The same three-phase-oriented therapy is indicated, but premature discussion about integration of the alters, and exploration of the trauma is not advisable, as this may frighten and re-traumatise the alters. Since the alters are child ego-states, the DID client is frequently and spontaneously age-regressing and therefore is oscillating in and out of a hypnotic age-regressed state. Formal hypnosis is, therefore, not advisable except for the purpose of providing a 'Special Place' for safety and containment. However, the therapist needs to appreciate that therapy inevitably involves working with the hypnotic trances that the client is drifting in and out of. For information on treating DID, the reader is recommended to consult the work of such authors as Chu (1998), ISSD Guidelines (1994), Kennerley (1996), Mollon (1996), Sinason (2002).

Last, but not least, the issue of iatrogenesis of DID is considered. Just as the creation of false memories by hypnosis has been very much exaggerated and misunderstood, so iatrogenesis of DID has been overestimated. There is no evidence that DID can be created in an adult who is not already highly dissociative with a history of trauma or severe neglect (Chu, 1998). Nonetheless, the corroboration of such histories can be difficult as clients reporting abuse may be fantasy-prone (Lynn and Rhue, 1988), show dissociative tendencies and make use of imagination in construing themselves and reality (Mollon, 1996). This does not imply that the memories are necessarily false, nor that the dissociative identities are always fake or created by the therapy.

It is extremely important for therapists to familiarise themselves with the guidelines and safeguards in therapy with these clients, as they are very vulnerable. When hypnosis is used with clients who have been traumatised and who are dissociative, then the importance of its proper use cannot be overemphasised.

ILLUSTRATIONS OF THERAPEUTIC WORK WITH HYPNOSIS IN SURVIVORS OF CHILDHOOD ABUSE

INTRODUCTION

This chapter is devoted to the experiences of four clients who are survivors of childhood abuse, and the applications of hypnosis in the course of their trauma therapy. Two therapists were involved in carrying out the therapy (one of them being myself). Each client was treated by one therapist only, but all four clients gave permission for their inclusion in this book. Their names in the text are not their real names, and some minor personal details have been changed to ensure anonymity. Otherwise all the details of the therapies including hypnotic and non-hypnotic procedures and also the responses of the clients themselves are accurately recorded.

The purpose of this chapter is to demonstrate the practical applications of the hypnotic interventions which can be successfully used to address many issues of these clients with complex PTSD and dissociative symptoms. The hypnotic procedures are very flexible and can be client-led and innovative. These four clients have had different histories, although they have all experienced child sexual abuse and sometimes other forms of abuse. There are also different degrees of severity of symptomatology, requiring therapy ranging from a few weeks to six years. The outcome for all four was positive.

LIFE EXPERIENCES OF ANNA

Problem Presented at First Therapeutic Contact

Anna, a 47-year-old divorced lady, complained that she got depressed at times and had a poor opinion of herself. She said she had been sexually abused by her father from age 8 to 16. She only remembered one event of abuse but knew that it was ongoing because her father would pay her money continually and told her not to tell her mother or it would 'break her'. She only remembered one incident of sex abuse, and that was because she remembered burning her knee badly on that occasion.

She had problems of bonding in her relationships, sometimes becoming aggressive and always having a fear of being hurt. She had feelings of low self-esteem and she became depressed at times.

She had symptoms of post-traumatic stress disorder, having flashbacks and nightmares about the abuse. She met the criteria of PTSD (DSM-IV). She reported feelings of being detached from others and had worries about her future. She was slightly claustrophobic and did not like closed windows or doors or blankets over her. She said it felt like someone inside her screaming to get out, although if she did come out, she would be vulnerable. She did not have problems of mood dysregulation, nor addictive behaviours, nor impulse dyscontrol, nor other symptoms, which might have suggested borderline personality disorder.

Her symptoms of PTSD first manifested after the death of her mother six months prior to her referral to the Psychology Department. Her mother had had a protracted terminal illness. During her illness, Anna had planned to confront her father once her mother had passed away. After her death, however, Anna refrained from doing this as her father had cared for her mother so well during her illness which lasted seven years.

Childhood History

Anna had a sister eight years her junior, and one older brother who had died about the same time that her father started abusing her. Another brother was born at about this time. Her mother paid a lot of attention to her younger sister and her baby brother. Anna felt rejected and turned to her father for comfort. In retrospect she believed that this encouraged his sexual abuse of her. At the time she accepted it, and thought there was nothing wrong with it.

At age 10–11 she realised from talking to her classmates that sexual activity at this age was not normal or acceptable. This made her feel very different from them. She then decided that she was going to protect her younger sister from her father's attention. Her sister later blamed Anna for taking her father away from her. When Anna explained the reason why she had been so protective of her sister, the latter told her to stop fussing about the past, and get on with her life. Her sister had no understanding of the impact of the abuse and the need for therapy in adult life. Anna felt once more rejected. As a child she was also abused by her uncle, which reinforced feelings of loneliness and 'being different'.

At school she could not concentrate and was disorganised in her work. She left school at 15 and took up several jobs in succession. Later she took further education and training to become a nurse, and worked in an acute admission ward in a hospital where she saw many casualties. It was then she began to understand traumatic stress.

Before Anna came for therapy, she had read a few books on child sexual abuse, and realised at a rational level that she was not different from many others, but this did not help her at an emotional level to come to terms with her past.

Relationships

Anna married in her twenties. Her husband turned out to be alcoholic and a womaniser. She had two daughters and a son by him. She had a good relationship with her children and was quite protective of them. She divorced her husband, but continued contact with him. When he sought help for his drinking problem, she supported him emotionally. Finally, he married another woman and he stopped contact with her. At about this time Anna's mother died and she expected some support from her ex-husband, as she had supported him with his alcohol problem. However, he never contacted her, and she felt very distressed and rejected again.

When Anna was first seen, she said she had a very supportive network in her family, as her grown-up children were frequently in touch with her. She also had support in her work environment, which she liked. She still felt lonely and had difficulty communicating with others, especially men.

When Anna was first seen she felt isolated because of her difficulty in relationships, and had low self-esteem. She had never sought therapy before and was not sure if she could be helped particularly with her symptoms of PTSD, which she did not understand.

The first session or two were devoted to explaining PTSD, namely that it is a normal response to an abnormal situation and to validating her and establishing a good therapeutic alliance. Phase-oriented therapy was introduced to her, so that she could gain control of her symptoms at her own pace, and then to feel more confident to talk about issues from the past which she may want to address. She would be able to do this, if she felt the need, at her own pace. Information about memory, traumatic memory and false memories was also given.

Phase 1: Stabilisation

Anna was first given coping methods for her flashbacks. These included the four-step approach to dealing with flashbacks (Dolan, 1991) and grounding techniques such as a phrase to bring her into the present. She was also introduced to hypnosis and it was explained that it could help her gain control by the creation of a vivid image of her favourite special place where she could relax and access good feelings. She agreed to this willingly. In fact she was very hypnotisable and it had a very calming effect on her. She chose a beach scene and her anchor to access good feelings of her special place was a coloured umbrella which symbolised protection. She could use the anchor word or symbol of security whenever she needed it.

Focusing Anna on the present was not a difficult task. Although she felt lonely, she did have support from some family members (her daughters) and friends, and she had artistic hobbies which she continued to pursue. She became future-oriented as well, by thinking of changing her career and taking up a course in counselling.

After 2–3 weeks of using self-hypnosis and the other grounding strategies, Anna felt ready to discuss her past; she felt she needed to and as she had gained sufficient control of her flashbacks, it seemed advisable.

At this stage, the value of hypnosis as an effective tool to help resolve traumatic memories was discussed with her. It was explained to her that it is client-oriented and she could select what she wanted to address. She would also have the experiencing dissociated hypnotic imagery so that she did not relive the trauma, but see it as 'out there'. The resolution of the trauma with changed imagery was also explained to her. The explanation of reconstructive nature of memory, and also understanding the way in which resolution can be brought about by closing the memory in a positive way, reassured her.

Phase 2: Memory Integration

The particular dissociated technique which Anna chose was the Bubble, as an appropriate time machine for travelling into the past. In hypnosis she responded to the hypnotic questioning (see Chapter 4 and 5) in the affirmative, to go back to some event which was important and significant for her, and necessary for her to recall for healing. Subconsciously she returned in hypnosis to her mother's death. She saw the event as follows. She had stopped work for a while to look after her mother at the end, and found that her suffering was difficult to bear. On this occasion she told her mother not to keep fighting so hard but to 'let go'. That night her mother died and Anna felt responsible for her death and felt guilty. She abreacted her feelings of grief and guilt in hypnosis. At the end of the hypnosis, the adult self was able to comfort the younger self. She was able to tell her younger self that she was not totally responsible and she had eased the process of dying for her mother. The hypnotic session was ended by the adult self and the younger self returning as one to the Special Place. After this hypnosis she felt much better. This choice of event surprised Anna as she thought she would select to go back to her childhood abuse. Nonetheless, she began to understand that she needed to resolve the guilt about her mother's death before she could face her childhood trauma.

The next session of hypnotic recall was using the Bubble again, and she responded to the hypnotic questioning in the affirmative. This time she focused on the departure of her ex-husband and her need to be loved. She abreacted feelings of loneliness, feelings of darkness and suffocation, and the feeling of being under a blanket. She could not say in hypnosis what this was related to but it was suggested by the therapist that she would, in her own time, understand why she had these feelings. Again the hypnotic session was terminated by her going to her Special Place and getting the return of good feelings.

In the third session of hypnotic recall the following week, again using the Bubble, she saw herself lying on a sofa as a child feeling her head detached from her body; she was very small and it was Christmas and she could see paper chains. She then began to have a claustrophobic reaction in hypnosis which she saw was similar to the feeling she had when having sexual intercourse. At this point, she could not say anything else about this event, but she showed no distress over it. She returned to her Special Place and hypnosis was terminated.

In the following session, she requested more hypnotic recall as she had felt the previous session gave her no answers. The same procedure was followed. She went back to age 16 when she had a relationship with a boyfriend but he never had sexual intercourse with her so she felt he did not love her. She had feelings of rejection and never being loved. She had a negative view of herself and believed she could not be loved. At this point the therapist entered the scene and gave her reassurances that she could and would see herself differently.

It was mutually agreed that she should have a break from the hypnotic sessions and re-commence focusing on her present life and her low self-esteem. She still was not ready to address the childhood abuse.

For the following five sessions she had cognitive therapy for her low self-esteem, and assertiveness training. Issues of self-blame and responsibility for what had happened to her were addressed. Hypnosis was used, but only for ego-strengthening and suggestions that she would recall in her own time and at her own pace what she needed to recall, and she would be able to 'put the pieces of the mosaic together'. This was a return to Phase 1: Stabilisation.

During this 5–6 weeks she began to have nightmares of trying to run away or being chased and something trying to stop her. She then wanted to have another session of hypnotic recall. The same procedure was used in this hypnotic session with the Bubble again, and she returned to an event of her choice. She related the one event of abuse for which she had had continuous memory. She had a burning sensation between her legs when her father molested her because he had some anti-burn ointment on his fingers. She knew she would have to lie to her mother about the nature of her discomfort. Feeling unable to talk was a great strain on her at the time and caused both psychological and physical pain. In hypnosis the adult part of her was able to comfort the child part and reassure her that she would be protected from further pain. Post-hypnotic suggestions were given that the adult part of her would always be able to comfort the child within, and they could come together as one to return to the Special Place and then to the present here and now.

Anna had two more sessions of hypnotic recall. In the next hypnotic recall using the Bubble, she went back to an incident when her uncle sexually abused her. The child self felt that she was worth nothing and said 'it does not matter if they hurt me'. The adult self told the child self that she is loved, and she (the adult) will always be there for her and this is not going to happen to her again. Post-hypnotic suggestions were given by the therapist to the adult self that she would be able to repeat this to the inner child whenever the need arose. This would boost her self-esteem. Anna felt a lot better after this session.

The session had clearly prepared her to address the remaining issues of the child abuse, and in the next session she was ready to have another hypnotic recall. This time she returned to the event of Christmas time when she was a child, and she was lying on the sofa. When recalling this event in hypnosis, she felt the weight of her father on top of her and she felt sick. She then realised why she had always felt sick at Christmas time throughout her adult life. She had previously blamed it on overeating. The sickness was clearly a 'body memory' of the past abuse. She abreacted much anger during this hypnotic session, but her adult self was able to rescue her child self and take her to safety, to the Special Place. Then the hypnosis was terminated.

The release of her anger resolved much of her past trauma, and she finally felt the need to forgive her father and asked the therapist how she could do this. She was at present caring for him and visiting him regularly. It was suggested that she could try to find out more about his background and upbringing, which apparently she knew little about, and this might help her understand some of his behaviour. Anna thought this was a good idea and spent some time talking to her father between sessions without actually mentioning the sexual abuse. She discovered he had been physically abused by his mother as a child, and got out of the parental home at age 13 to go to sea. He refused to talk about his life at sea, but Anna suspected he might have been sexually abused by the sailors. She concluded he had had no love and nurturing, but she felt he searched for love, and he used to buy a lot for his wife when Anna was a child. Anna now felt she could understand where he came from psychologically and she could 'put the past into a box', and not have it intrude on her life.

Anna had four more sessions which did not include hypnosis. She addressed the anger she felt about her ex-husband. This involved talking, writing angry letters to him (not posted) and painting (art work). She then felt she could 'let go of him', and let him get on with his life and she could get on with hers.

At this point in time she had had 8 hypnotic sessions, 6 of which were hypnotic recall of the past. There were 18 sessions devoted to psycho-education and issues of the present.

Phase 3: Rehabilitation and Further Integration

Anna agreed to attend the therapy group for Survivors of Child Abuse (see Chapter 5). This enabled her to talk to fellow sufferers and to facilitate further cognitive changes. She reported she did not now feel so different from others, and felt less isolated than before.

The hypnosis had facilitated ventilation of her feelings, the transformation of fragmented traumatic memories into a narrative, and empowerment of the adult part of her to comfort the hurt inner child. This in turn enabled her to view it all differently, and brought her out of the core of the trauma and able to focus on survival and the future.

The group therapy helped towards rehabilitation, but Anna still needed to address issues arising from the abuse, mainly concerning her relationships with men. This prevented her from socialising. If she had the love of a man, she believed she also had to have their abuse. Therefore, she was unable to accept any commitment, and was not happy with this; she still felt very lonely and wanted to change.

Hypnosis was again used to help her make appropriate changes for herself and call on her own resources. Post-hypnotic dream suggestion was used (see Chapter 4); it was suggested she would have a dream, which would throw light on her problem, and she would find a possible solution with help from the therapist. She had a night dream following this hypnotic session.

The content was about a little girl terrified by an attacking ostrich. This made her choke, sneeze and vomit, and then she felt cleansed. Anna did not understand the dream, so dream elaboration in hypnosis was offered, she then went back (during hypnosis) to another memory when she was a little girl and she was abused and hurt by her father and she shut herself away in a shed. She then commented in hypnosis that this little girl had been shut away for too long in the dark and wanted to come into the sunshine, but she was too frightened. At this point it was necessary to resolve the trauma. Anna the adult self then entered the scene and told the child self that she would always protect her and keep her safe, so she could come into the sunshine.

Anna felt a lot more positive after this session and was more confident to try and expand her social life. However, during the following few weeks she was persuaded to take sick leave as she had over-stressed herself at work and had not paced herself. She had also been over-committed to the demands of her family. Little progress was made during this period though she began to gain insight into the reasons for taking on so much work. She could avoid focusing on her own needs and her social relationships, which she was afraid of pursuing. She did not want to move from the familiar areas into new ones; she believed something was holding her back, but she did not understand what. There was some fear and some anger remaining. Some of the letters suggested by Dolan (1991), such as 'Write, Read and Burn' began to help her. The Rainy Day Letter also helped her focus on herself, her needs and gave her some sense of identity and confidence, but she still felt 'blocked', as she put it.

Hypnosis was again used for a post-hypnotic dream suggestion to throw more light on her continual social withdrawal. This hypnotic session was to facilitate a dream or thought during the day or night after the session. However, Anna voiced her fears as well during the hypnotic session. She spontaneously revealed that she felt that letting people near her was like going over a precipice – would she be a different person? She could not answer this. The hypnosis was terminated with a return to the Special Place.

In the following session, a week later, she reported having had two night dreams; in the first dream she was in a castle under siege, which she did not understand. She was then given hypnosis for dream elaboration. She related the dream in hypnosis as follows: she was looking out of a window of the castle and she heard people singing in the fields and she wanted to get out and join them. She was frightened to go out, but someone picked her up to carry her down and she was frightened no more. She was then outside and the sun was shining. She wanted to walk into the fields to join the people, but felt she had to stay near the castle walls. How could she get to the people if she wanted to be safe? She tried travelling in her protective Bubble through the fields to the people. The sun was shining and it was getting brighter and brighter.

The second night dream was about a castle on a mountain, and marauders were trying to get in, but there was no way in as she had blocked all the entrances. During another session of hypnotic dream elaboration, she said she had been in the castle too long and she had to get out. She decided to get into her protective Bubble and go over the top of the castle and travel towards the light. She was then high in the sky and the light was very bright, and she was safe up there. Now she should come down into the light below, which she could do in her own time and at her own pace, using her protective Bubble when she needed. Anna felt considerably better after this session. She was subsequently able to bring herself out of a nightmare or panic by using the Bubble. This gave her added confidence in her own resources.

It is interesting to note that Anna had two night dreams which subconsciously reflected her problem of isolation and fear of relationships. She nonetheless could not understand them consciously. However, with dream elaboration in hypnosis, she was not only able to understand them, she was able to resolve the problem by using the hypnotic imagery of the safe Bubble. No suggestions or cues were given by the therapist. It was totally her own inner resources she had accessed.

The following week she had had another night dream about a clock ticking away threatening her. She said in the dream, 'I have to get out and I can take the Bubble.' After this dream she felt a lot more positive to take the risk to socialise more. She also went back to work and paced herself better at work.

Anna was given a last session of hypnosis with ego-strengthening suggestions.

These subsequent hypnotic sessions seemed to motivate her more to experiment in her social life to make changes and take her out of her isolation. It enabled her to have more concern for her own needs and she was motivated to return to the cognitive therapy which she had started during Phase 2 in her assertiveness training. In doing this, she realised that she had focused on all the negative statements made to her by others, and dismissed all the positive statements. The hypnosis combined with the cognitive therapy helped her to come out of her life-long tendency to social withdrawal and a lifestyle of chores and no pleasure. She began slowly to feel a sense of happiness, freedom and light, as she put it. She began to enjoy her life more, and went on trips to the seaside with friends, which helped her reclaim her lost childhood.

There were 13 sessions of hypnosis and 26 sessions in total over a period of seven months.

In conclusion, Anna finally resolved her traumatic memories and had no more symptoms of PTSD and was successfully moving on in her life. This was achieved by employing the three-phase-oriented approach in the trauma treatment and establishing a good therapeutic alliance.

In *Phase 1*, Anna stabilised herself by adopting techniques to control flashbacks and to focus on agendas in the present. The hypnotic Special Place with anchor word was particularly helpful.

In *Phase 2*, the hypnotic dissociative technique of the Bubble selected by Anna for the purpose of hypnotic recall of past abuse, enabled her to resolve a number of traumatic events, some of which she had not consciously identified. Issues affecting her in the present, such as low self-esteem and lack of assertiveness, were also addressed in Phase 2. This built up her confidence to complete the resolution of her traumas and to make meaning for her with a coherent narrative of what happened to her.

Phase 3 involved motivating her to break her old habits and beliefs about relationships, and her social withdrawal. These changes were made by the use of Hypnotic Dream Suggestions. This not only uncovered the nature of the problem but also how to solve it and break through the subconscious barriers. This hypnotic intervention also enabled her to access hidden resources she did not know she had. All these hypnotic interventions were client-led. Apart from setting up the hypnotic script, all solutions were initiated by the client and not by the therapist.

No false memories were created. The resolutions of the trauma memories involved change of the ending by hypnotic imagery, which was fully appreciated by the client and it merely assisted her in realising she survived and put the 'past into the past'.

At the end of Phase 2, only two ego-states, namely the adult self and the child self, were involved in the resolution of the trauma and integration. No other ego-states appeared. However, it could be argued the hypnotic dreams in Phase 3 indicated two parts of the client; the part that was fearful of relating to others, particularly men, and the part that wanted to be loved, and to take the risk and develop a relationship. This seemed to reflect two different attachment patterns belonging to two ego-states, one being insecure and avoidant, and perhaps the other being insecure and ambivalent. One might also label them Emotional Personality (EP) and Apparently Normal Personality (ANP) respectively. Ego-state therapy could have been used. However, the dream solutions seemed to bring about integration, and Anna did not appear to be in conflict afterwards.

Follow-up

Five years later, Anna was contacted and she had followed a career which she enjoyed, counselling. She had married again, which she had said she would never do because of her problems. She presented as a confident and happy woman. She said that whenever she faced a problem or difficulty, she imagined it like a wall and used the Bubble to take her over the wall. This gave her strength to work through the problem and helped her access her inner resources. Finally, she gave the therapist a 'letter' which expresses her feelings, and which she hoped would give encouragement to other survivors. This 'letter', she labelled 'Message in a Bottle' (see below).

Message in a Bottle

Many years ago, I recorded a programme that was shown on television. It was a short story about a shy lonely girl, who had been mentally abused by her mother. In the story, she put a message in a bottle and threw it into the sea. That message touched something inside me and I wrote it down.

The message was. . . . . .

THERE IS IN CERTAIN LIVING SOULS A LONELINESS UNSPEAKABLE, SO GREAT IT MUST BE SHARED AS COMPANY IS SHARED BY LESSER BEINGS.
SUCH A LONELINESS IS MINE AND KNOW BY THIS, THAT IN IMMENSITY THERE IS ONE LONELIER THAN YOU . . .

I had always felt so alone. No one could understand how I felt. No one was like me and yet here in a simple television programme was someone expressing the feelings I had experienced all my life.

As a child I did not belong. I did not fit. I was a grey Non-descript person. I was not like other children more an Adult/Child or a Child/Adult. I did not understand why I did not fit but I knew instinctively I did not. This feeling of not belonging went on into adulthood. I was a part of society but not a part of it. Do you know what I mean? I could be sitting at a table with a group of friends, but not there. It was as though I was on the outside looking in at them enjoying themselves and feeling left out.

I had from a child, by necessity built a wall around myself, this was my survival kit, my way of dealing with the pain from my past.

CLOSE MYSELF OFF.
DO NOT LET ANYONE IN TOO CLOSE.
SHUT OUT THE PAST.
PRETEND IT DID NOT HAPPEN.
PRETEND IT DID NOT AFFECT ME.
PRETEND TO BE HAPPY.
DO NOT LET ANYONE KNOW YOU ARE SCREAMING INSIDE.
HIT OUT BEFORE THEY HURT YOU.
TRY VERY HARD TO BE PERFECT.

These and many others were part of my survival kit. I felt worthless, less than worthless, I felt I was nothing. I did not deserve to be happy. I did not deserve to be loved. I was unlovable. After all hadn't I been taught that I was only fit to be abused. What was I good for?

All the things I had achieved in my life did not matter, all the things I had done to prove I was worth something. I still felt worthless.

Then something wonderful happened. My Mother died. I'm sure you are thinking how could this be wonderful, in a way you are right. I loved my Mother very much and could never have hurt her in any way. She never knew about my abuse from my father. She became an invalid and gradually gave up the will to live. She was ready to die not wanting to go on the way she was.

I always believed when she died I could face my father and hate him for what he had done. But when my Mother became ill this horrible man who had been a dreadful husband and a worse father became a paragon, a saint. He devoted his whole life to her; caring for her, waiting on her hand and foot, in fact doing everything he could to make her life comfortable. Consequently, eight years later when she was dying, she asked me to look after him and because he had been so good to her, I found I was unable to say or do all the things I had imagined I would.

I really don't know if I would have, even if things had been different. This caused me a lot of heartache and suffering, so much so, that I became very depressed to the point of suicide. My work suffered, my family relationships suffered and life seemed to take a downhill turn. A work colleague suggested and encouraged me to seek help and got in touch with a Psychotherapist who agreed to see me.

I am not saying it's been easy. It hasn't it's been a lot of hard work, therapy, hypnotism, self-evaluation, studying, time, heartache and tears. But it has been worth it. Now I know I am a valuable lovable worthwhile human being who was cheated out of her childhood by an abuser through no fault of her own and SURVIVED.

I can say it . . .

I AM A SURVIVOR.

I'll repeat that. I AM A SURVIVOR.

YOU ARE A SURVIVOR . . .

If we were not survivors we would not be here today. We have an inner strength that we are not aware of. If we had not, we would not have survived.

It's remarkable what you can do once you start to realize your worth. It doesn't happen overnight. It gets better only if you work at it, only if you are willing to go through whatever it takes to make it work for you.

I can now see the sun. I am now part of humanity. Now I belong.

I have not forgotten, I have not even forgiven. But now I can move on safe in the knowledge that my future depends on me.

I still have my down days, I still get sad, I still wish I could change the past. Who doesn't! But it's far less now than it used to be and improving all the time. I don't sit and wait. I do something about it.

I am now part of the human race. Consequently I realize everyone would like to change something from their past. But now I know.

I AM NOT ALONE ANYMORE.

YOU ARE NOT ALONE . . .

End of letter, 'Message in a Bottle'

LIFE EXPERIENCES OF BERYL

Problem Presented at First Therapeutic Contact

Beryl, aged 42 and married with two daughters, was initially referred for psychosexual counselling. She had suffered anorgasmia for the whole of her married life. She had never told her husband that she did not enjoy sex, but she now felt she should and seek help for her problem. Other than this, she claimed there were no problems in her life today.

Childhood History

Beryl was the eldest of five children. She and three of the other children were taken into care when she was aged four. She was not sure why they were taken into care, but she had big memory gaps and felt she had lost her childhood. She and her siblings were returned to the parents when she was 13 years old. Her mother then brought men into the home and neglected the children and sexually abused Beryl. Her father also sexually abused her and another sister. The family lived in different lodgings throughout the next few years, Beryl was also sexually abused by one of the landlords for a whole year. Her father used her as a prostitute for male friends of his, who gang raped her. She remembered she had to pose for them. During her adolescence she ran away from home and lived with a distant relative and her husband. This was only for about 18 months but Beryl felt for the first time she had been cared for and nurtured. She eventually had to return home and then married her first boyfriend at age 18 to get away from her abusive parents.

Marriage and Relationships

Beryl admitted that she had never told her husband about her traumatic early life. She was too ashamed. She had also never admitted to him that she had only had sex with him to please him, and to have the children. She said that she had only twice experienced an orgasm throughout her married life. Nonetheless, she cared very much for her husband and they had had a harmonious relationship until recently when she had refused sex, because she did not want to pretend she enjoyed it any more.

Her relationship with her daughters was good, but she had had problems showing them affection in a demonstrative way, such as kissing and cuddling them, especially when they were young. She could hug her husband, however.

Beryl reported that she had difficulty in trusting people in general, because she felt she would eventually be let down and hurt. However, she had learned to trust her husband, and she said they had communicated well over the years until recently when she had started to refuse sex. This had caused rows between them.

Over the 24 years of marriage, Beryl had been a conscientious wife and mother. She had had a very abusive family background and she was determined her children would not suffer the same. Her daughters were well educated, and had no emotional problems. Although she herself had had a very disrupted schooling, and had no qualifications, she wanted to give her children a good start in life. She also wanted to improve herself, and as her children grew up she decided to start working in a part-time job. She was able to relate well to the people in the work place, and was a sociable, caring person outside the home as well.

When Beryl was referred for therapy, she considered that she had put the past into the past and did not need to talk about it any more. Now her own children were grown up and had left home (one of them was married), she wanted to be able to improve her marital relationship and be able to have intimate contact with her husband and enjoy it.

First Therapeutic Intervention

Couple therapy and psychosexual counselling were commenced for both Beryl and her husband who were seen together. It soon became very clear that Beryl's concern to keep secret her past traumatic childhood was preventing her being direct and honest about her true feelings and communicating these to her husband. Beryl then told the therapist that she wanted to divulge her past to her husband in the presence of the therapist in order to have emotional support. This was arranged, and her husband's response was very understanding; in fact the disclosure created a better bond between them. She became less depressed and less emotionally withdrawn. The sexual relationship improved. She decided to terminate the therapy after they had had weekly sessions for three months. However, she returned for further help as the renewed intimate contact with her husband was causing flashbacks to the abuse. She also had developed irritability and hypervigilance and felt despondent, as she believed there was nothing more she could do about the past abuse affecting her this way. It was apparent she had symptoms of PTSD as the sexual activity was also triggering traumatic memories of the abuse.

A full explanation of PTSD was given to the couple. Beryl was reassured she did not have to live with it for the rest of her life, and that she could resolve traumatic memories with help from an alternative therapeutic approach and finally be able to have satisfactory sexual relations with her husband.

As with all survivors of trauma, Beryl received the appropriate psycho-education about the nature of trauma memory, and how it can be resolved by becoming a coherent narrative. The three phases of trauma therapy were also discussed. Beryl accepted this and seemed relieved that something could help her to recover from her painful mental state.

The value of hypnosis, and its use in resolving traumatic memories in a painless way was also put to her. She agreed to this willingly. She also learned about the reconstructive nature of memory, and that false memories would not be created.

Phase 1: Stabilisation

Beryl attended alone for her trauma therapy. She received further information about hypnosis and how it could be used to help her gain control over her symptoms, particularly flashbacks, and mood swings. She accepted this idea as well. Her first session of hypnosis was her Special Place (see Chapter 4). She chose a cottage with roses round the door in the countryside. It was sunny and warm and miles away from any town. Her anchor word to access the good feelings was 'cottage'. She was very hypnotisable and hypnosis calmed her and enabled her to use the anchor word to control flashbacks. She was also given Dolan's four-step approach to dealing with flashbacks (Dolan, 1991, p. 106).

These two coping strategies were successful in stabilising her, and she understood that she was not to attempt any intimacy with her husband until much later in the therapy. This was also accepted by her husband. She practised self-hypnosis every day to reinforce the anchor word and the good feelings of the Special Place. She benefited a lot from this. After three weeks, Beryl seemed ready to address the past trauma. As she had agreed to having hypnosis for this too, she was offered a choice of methods that could be used. She chose the Bubble. The whole procedure was discussed with her first, and also how she could resolve the traumatic event if she chose to visit it in the Bubble. The hypnotic questioning was also discussed which gave her choice together with safeguards so that she only visited what she needed to in order to heal. The way to resolve the trauma by reconstructing the ending was explained too.

Phase 2: Memory Integration

In the first session of hypnotic recall, she responded to the hypnotic questions in the affirmative and subconsciously selected a time when she was sexually abused by the landlord, where the family stayed after she was taken out of care at age 13. She related how the landlord threatened her that if she told her parents, they would throw her out of the house. This sexual abuse continued for one year. She recalled how her father also commenced abusing her sexually, saying that he could use her as a prostitute to get money and therefore did not need to work. Beryl ventilated feelings of anger and despair during hypnosis. She expressed feelings of hate towards her parents; first for putting her into care and then abusing her. The total lack of real care and affection, the emotional and verbal abuse and rejection greatly distressed her. No one, she said, ever listened to her, and she never experienced anything good in her childhood. She cried, 'I am angry; I do not know who I am; I am put here and I am 42 now and cannot remember any nice times.'

To resolve this traumatic memory, the 13-year-old part of her needed someone to love her and someone to cuddle her. However, Beryl the adult part, was unable to get an image of her child self at this age. She was therefore encouraged by the therapist to imagine another 13 year old with similar experiences standing before her (the adult self) while she listened to the child's story. She could listen to her and believe her, although she (the adult) still felt unable to offer the child words of comfort or cuddle her. This was just one step towards interacting with a hurt and angry child. She returned to her Special Place before ending the hypnosis.

Beryl had tried to block out her memories of child abuse for so long and pretended it happened to someone else. She could not now access the child part of her. She did, however, access feelings which were very strong, and overwhelming. Therapeutically it seemed important for her now to deal with the feelings.

For several sessions after this hypnotic intervention, she kept a diary of her feelings of anger, hate and despair, which surfaced from time to time; she also did drawings of herself in a prison. She released a lot of her anger by doing the 'stomp walk' in her garden. Sometimes she found herself spontaneously trying to stop the anger or dissociate from it. From her diaries, it was clear she had difficulty connecting some of her feelings to events, and she thought she had more to remember. She wrote in her diary that the art work, the writing, playing music and doing self-hypnosis helped her deal with the feelings, and that she had belief in hypnosis helping her to access the inner child. She also considered her self-hypnosis helped calm her down and the anchor word gave her some control. Her husband was also very supportive during this time. This was a period of returning to Phase 1: Stabilisation.

One Saturday evening she went out with friends and they were taking photographs with a flashbulb camera. She became very agitated by this and did not know why. She began to cry a lot; she thought she was mourning her lost childhood. This seemed to be the right moment for her to make the connections between her feelings and events and piece together these fragmented memories.

At this point, the therapist gave her a choice of the hypnotic interventions. She preferred not to select the Bubble or even an Affect Bridge, but rather a post-hypnotic suggestion to have a night dream about an event she had not resolved (see Chapter 4). At the next session she brought the written account of two dreams she had had on two consecutive nights. The first dream she was in a dark room, and there were lights flashing like a camera, and some people were talking very loudly. Someone was there trying to comfort her. She woke up at this point screaming. She could not go back to sleep after this although her husband comforted her. In the second dream on the following night, she was locked in a room with no lights, and she was banging on the door to get out. Then she awoke.

In hypnotic dream elaboration, she chose to run the second dream first. She said she was outside the dark room and could not see into it, but heard male voices talking (this was a slight modification of her second dream). She believed she would scream if she went in there; she had always been afraid of the dark. She thought the men inside wanted to take her into the room. Then she kept seeing the flashing lights from a camera, and she did not feel safe. She thought she was very little then, but she commented she had difficulty remembering she had ever been a child. She felt she needed to understand what this room was about. A post-hypnotic suggestion was given that she would see this in her own time and at her own pace. She did not want to run through the first dream. For the next two sessions she felt there was a wall or barrier preventing her from understanding this dark room. She was very distressed and agitated that she did not know what was stopping her from understanding her dream fully.

During these two sessions, which were spent discussing possibilities, she said that part of her does enjoy sex and another part of her does not want to go there. She came to her own conclusion, without any suggestions from the therapist, that this part of her was 'the child in her'. She said she felt ready to access this inner child, but chose a hypnotic dream to do this, rather than ego-state therapy. She felt she could see herself as a child in a dream. At the next session in hypnosis she was given a post-hypnotic suggestion that she would have a dream which would throw light on the meaning of the dark room from her previous dream.

The third dream she had a few nights later. She presented it in writing at the next session. She dreamt of a dark room in which there were flashing lights. She was outside crying and she did not want to go in. Her mother gave her sweets and pushed her in and left her there. She saw two men and her father who took a picture of her. She was undressed and the two men had sex with her. Then the dream switched and she was taken to hospital in an ambulance. When she was better she was taken to a home and her parents did not see her. A policewoman then came to see her in the home. This was all she could remember of the dream.

In hypnotic dream elaboration she saw herself screaming as this event unfolded. She wondered why her mother did not come when she screamed. ('Why doesn't someone come and rescue that screaming child?' she said in hypnosis). She could not believe no one was there to help her, nor could she believe that her father would undress her and take her clothes off. There were three men there and no one would help this child who went on screaming. She believed, as an adult observing this event in hypnosis, that the men were sick in their minds. Resolution of the trauma was then carried out by the adult/child interaction. It was suggested to her that she might offer the child whatever she needs. She said she needed to be brought out of this place and cuddled, but she (as an adult) did not feel safe to enter the scene to do this. The adult part felt she might kill the parents. Instead, she brought in the police woman to do it. She also did not feel able to cuddle the child, but she did tell her it was not her fault and she would get away from her parents. The adult self and child self returned to the Special Place again before ending the hypnosis.

Beryl felt relieved after this, as she had now made sense of her previous over-reaction to flashing lights at the Saturday night social, namely that the dark room in her dreams was related to the abuse. One might argue that this was only a dream and her fantasy, which did not necessarily reflect what actually happened to her as a small child. She had very few memories of her early childhood. The content of this dream, nonetheless, was consistent with what she described happened to her in adolescent years for which she had had continuous memory. Furthermore, this dream helped her to connect with her deep feelings of hurt and anger and to relate them to this horrific abuse. She had at last accessed the inner child. For the next two sessions, she talked about her anger and hurt, and wrote angry letters to her parents (not posted), and released some of her feelings by pillow beating.

Some degree of dissociation still remained. She commented that she still felt this child who was screaming in her dreams was someone else and not herself. She therefore could still not integrate the child sexual abuse into her autobiographical memory. It is interesting that in one of her angry letters addressed to her mother, she wrote that because of the abuse, she had gone through the whole of her life 'being someone else because I cannot bear the shame'. Later in the letter, she wrote 'I get down and cry and I cannot comfort the child in me, because *you* never comforted me.' These two insights threw light on the nature of her difficulty in re-associating with her childhood feelings and events.

One more hypnotic recall, using the Bubble, was successful in enabling her to identify more with her inner child, the part of her that held so many memories of the abuse. Beryl selected the Bubble to help her with this task.

First, she chose to regress to age 4. She felt very insecure and confused trying to talk to her parents. She particularly wanted to talk to her mother but could not do so. As the adult self, she 'mind-read' her mother and father as people who have no care or affection, and she did not even know where they came from. She felt there was no point in trying to talk to them. The adult part of her then decided to take the child out of the scene and into the Bubble. The adult told the child that she would survive and it would not happen again. She was then able to take the child in the Bubble back to her Special Place. This was the first time she said she was really able to contact the child within and re-appraise the situation. She said afterwards the 'shame and blame is theirs, not mine'. This re-association with her childhood abuse triggered more anger, crying and sadness and she adopted more coping strategies such as the 'Hand Scream', 'Power Stomp' and 'Beat Pillows' (McClure, 1990). When she felt more stabilised two weeks later, she decided to have another hypnotic recall as she consciously felt there was something more to address.

This next hypnotic intervention was also the Bubble. She 'travelled back' to a later time when she was put into care, and related the physical abuse which she also suffered there. She felt that no one loved her and she could trust no one. The adult part told her one day she would be loved and she would learn to trust. The adolescent did not believe this totally, but at least she realised that this child was herself and that the younger child was also herself. There was further positive talk between the 'adult' and the 'adolescent' in the same hypnotic session, when the adult told the adolescent she would one day learn to laugh, she would gain friends, things would change and she would survive. The 'adolescent' and 'adult' returned to the Special Place together. Beryl could now accept and acknowledge the hurt and angry feelings and understand them. A post-hypnotic suggestion was given that she would always be able to reassure her inner child in this way.

The following week Beryl felt she needed another hypnotic recall. In the Bubble she went back to being 5 years old. She could not talk to anyone, and she was terrorised and speechless. She was thinking of ways to get out. She was having photos taken of her, and she was feeling dirty and no good. The same men were there and it was like a nightmare, because if she told anyone, they would not believe her. The adult self listened to the child's thoughts, and told her it would all come to an end and she (the adult) could take the child self into the Bubble to safety. The child self said she felt confused – where would she be taken? The adult self replied she would survive and come out of it completely.

Following this part of the therapy she was able to do more letter writing and come to terms with what had happened to her. She became more empowered, felt in touch with her feelings and able to deal with them. She had 15 sessions in total, 9 of which involved hypnosis. This covered a period of 8 months.

Phase 3: Rehabilitation

Beryl was now ready to re-embark on psycho-sexual counselling together with her husband. This was a particularly slow process, because of the violent sexual abuse she had suffered. The methods of Dolan (1991) and Maltz (1988) were used before any introduction of the more traditional sensate focusing. Getting in touch with her own sexuality was the last hurdle for her. Otherwise, she had achieved a sense of her own identity, namely a woman who had survived a horrific past, but had been able to have a family of her own with daughters who were well-adjusted and a loyal caring husband. As she re-associated with her feelings, she became more assertive and related to others in a way she had not done before.

She had also acquired a good sense of humour, and has shown herself able to deal with some more recent stresses in her life, such as bereavement and loss of some good relatives near to her. Her father had died some years ago, but her mother had survived and she met one of her sisters again. This meeting made her realise how far she (Beryl) had travelled down the road to recovery. Her sister still lived in an abusive situation with her mother, and was still strongly influenced by her mother. Beryl then decided never to return to her home town and re-visit her mother, as she felt she had left all this behind her; she had walked away from it both physically and psychologically, although she could now remember it as an essential part of her own history. This had given her a sense of empowerment, and belief in her own courage and inner strength.

Regarding the sex therapy, this was a very slow process, largely because Beryl's husband did not appreciate the importance of a graded process. He also had to learn about the possible triggers to memories of her abuse. The couple also needed a lot of help in communication, as intimate issues had never been discussed before. Furthermore, in order to move on, Beryl felt she had to grieve her lost childhood, and she had not totally resolved the anger over her abusive parents. She required two more hypnotic sessions of silent abreaction (see Chapter 4, 'Moving On'). In retrospect, the engagement in couple therapy and sex therapy should have been delayed to allow for her grieving process. This was the first time she had ever engaged with her lost childhood. She had, however, recovered from her PTSD, in so far as she had no more flashbacks, dissociation and hyper-arousal. Eventually, the couple had a satisfactory sexual life and communicated better. Several more sessions were needed for the couple together.

In Conclusion

The therapy of Beryl demonstrates the importance of hypnosis in helping a severely traumatised client with a considerable degree of dissociation, to re-associate with her feelings, to facilitate control of these feelings, and also to link them to specific events in the past, thus making meaning for her. In order to achieve this integration of traumatic memories, she had to relate to the child part of her. For many years she had pretended she was someone else. This powerful defence which had been so vital for her survival, had hindered her recovery. Hypnosis proved to be an invaluable tool in slowly breaking through this barrier. She was able to see how effective the dissociative experience of the hypnotic state was in achieving this. What causes the splits (dissociation) can also heal the splits (re-association) (Brende, 1985). She had been fighting the ego-state of the hurt inner child. Once this became integrated with the adult self, she started to make a good recovery. Similar to Anna, Beryl also found different hypnotic interventions helped her in different ways at various stages of therapy (e.g. the Bubble; hypnotic dream suggestions and hypnotic imagery).

At follow-up several years later, she has a good job working with children as a teaching assistant. She is well appreciated in her work. Her own children are grown up and married. She has a happy and close relationship with her husband. She feels she is a woman in her own right with a good sense of her own identity.

General Comments on the Experiences of Anna and Beryl

Both these clients had somato-sensory fragmented memories, namely sickness with pressure on the abdomen in one case, and flashing lights in the other. These were linked to past events for which they had no narrative memory. These events were recalled later; one in a hypnotic session, and the other in a post-hypnotic dream. No suggestions were given by the therapist as to what events these body sensations were related. In both cases traumatic memories were transformed into a narrative in hypnosis. Although there was no corroborative evidence for these memories, the clients' narratives were consistent with the continuous memories they had already, enabling them to make meaning out of their experiences, incorporate them into their autobiographical memory, and realise their own inner strength and resources in surviving.

The importance of integrating body memories into the trauma narrative has been emphasised by Babette Rothschild (2000). This can be a major challenge in trauma work and a slow process. Hypnosis can be one way to facilitate this process by accessing the implicit trauma memories (Spiegel, 1998).

Both of these clients had partial and incomplete memories of their past abuse; both had some continuous memories throughout their adult life, but apparently never had a period when they had total amnesia. Beryl successfully managed to put her childhood abuse out of her conscious awareness for a few years, by pretending it happened to someone else. This did not appear to be the same as dissociative amnesia; she deliberately did not tell her husband of her past abuse as she was so ashamed. The gaps in their memories for the abuse were filled in with the aid of hypnosis. As explained in Chapter 1, this does not mean that false memories were created. The procedures involved the reconstruction of fragmented memories which were already there.

LIFE EXPERIENCES OF GILLIAN

Problem Presented at First Therapeutic Contact

Gillian was a 27-year-old woman who presented with recurrent depression and anxiety. She had had several episodes of depression on and off since a teenager and had always felt shy and anxious. She was a clerical worker in an office and quite enjoyed this most of the time and got on well with her colleagues. She lived alone but had several girlfriends. Most of her history emerged gradually throughout the first couple of sessions, as the therapist engaged with her and established a therapeutic alliance. Her history of abuse was only disclosed after rapport had been built, and at no time was she pressed for details, allowing her to disclose whatever she felt she needed to in her own time.

She was first asked what had made her decide to seek help at this stage. She stated that she had had difficulty coping with a recent appraisal of her work as a clerical officer, and the increasing workload. This had triggered feelings of depression for which she had seen her GP. She was reluctant to take medication, as previously it had made her feel unreal and spaced out, and it was suggested that she seek therapy as an alternative.

She stated that she had had several episodes of depression on and off since she was a teenager and that she had always been shy and anxious. She was asked if she could give a *Readers' Digest* version of her life.

History

She was an only child and had had an unhappy childhood, which she did not elaborate on at this time, and although she had quite enjoyed school, she had never achieved a lot academically. Her parents had divorced when she was 14 and she had not seen her father since. He had subsequently died some years later. She had got on reasonably well with her mother who had had various boyfriends since, although for much of her teenage years she had stayed with her grandparents. Gillian had been in the school netball team and been one of their star players. She also enjoyed tennis, which she continued to play occasionally. Her grandparents had died a few years ago and she had felt very low for a while as she had been very close to them. She had left school at 16 and done various jobs until she joined her current firm 6 years ago.

She had had a couple of boyfriends but had not found relationships easy because of her shyness. She enjoyed her work but had been upset by various things said to her at her appraisal, and felt she was being given too much work to do with little support from her manager. She had several girlfriends from work and enjoyed going out with them occasionally. She had left home when she was 20 when she had inherited some money from her grandparents, and had a small flat which she was very proud of as she had decorated it herself. She enjoyed listening to music, although she could not play anything herself, and enjoyed keeping tropical fish, doing cross-stitch and cooking.

She talked about what she wanted to achieve by coming to see a therapist and she said she wanted to feel better about herself, to feel more confident and happier.

It was obvious from talking to her that Gillian had feelings of worthlessness and poor self-esteem, so one of the first interventions was to ask what her internal dialogue was like. The therapist discussed ways she could disrupt the 'I'm useless, worthless' type dialogue by changing the voice tone, maybe making it sound like a cartoon character or helium-ising it. What she had already achieved was discussed and then an exercise which is very useful in getting people to experience that they have abilities and resources that they forget about (from Danie Beaulieu).

The therapist took a pack of playing cards – ace high, 2 low and asked her to pick a card that she thought represented her, in this case a 3. This was placed face down on the desk and she was asked what card her grandmother would give her? – a 10; then grandfather – a Jack; her friends – a Jack; how would she rate her ability at playing netball when she was at school? – a King; how would she rate her ability at doing cross-stitch? – a King; how would she rate her ability at cooking? – a Queen; how would she rate her ability as a homemaker? – a 10: her ability to organise – another 10 . . . each time placing the card chosen on top of the first one. The therapist then picked up the cards she had selected in a pack with the 3 on top saying 'This is what you told me you are', and then as all the other cards are fanned out the therapist says, 'But look at all these you have forgotten about!' She laughed and said, 'Please can I keep the cards? I will put them on my fridge door to remind me!'

She was taught a way of doing self-hypnosis using her breathing as a focus and she developed her own special place imagery which was on a beach. She was introduced to the idea of a pool of resources that she could use to give herself positive suggestion. It was suggested that she find her way to a still calm pool of water and that as she sits and gazes at the water, she will notice that on the bottom of the pool are various stones and pebbles. These represent all the strengths, abilities and resources she already has, and she can feel pleased and encouraged as her unconscious mind identifies each resource, even though her conscious mind may not know what they are. Some she may have forgotten about and others she may not even know she has yet, and she can begin to feel excited at all the things she can begin to achieve with all these resources.

Around the edge of her pool are various stones that represent other positive feelings or resources or those that she may want even more of . . . She was asked to pick up a stone that represents 'calmness' (your unconscious mind will let you know which stone is the right one). She was asked to study it carefully, noticing its shape, texture, colour and weight . . . and then to drop it gently into her pool, watching it drift down through the clear water to settle safely on the bottom and to give a nod when it was there. It was repeated with another pebble for confidence in herself and in her abilities to be the way she wanted to be. When she was ready, she was asked to make connection with her pool in some way; maybe dabbling her hands and feet in the water, maybe swimming in it and to become fully in touch with all those resources within her. She said later that she had enjoyed diving into her pool and swimming in it.

It was suggested that she do five minutes' self-hypnosis a day and discuss when would be best for her to schedule this. This increases the likelihood of the client actually doing self-hypnosis regularly.

Session 2

Gillian reported that she had been practising her self-hypnosis and was feeling calmer at work. She had noticed sometimes when she was 'doing herself down' and had changed it. It was discussed how believable the negative self-talk can be and what feelings it engenders. She was obviously a good friend and she agreed that if a friend was in trouble she would support and encourage them in a compassionate way. It was suggested that in the same way as encouragement rather than criticism can help a child to achieve, that maybe she needed to listen to what that strong compassionate part of herself would say about the situations in which she 'Did herself down'. It was suggested that she close her eyes and review a couple of recent situations in which she said that she had 'beaten herself up' and listen to that compassionate part of herself. She then gave feedback on how that had helped and suggested that she might like to do this every evening.

Gillian then said that there was something else she wanted to say. She said that she had been abused on several occasions by her father and she felt she needed to 'sort it out' as she thought that a lot of her problems could stem from it. She said that she had always known about it, but had not allowed herself to think about it until recently. She had put it all 'Behind a door marked with a no-entry sign'. When she was about seven or eight he had started by touching her inappropriately, usually when he had been drinking and had abused her on several occasions up until she was 13 years old, threatening her to keep silent. She thought that maybe her mother had guessed what was happening and that was what had led to the divorce, but she had felt unable to talk to her mother about this. She felt ashamed and guilty as well as angry and confused.

Gillian became increasingly upset as she was relating this and the therapist said that she did not need to know the details unless she felt she needed to tell them. It was suggested that she close her eyes and go to her special place and she was congratulated on her courage in talking about events that had been so difficult for her. The therapist asked how the adult compassionate part of her would feel about these events if she heard they had happened to someone else? Would she think the child was to blame? What did her younger self need in order to heal and grow through the traumatic things that had happened to her? Could she perhaps imagine putting her arms around that younger self and comforting her? If not, perhaps she could imagine some strong, wise, compassionate older higher self or friend giving her the love and comfort that she needed. Maybe a special animal would come to her special place and give her the comfort and love that she needed just now.

The therapist suggested that over the next little while they would work together to help her resolve her difficulties, but that just for now perhaps she could put her problems back behind her door where they would not disturb her consciously and that each day when she went to her special place, if it was appropriate and she wanted to, she could imagine meeting up with that younger part of herself and begin to give her the love and comfort she needed in just the right way for her.

Session 3

This involved interventions which would stabilise her. The third session included also talking about appropriate and inappropriate guilt, forgiveness and payback and the need for the younger part of herself to express the anger that she felt towards her father. It was necessary to separate the behaviour from the person and that her father had acted in a way that a well balanced and emotionally mature person could not possibly have done. This was not to excuse him for his actions but to begin to get Gillian to see that her father was acting in the way he did because of his emotional circumstances and development. Gillian was taken through 'silent abreaction' (see Chapter 4).

It was suggested that Gillian take herself into hypnosis and give a nod when she was ready to proceed. After a few moments she gave a nod and she was asked to take herself far, far away from anywhere to a rock place, maybe a cliff or a quarry. There she was to select a boulder or rock that was to become her anger and project the anger that she wanted to get rid of at this time into it and mark it in some way so that she knew what the rock represented. She was then to look around and find some way of smashing up the rock; maybe a pickaxe, maybe a hammer and chisel, a pneumatic drill or some dynamite. She was then to really enjoy smashing up the rock into tiny pieces and give a nod when she was finished. When she gave a nod she was asked what she wished to do with the little pieces left. She wanted to sweep them away, which she then did. It was then suggested that she should go to a calm place and really connect with it, maybe trailing her hands in a stream or touching the bark of the trees, or in any other way gather up the calm feelings of that place to replace the anger that she had released. She came out of hypnosis smiling and saying she had 'enjoyed that'.

It was discussed with Gillian about the kinds of payback in other cases where the younger part has had the perpetrator strip or been otherwise humiliated in front of others. Whatever comes into her mind is alright so long as she knows it is only imagination and fantasy.

Dissociative ways of helping to resolve traumatic past memories were then discussed, and the fact that one cannot change what happened in the past but one can change the emotional feeling that that memory has in the present. Memory was also discussed; and that 'memories' when they come to mind in therapy are not necessarily historically true, but maybe a symbolic representation of whatever her mind needed to work on would be effective. This was in preparation for Phase 2: Memory Integration. The time road and cinema technique were talked through and she was asked which she would like to work with today. She chose the cinema and it was suggested that she take herself into hypnosis and give a nod when she was ready.

She was asked to imagine sitting on the second row in a cinema, one she remembered or an imaginary one. The cinema is empty and she is looking up at a blank screen. She was asked to tell the colour of the seats and she said 'red' which confirmed that she was succeeding with the imagery. She was then asked to imagine leaving her body comfortably sitting there and float back to the projection room and look through the glass to see the back of her head in the second row watching the empty screen. The projection room is entirely safe, the glass screen is toughened and bullet proof, the doors are locked and she has the key and is in charge of the projector. (*Double dissociation.*) She was asked to allow an image to form on the screen of some happy event that she was involved in and play it through over a couple of minutes. Then she was asked to float down into the image and really enjoy experiencing the good feelings. Then it was suggested that she float back to the projection booth and make a button on her remote control that, if pressed, would immediately put her in the happy scene. She was asked what colour it was and she told me 'green'. She was told that if the therapist ever asked her to press that button she would do so immediately and find herself in the good event. If she wanted to press the button at any stage she could do so but she was to tell the therapist that she had done so. She was then asked to check that the button worked and enjoy her happy scene for a few moments. (*This is a visual image used as a safety anchor.*)

The therapist then asked her to ask inside if it was alright to work on the events from the past and to give a nod if it was or to say if there was a hesitation. (*Permission at an unconscious level to work on the material.*)

Gillian gave a nod so the therapist proceeded to ask her to project a still image of herself, just before the significant events on which she wished to work, onto the screen. (*The therapist did not suggest what she should work on, as the unconscious mind was trusted to do what it needed.*)

It was suggested that she may like to make it an old black and white film, maybe a bit scratchy and jumpy as old films often are. Then she was asked to play the film of the events through for approximately two minutes and nod when it had finished, reminding her that she was safely in the projection room, watching herself on the second row, watching the film. As she played the film she became a little distressed so the therapist continued to remind her that she was quite safe here in the projection room watching that old film and that soon she would not need to feel that distress again. When she nodded she was asked to score the emotional response of watching that film on a 0–10 scale with 0 being not distressing at all and 10 being the worst experience she could imagine. Gillian rated it a 10.

She was then asked in a few moments to rewind the film and reminded that as it is rewound the sounds and actions go backwards and look and feel totally different. Gillian rewound the film quickly as the therapist said, 'Whoo . . . ooo . . . ooo . . . sh'. It was then suggested that she play the film backwards and forwards about three times and then give a nod when she had finished and to tell what number the score *had fallen to*. (*Embedded command.*) In Gillian's case it had only fallen to about 8.

It was then suggested that she play the film through again but this time she could stop the film at any time to give comfort, love and support to that younger self. Gillian, better than anyone else, knows what that younger self needed, and she can really make sure that that younger self knows that, however bad those times were, she survived, she came through, because she is from her future. Maybe that younger self needs to have some kind of payback; maybe an older self or a supportive friend figure can say what needs to be said to the people in the events. If she felt stuck and wanted help she could ask but otherwise it would be left to her to do what she needed to do. When she had finished she was asked to rewind and then replay the film and tell the score. It had fallen to 5.

It was now suggested that she was the director of the film and could re-make the film – keeping the main events but changing things as her creativity suggested. For instance, she could make the people in the film cartoon characters, change images (she was told of a case where someone held at gunpoint had changed the gun into a banana) or make any other changes that seemed appropriate, while keeping the same basic events. It was sug-gested that she make some changes and then rewind the film.

She was asked to run the film with the changes and score the film again on a 0–10 scale. The score had fallen to 3 and she was asked if this was alright or if she needed to reduce it further. She said it was alright so she was asked finally to rewind the film but that as she did so, she would inadvertently press her green button so that the film rewinds back into the happy scene. *(Collapsing of anchors.)*

She could now enjoy her happy scene for a few moments and then float back to the projection room and from there back down into the cinema seat on the second row. *(Reintegration.)*

Gillian was asked to thank her unconscious mind for the good work it had just done and suggested she return to her special place and her pool of resources where she could pick up a pebble to represent the work she had just done and add it to her pool before swimming in her pool and really connecting with all those resources within her.

The session was finished by giving Gillian an opportunity to talk about anything that she felt she needed to and she was congratulated on the work she had done. *(The therapist still does not know, or needs to know, what Gillian was working on in the cinema.)*

Session 4

Further memory integration was addressed in this session. Gillian had been feeling much more optimistic since her last session, she felt 'lighter'. She said that giving her younger self a cuddle in her special place had been very helpful. It was suggested that she use the time road metaphor to help her resolve remaining negative feelings from the past and to look at where her ideas and beliefs about herself had come from and whether the time had come to help herself change these perceptions.

Having induced hypnosis and set up the time road imagery she was asked to float way up high above the present and ask inside whether it would be alright to let go negative feelings from the past so long as she learnt whatever she needed for her protection . . . that negative feelings were there as a message and a protection but that once she had learnt what she needed they no longer served a purpose. She nodded and so the therapist asked her unconscious mind to look at the past and sort out past events of significance onto either side of her road. On one side events with good feelings attached and on the other those with not so good feelings. She was told that she may get visual images or she may just get an internal awareness of when that had been completed and to give a nod when she had completed this. She was then asked to float down into the good feeling memories and really connect with the good feelings as they could always be there at the front of her mind, helping her. Then she was asked to float from above her earliest not so good memory and floating up high, allow her unconscious mind to learn what it needed to let the feeling go. It was suggested that maybe that the younger self down there needed help, comfort, love and support in order to feel comforted and loved. She could float down within a protective bubble of love and calmness (she imagined this as a golden aura around herself) or imagine an older wiser self from the future, her higher self or some supportive friend figure going and helping her younger self in whatever way was best or maybe she could imagine a universal source of love and strength sending down a supportive light through her and down to her younger self on the time road.

She was to really make sure that the younger self knew her, and that however distressing the event was, she survived, because she was from her future. When she felt that she had done what was needed she was to let the therapist know with a nod. She was then asked to float back up if she was not already there and look down and check that that feeling had gone and that there was nothing else that needed to be done. She was then asked to float back towards the present dealing with all the not so good memories in the same way, to say if she got stuck and to give a nod when she had finished. She was asked whether she wanted to do anything with the not so good images as they had served their purpose and were no longer needed and she said she wanted to blow them away, which she did. She was then asked to float back over the good feeling memories and really connect with those good feelings again.

Having congratulated her on the good work she had done, the therapist suggested she spend a few moments enjoying her special place before returning to the here and now.

Self-esteem was then discussed and how a person develops beliefs about themselves. Time road imagery was set up again and it was suggested that she float back above her time road and look at herself when she was a baby, when she had no idea of herself as a separate individual. It was then suggested that she look down and notice where her beliefs about herself came from. She noticed that, as she grew older, she responded to the response and behaviour of others around her (who were themselves labouring under their own emotional baggage and difficulties) and thus made various assumptions about herself. It was suggested that with her adult knowledge and experience she could examine these and see whether they served her well or whether it was time to change them and put them where old beliefs are kept. When she had completed this to her satisfaction she gave a nod and she was asked to float a little way into the future to see the self she was becoming, the self that accepted herself as she was, with things she needed to work on, but with abilities that she could be proud of, with more self-confidence, calmness and an internal knowledge that she was a worthwhile, loving and loveable individual. Having seen her future self, she was asked to float down into that self and really get a sense of how that would be, to connect with the feelings and allow her unconscious mind to make any internal adjustments necessary to allow this future to be her reality. When her mind had done this she was to return to the here and now.

This could be considered part of Phase 3 in phase-oriented therapy.

Session 5

Gillian said that she had been feeling much better since the last session and had surprised herself by going and talking frankly with her mother. They had had an emotional conversation and her mother had said that she had no idea of the abuse and was very distressed about it. Gillian said she had ended up comforting her mother and felt generally much stronger and better about things.

The therapist and Gillian discussed what happened when Gillian began to feel depressed and she started to realise it was whenever she suppressed her feelings. She had started to recognise the kinds of thoughts she would have and how these ruminations would spiral her down into depression. There are different kinds of interventions she could use when she noticed her 'smoke alarm' such as exercise, thought stopping and mindfulness techniques. This latter is often used as a way of training someone to be in the present moment observing their thoughts and feelings rather than evaluating them and starting to build on them. Gillian was already beginning to find herself more able to take a step back and look at things. The metaphor used was standing on the bank of a stream rather than being in the stream itself.

It was explained how self-confidence is built by doing, while self-esteem is more about being. She decided to set a confidence anchor, which in her case was the image of a bird soaring above the clouds. She also decided on some goals for the future, phoning a friend to ask her out, and saying yes when she was next asked out herself. She also felt that she could deal better with her appraisal as she would remember it was something she had done that may be criticised, not her own self.

She was then taught positive mental rehearsal which she could do for herself whenever some event was worrying her. This involved closing her eyes, imagining herself the way she wished to be in a particular situation, stepping into the image and feeling how it felt while saying something appropriate to herself, then opening her eyes. It was suggested that she repeat this a few times and maybe also see herself after successful completion of the situation having done her best and connect with this.

It was ended with a short hypnosis session with ego-strengthening and future age progression, confirming and acknowledging the progress she had made and focusing her on the future her, thinking, feeling and behaving the way she wished to think, feel and behave.

She was encouraged to come again in a few weeks and reassured that a schedule could be planned for further sessions if needed. Gillian has been seen on several occasions over the last two years but neither the therapist nor Gillian has felt that she needed further sessions. Sometimes she has been reminded of things discussed that would be helpful to her and she does her self-hypnosis fairly regularly. Recently she has been in a relationship which seems to be progressing well.

Hypnosis was used in this case along with various non-hypnotic techniques to help Gillian resolve traumatic feelings from her past and build her self-esteem and self-confidence.

The various hypnotic techniques have been described in some detail as they occurred to demonstrate how such techniques as the Cinema and Time Road can be adapted by the therapist to suit their own style, and the responses and needs of the client. They can also be adapted to deal with issues arising in all three phases of Trauma Therapy. In this case very few sessions were needed.

LIFE EXPERIENCES OF KATE

Problem Presented at First Therapeutic Contact

Kate, age 38, was referred for therapy in order to address issues related to child sexual abuse. She had already had therapy for one year, but her therapist had left for another post. Kate reported at the first session that she had flashbacks and panic attacks which she wanted to understand. She knew the symptoms were related to her childhood abuse, and she wanted to work on the abuse memories although she did not feel that she would ever be able to deal with them.

She stated that she experienced age regressions and she felt she was reliving the abuse. She regressed to three different ages; 4, 6 and 12 years old, and when she regressed to any one of those ages, she felt she was that particular age and only had the skills she possessed at that age. For example, when the '4 year old was around', she literally could not read. When one of these younger parts of herself was about to emerge, she got 'a sense that something is coming' and would experience a panic attack and be aware that a part of her was very scared. Each part of her, the 4, 6 and 12 year old had different feelings. The 4 year old was upset and confused, and it felt as though it was the first time the abuse occurred. The 6 year old was petrified, and accepted what was happening but knew it was wrong. The 12 year old held all the memories, but also was full of anger. Kate remembered that at age 12 she had told her mother about the sexual abuse by her paternal uncle. Her mother had not believed her.

These child parts of her did not emerge very often, perhaps twice over the previous two months. At the times when it happened, she experienced very vivid sensations and feelings which made her feel she was living through the abuse again. Afterwards, she said her body felt bruised and she was unable to walk properly.

Kate also had bouts of depression and feeling unable to cope with everyday events, such as looking after her 12-year-old son, and doing household chores. She claimed the adult part of her was quite confident and assertive, but was unable to have any control over the child parts. It was when she felt safe and in control, that one of the child parts would surface. She reported that, on one occasion when she was seeing her previous therapist, she saw a small child standing beside her. As it felt unreal, she asked the therapist if there was this child beside her. He replied that there was no child there. She then thought she was going mad. However, when she got home she decided to look up some old photographs of herself as a child, and found one where she was wearing the same dress as she had seen on the child she hallucinated in the session. She realised she was 4 years old at the time of the photograph and realised she had hallucinated herself. From that moment she experienced a younger part of herself, aged 4, inside her head. This was the first emergence of the 4 year old part of her.

Childhood History

Kate had a sister four years younger than herself and a brother eight years younger than herself. They lived with their parents into adulthood. Kate said she remembered nothing of her childhood except that she was physically abused by her mother. She did not recall the sexual abuse of her uncle until later in her adult life when her son was 12 years old, the same age as she had been when she disclosed the sexual abuse to her mother. She had been taking her son to school across a park and she began to feel frightened of the trees and then felt very small, and she said it felt as though she had a blackout. She later found out that she had been abused in the park. This was the first flashback she had and the 12 year old part of her emerged for the first time. She no longer had dissociative amnesia for the sexual abuse. This breakthrough occurred after she started art therapy on her first referral to the Mental Health Service (see below under Therapies).

Kate then recalled that she was age 4 when the sexual abuse began (at least as far as she could remember). She remembered growing up believing this behaviour was normal and that all her friends were treated in the same way. She nonetheless felt scared and confused, and believed it was wrong. At age 12, she told her mother who did not believe her, but she managed to fight off her uncle. She would also stay close to her mother so he could not get to her. It is possible that her uncle also abused her sister and brother, as the former developed mental health problems later in life, and her brother later sexually abused Kate's son, and confessed to it.

Adult Relationships

Kate married a man who was very abusive to her, both sexually and physically. The marriage lasted four years as he was killed in a car accident, and their son was only two years old. Eighteen months later Kate began a relationship with another man, who finally rejected her as he could not accept the fact that her son was of mixed race (his father being black). Kate moved back to an area near her parents for support. Here she met her second husband, whom she said she married for stability. Soon after this Kate's brother sexually abused her son, and initially she did not know about it. Five years after this marriage, her husband left her for her sister, with whom he had had an affair. Kate began to have difficulty coping and felt she needed help. Her mother became more understanding and confessed that she too had been abused as a child, though she did not say in what way.

Therapies

The first referral to the Mental Health Service which Kate had was to group therapy which included art therapy. She claimed that she began painting images which were disturbing to her and she did not remember actually painting them. This procedure nonetheless facilitated her recall of her past history. The 12-year-old child part of her was the first to emerge, and then the 6 year old. When she was referred on for individual therapy, the 4 year old surfaced, as already described.

The third referral was for further individual psychotherapy to facilitate resolution and integration. After providing all this information over a few sessions, Kate expressed the need to control her 'children'; by this, she meant the child parts of her, not her own son. She was afraid they would come out and 'take over', meaning overwhelm her. She was afraid of getting in touch with her feelings. She said her 'children' had all the feelings, not the adult part.

Further Assessment

Kate was administered two questionnaires: the Post-Traumatic Stress Diagnostic Scale (PDS) by E. Foa (1995), and the Dissociative Disorders Interview Schedule (DDIS) by C. Ross et al. (1989). From the PDS results, Kate had severe Post-Traumatic Stress Disorder and severe impairment in functioning. She attributed the cause to the sexual abuse by her uncle between the ages of 4 and 12 years old. The DDIS placed her in the diagnostic categories of Dissociative Identity Disorder and major depression. She almost met the criteria of Borderline Personality Disorder as well.

This diagnostic picture is consistent with the clinical presentation. The ego-states or 'alters', which were all child states of different ages, did not know each other. Kate as an adult also had no control of the 'alters', and when one of them 'came out', she became amnesic for the part of her life *after* the particular age of that child alter. She could not drive her car, nor carry out any activities which she had learnt after that particular age. She could not even recognise her friends if she had first met them after that age. The 'alters' themselves also could not recognise Kate as an adult, except the 12 year old who seemed to be more integrated, as this was the age when she first disclosed the abuse, and asserted herself with her uncle and managed to prevent the abuse recurring.

In view of the diagnoses, it was advisable to follow the guidelines for treating DID produced by the International Society for the Study of Dissociation (ISSD, 1994), with particular reference to the use of hypnosis. As stated in Chapter 3, in cases of DID, the 'alters' are child states to which the adult part has age regressed. So the person is in a state, similar to hypnotic age regression. The 'alters' are like trance states. The DID client will frequently enter a trance state even when the therapist has not performed any hypnotic induction procedure. However, paradoxically, hypnosis can be used to help the client re-orient themselves to external reality when these trance states occur uninvited. Hypnosis can also be used for ego-strengthening, for the safe expression of feeling (silent abreaction, for relief of somatic memory pain, for skill building or to help communication between alters). Essentially, the aim of the therapy is to facilitate integrated functioning and a sense of connectedness between the different alters. The degree of integration may vary, but it is important that the therapist and client appreciate that getting rid of an 'alter' is *not* part of the agenda. It is also essential not to state the target to be total integration of all the 'alters' into one personality. This can produce fear in the 'alters'.

Although Kate had had therapy already, the same information and introduction was given to her, as in the case of all trauma clients. Normalisation and validation was necessary, particularly since Kate had a fear of becoming psychotic, in view of her hallucination of herself at age 4, and also her child states manifested sometimes as inner voices. Explanations of trauma, PTSD, and ego-states were given. Hypnosis was discussed in terms of helping her understand her dissociated states, and helping her gain control and communicate with them. Each child state was like a hypnotic state. The reconstructive nature of memory and the difference between this and false memories were very helpful points of information for Kate, as some other family members had already accused her of having false memories and living in a world of fantasy. Her abusive uncle in particular had warned her that if she divulged anything to the family about his sexual advances, they would never believe her and she would be thrown out of the family.

Kate would clearly need more sessions to recover than some of the other trauma cases. It is recognised among therapists that it may take years not months, with regular appointments, to help DID clients to resolve their problems and have a manageable degree of integration. Kate was very motivated to move on in her therapy and accepted all the information given to her. It was 3–4 weeks after her first session that it seemed opportune and appropriate to start on Phase 1.

Phase 1: Stabilisation

The first priority for Kate was to be able to control the 'children', so that they did not keep 'coming out', when she, the adult, was not in a position to deal with them. She was also afraid they would overwhelm her with their feelings. Hypnosis with the Special Place (see Chapter 4 – Establishing Hypnosis and Building Resources) would help her calm herself as an adult and could also be modified to help the 'children' too. This was accomplished by starting the hypnosis with the travelling vehicle, The Bubble (see Chapter 4) and she took the 'children' in the Bubble to the Special Place which was a garden. She then let the 'children' out to go into the garden and left them there closing the garden gate behind them so they were kept safe, and telling them she would speak to them later, while she stayed in the other part of the garden. At this point in time the 'children' did not know each other but she, as an adult, knew them, so she was able to use this imagery. Later, after she had learned to use self-hypnosis with this imagery, she decided that she wanted another Special Place for herself the adult, and to keep the Bubble and the garden for the 'children'. Being hypnotisable she was able first to use this imagery wherever she was, and it became effective in giving her control of the 'children'. She would just put them in the Bubble and take them to the garden, and then get on with everyday activities. The Special Place for her adult self was a castle in beautiful grounds, and she would practise self-hypnosis for her adult self in this way to calm herself.

After several weeks, she felt much more empowered and in control of the 'children'. She was in fact able to have inner talk to a child state, and the latter would obey the adult's wishes. One day she was entertaining some friends, and she went into the living room where they were congregated, and said 'Do I know you?' They laughed and obviously thought that she was joking. Their response made the adult part of her realise that one of the child states had taken over, so she had no memory of her adult friends in front of her. She, the adult, left the room, saying she would be back in a few minutes. She then went to her bedroom, lay on the bed and told the child state, whom she recognised as the 12 year old, that she could not talk to her now, but she would talk to her later (Kate called this 'talking down the children'). When she returned to the living room she knew the names of all her friends, and also recognised them all. The adult self had taken over.

Having gained control of the child states, she then began having flash-backs to an event in her adult life when her first husband raped her. The 12-year-old child state was very angry that this happened. (The 12 year old held all Kate's anger.) She felt she had to resolve this trauma before pursuing any other goal. Although it had not been planned to use the Bubble as a safe remembering technique for resolution of her childhood abuse, but rather to facilitate communication and connectedness between the child states, it did seem an appropriate intervention to help her resolve her adult trauma. She was familiar with the Bubble and it had been successful in keeping her child states safe, and it might help her resolve a traumatic event in her adult life. Kate agreed to it.

Phase 2: Memory Integration

She was given the Bubble intervention for safe recall of this traumatic event (see Chapter 4). She regressed to the day her abusive ex-husband raped her, and she resolved the trauma by having her adult self enter the scene and convince the younger adult self that she survived, and that he later died and was no longer there to abuse her. This was successful in resolving the trauma, and she had no more flashbacks about her ex-husband.

This intervention was part of memory integration in her adult life, which was necessary to address before she had the full inner strength to deal with the issues of her child states. Kate was also much more stabilised after this session.

She was now engaged to be married for a third time and was happy about preparing for the wedding. She felt that the 'children' who had come out trusted her more, and she had good control.

After her wedding, which went off very well, she said the 6 year old was very happy. The next step in the therapy when she returned from honeymoon was to map out her child states as follows:

- *4 year old* – knew the 12 year old and was playful with her, communicated well together.
- *6 year old* – was numb and withdrawn, and never mixed with children, and knew she had been abused, so was having difficulty relating to others.
- *8 year old* – had many feelings about the abuse, but the abuse had temporarily stopped as uncle went into the army.
- *12 year old* – is very protective of the others, but cannot talk to them because they do not know her, except for the 4 year old.

Kate felt that there would not be shared communication between the child states until the 6 and 8 year old could talk about their abuse. She also felt she, as an adult, needed extra safety measures by having a transitional object which was a key-ring with a picture of her present husband. She also began to realise that her child states not only had the vulnerable side of themselves, but also each had a 'false front'. This was a barrier for protection. The original purpose of the false front was so she could mix with the adults when she was a child and if her uncle took her away, she would be missed, and the adults would go looking for her and she would be rescued. So now all the child states had preserved their false fronts as protection.

Another child state emerged one month later who was 10 years old. She had been raped by her aunt's boyfriend and locked in a cellar. Kate commented that now she understood why she had felt as claustrophobic over the previous two months.

Kate was also getting body memories, which was the precursor to the emergence of a 7 year old who had been put in a box and tried to come out but could not. Now she felt free and enjoyed childish activities. Then a 3 year old came out who had a lot of inner pain. There were now seven child states; 3, 4, 6, 7, 8, 10 and 12 year olds. Kate was able to put the 'children' into the garden (the Special Place), and to use the Bubble just for their protection.

So she felt in control and could listen to the 'children' as an adult, although not all of them knew each other.

It was important to note that Kate saw her therapist always in the same room at the same time and same day of the week. This apparently helped to build up trust in the child states, and they always listened to the session and felt comfortable. This in turn helped Kate to communicate with them afterwards. If the room was different the 'children' did not come out. This had been tried before at one stage in the therapy when there was a shortage of rooms, and the children did not come out. When they did consistently come out in later sessions in the same room, it was as inner voices. The sessions she had in the same room facilitated her communication with the children, which she was able to pursue outside the sessions, as well. She had adopted several coping strategies for gaining full control:

- She learned to clench her fist and thereby shut an imaginary door, behind which the children stayed till she opened the door by clenching her fist again.
- When she woke every morning, the 'children' saw her and knew her, so she told them they would have to stay quiet and she would speak to them later. It was not her choice, but circumstances dictated it.
- If she panicked because feelings were surfacing, she did deep breathing to calm herself, so she could consider what coping strategy to use.
- She used the Bubble to protect herself as an adult. She also used it to put the 'children' in to protect them. The garden, which was her Special Place, was also a place where her 'children' could play, and she shut the garden gate if she needed them to stay there for a while. She, the adult, could also stay in the Bubble to watch them and monitor them.

These coping strategies were all part of the stabilisation phase which alternated with communication with the 'alters'.

About one year after her first being referred to the present therapist, she and her husband planned to go to Scotland near his family. This was meant to be a permanent move, but unfortunately her son, who had been sexually abused by Kate's brother as a child (unknown to Kate at the time), had become a perpetrator himself. He abused a young girl and had been expelled from the school. So Kate and her husband decided to return to England and to ensure he got appropriate treatment. This was devastating news for Kate who herself returned to the therapy.

Kate said that since that event, one of her 'children' was screaming and she had to shut off all her 'children' in order to deal with this new trauma. When she shut them off like this, she dissociated from her feelings and also suffered many physical symptoms as a result. It took considerable energy to keep the 'children' safe in her imaginary garden. She became very panicky also if another child state emerged. At this point, it seemed appropriate to allow the 'children' to come out and to play childish games with them, and buy toys, so that the child states were validated without opening any wounds (a return to stabilisation). Kate was, however, reminded that the ultimate goal was to share communication and knowledge so the child states could grow up. The 12 year old had already come to know the 10 year old.

During her therapy, Kate suffered a number of physical problems, some of which were serious. She was naturally worried about her physical health, but also concerned whether it would impact on her progress in communicating with the 'children'. There were various hypnotic approaches with the 'children' and her adult self, which helped her through the dilemmas. Some of these will be described.

She was diagnosed with breast cancer and had to undergo chemotherapy. Kate said that as a child she liked being ill because she was then cared for by adults in the family. She now used hypnosis to talk to the children about her illness and asked them to support her, and some of them understood. The 12 year old and the 8 year old now knew her as an adult. She could talk to them quite a lot and it gave her peace of mind. The 12 year old particularly gave her strength. The 4 year old, however, was distressed and some of the 'children' were scared. Her mother and members of her family, in reality, were quite unsupportive, as they believed she was faking it, just as they thought she lied about the sexual abuse. Not surprisingly, this prompted the emergence of another child state, who had much anger. Kate felt she wanted to return to artwork in order to express the anger. She also needed more grounding techniques and she bought herself a small toy bear as a grounding object. She also played a lot with the 'children' outside the sessions.

During the time when she was receiving treatment for the cancer, she attended sessions of art therapy as well as monthly sessions of psychotherapy. This seemed to help her cope with her feelings and keep stabilised. The art work was particularly helpful in enabling her to see what the 'children' had suffered. She perceived this in a dissociated way, as though someone else was talking to the 'children'. Finally, in addition to the painting, she did some paper sculpture. She made a skull which she said symbolised the death of dissociation, and the integration of all the child states. The skull she said had no pain and no anger. In the psychotherapy sessions, she said that the therapist's voice had become a trigger for the 'children' to come out. The 12 year old had now taken on the role of mother for all the other child states. This seemed an important step forward to integration.

Following the treatment for breast cancer, Kate was also told she had to have a hysterectomy. She was diagnosed as well with irritable bowel syndrome. The hysterectomy was planned for 5 months time. Kate drafted the agenda for preparation for the operation with the therapist. She knew that the 'children' had to be included in the preparation, which was as follows:

- She needed to explain to the nurses and surgical staff that she was a survivor of child sexual abuse (her oncologist already knew), and that she may come out of the operation as a child state.
- It was also necessary for her to explain to the staff that she would be doing some self-hypnosis before the operation.
- There were several purposes for self-hypnosis. Firstly, it could be used to stop body memories of the abuse and pain. Secondly, she could go to her Special Place, the garden or stay in the Bubble. Thirdly, another hypnotic procedure could be used so that she did not feel the canula in her arm when she was being anaesthetised (pain of any kind brought out the 'children).
- For the benefit of the adult self, she decided on some cognitive self-talk; firstly she could see this as a journey to goals for a better life; secondly, the day before the operation (or week before) she can say 'this time tomorrow (or next week) it will all be over'.
- She also decided to practise self-hypnosis with eyes open so she did not miss signals just before the operation.

Hypnosis for Anaesthetic

The hypnotic intervention for the adult self to prevent any sensation from the canula had to be learnt and practised in self-hypnosis well before the operation. This involved first a hypnotic induction and deepening, followed by a test for sensation in the right arm. A hypnotic suggestion was then given that her right arm would feel separate from her body and with no sensation. A re-test of sensation in the right arm by using a pin prick was then carried out. There was absence of response in the right arm, but not in the left arm. A post-hypnotic suggestion was then given that she would be able to carry out the same procedure when needed in either arm. Lastly, the suggestion of anaesthesia in her right arm was reversed, so there was the return of sensation in the right arm and both arms felt the same and feeling normal. Then the hypnosis was terminated and she had to try it herself in self-hypnosis. This worked very well for her; she felt the right arm was separate from her body and did not feel any pin prick after the first suggestion. She continued to practise this self-hypnosis, which gave her a lot of confidence. As she was well used to dissociative experiences, it is not surprising she was well able to use hypnotic dissociation for the purpose of coping and healing.

The operation was successful from a physical point of view. However, the 'children' did not recognise the faces of the 3 and 4 year olds because she said at that age she had pretended the abuse had not happened. Since her operation, she also heard the internal screaming of the 'children', and she also recovered a memory of her sister being abused, but she was not going to tell her, as the latter had always denied it.

The 12 year old had now grown up and had integrated with the adult Kate, but she did not know what to do with the other children who now did not know each other. So Kate decided to look up the photographs of herself as a child at different ages which might facilitate communication and recognition. The 'children' were also becoming confused, and thought her husband was the abusive uncle, although he (the husband) had not abused her at all. This confusion did not last, but it was worrying for her at all levels.

Kate started to focus on the present and took up her interests in sewing, painting and joined a gym. She took up links with her parents again, and when her sister's marriage broke down, she was there for her. Distress of any kind would make the 'children' believe that her abusive uncle was around. The 'children' also felt ignored as she was too focused on her adult life in the present. She needed to balance the time she spent for the adult self, and the time she spent on communicating with the child states. Kate also started getting flashbacks of herself as a child being in a children's park with her uncle. She was on a slide, and he asked her to take off her pants before going on the slides. This was not the emergence of another child state, it was a case of the adult recalling a memory of herself as a child. There was less dissociation in this traumatic memory. It seemed, therefore, appropriate once more to attempt resolution of the trauma by the safe remembering hypnotic technique (Chapter 4) and enable the adult self to comfort the child self in hypnosis.

Using the Bubble technique for the purpose of travelling into the past, Kate went back to seeing herself at the age of 9 years in the park with her uncle. When the child was asked what she needed she said she needed an adult there. Kate, the adult, went out of the Bubble, and the child self said 'There is a lady there now who cannot rescue me, and I do not know who she is.' Here Kate the adult self spoke to her and said 'What this man is doing to you is wrong, but I will always be here for you.' The child self was confused but felt safer, and happy that the lady believed her. The 9-year-old self was clearly more dissociated than anticipated, since she did not emerge initially as a separate child state. Also she did not recognise the 'lady' as her adult self. However, Kate had no more flashbacks to that event in the park.

As Kate spent more time communicating with the children by positive play activities, and also taking up more artwork again, they came to know each other better. Their pain and hurt was not completely resolved, in spite of Kate talking to them. No other child states emerged, but all that had come out expressed a great need to have reassurance from their mother. Kate as an adult was not able to do this for them in the way she had done it for the 9 year old. Kate stated that there was only one way to help the 'children' and that was to have her mother acknowledge that the abuse occurred, and that she would understand the inner 'children' and apologise for never having believed them. This would also help Kate as an adult to have a better relationship with her mother than she had ever had. In other words, the needs of the 'children' were the same as the needs of the adult self. Kate requested that the therapist might spend one session with herself and her parents in the same room where the 'children were also comfortable in 'coming out'.

Session with the Parents of Kate

This session took place in the same room as Kate had her therapy sessions. She was present with her parents. The parents were introduced to the therapist, who explained as simply as possible Kate's problem of dissociation and of inner child states. The purpose of the therapy was to help Kate have communication with them all so that they become more at one with the adult self; that is, mutual recognition, re-association with her past experiences and acceptance. It was then explained that these inner child states needed to say some things to help them (the parents) to understand more, then there would be better contact between the parents and Kate herself as an adult and her inner child states. After the session, they (the parents) could take with them what they wanted or leave behind what they did not want.

This information seemed to be accepted by the parents and the session itself provided an opportunity for the child states to come out and communicate through adult Kate what they really needed. The first need was to be believed. The second need was for the children to be accepted as part of their daughter Kate, and to consider the welfare of all of them. The reaction of the parents was positive. They believed the sexual abuse happened, and the mother in particular said she understood a lot better about the 'child states' and started to accept Kate's behaviour when a 'child' came out. The father also became more concerned about Kate as an adult. The 'children' felt much safer after this session.

Unfortunately the rest of the family remained 'non-believers' regarding the sexual abuse, and this always made them (the 'children') feel less safe. However, Kate's communication with her parents improved and her mother started accepting the child states and talking to them, apologising for the past disbelief. The 'children' also shared their childhood pain with Kate and accepted her adult self. Kate also played with them and bought toys, and was in her own way reclaiming her childhood. At the same time she was giving herself time to deal with everyday matters, and to plan her day. She had more contact with her friends and pursued her interests again.

Kate's husband took a job in another part of the country and this meant that her therapy had to come to a close or she had to be referred on to another therapist. This move was not to be before a few months time. Unfortunately, she developed more physical problems for which she had to have an exploratory operation without anaesthetic. She was considerably worried about this since it would worry the 'children' who were so sensitive to any bodily intrusion. There were different requirements for the use of hypnosis on this occasion. She had to remain conscious, to experience the sensations and be able to report on them. The solutions were as follows:

- Put the children in a safe place in hypnosis and keep them there throughout the whole procedure.
- Have another special place for herself as an adult, where she could be safe, but responsive to sensations (relaxed but vigilant).
- Incorporate the clenched fist technique to shut the door behind the 'children' and repeat that she would later let them out at the end of the procedure.

Hypnosis for Medical Procedure without Anaesthetic

Following a hypnotic induction, Kate took the 'children' in the Bubble to their safe place, the garden, and told them to be quiet and she would come back for them after a short while. She then clenched her fist to close the gate behind them.

She then went to a Special Place for the adult self. This was the castle near a Scottish loch. There was a green wooded area where only good things happen. If she felt any discomfort or pain after the exploration, she could practise a way of dissociating in her Special Place as follows.

She would sit down on the loch side where there was a lot of mist which covered that part of her body, and she would feel a numbness or coldness coming over her body from the toes upward. She could then use the warmth of the sun to burn away the mist, and then come out of the hypnotic state. Any soreness afterwards could be attributed to sitting on the grass. She could then clench her fist to open the gate and let the children out. She naturally had to inform the surgeon about her self-hypnosis as previously.

This hypnotic intervention also worked well for her and she had no problems with the children. Her physical problems, however, were not over. She was later diagnosed with irritable bowel syndrome and food intolerances. She received medication for the IBS, but she also felt that hypnosis might help her again, as it has been used often to alleviate IBS. A standard procedure was used with suggestions of hand warming and transferring the warmth to the abdomen (Hammond, 1990, p. 281), which has been very successful. Kate did not need to change anything in the procedure nor modify it in order to contain the 'children'. She carried out the self-hypnosis regularly and was also working with the 'children' to facilitate more integration. She was, however, warned against nurturing the 'children' too much, as they had to be allowed to grow up, otherwise it would be more difficult to integrate them if they stayed at the same child age.

More Ways towards Integration

There were a number of ways in which Kate now worked towards integration. She allotted time for the 'children', as well as for the adult self and her present duties. All the 'children' now knew her, the adult, and recognised her. If and when a 'new child' came out, she (the adult) used self-hypnosis to take her to the Special Place, the garden, to show the new child where she was. When Kate terminated this hypnosis, she then re-oriented herself by looking round the house. She had a number of photographs of herself as a child at different ages. She would then look through these for the new child to see that she is part of the others. Then she, the adult, would look in a long mirror and see herself as an adult, so the 'new child' could see she had survived. Kate had also decided not to shut the children away again, but first keep them safe in the Bubble.

She had a 10 year old emerge (first in a dream) and then a 14 year old. The above routine worked successfully with these 'new children'. Kate discovered that once they recognised her as the adult self, they started to integrate, and to grow up. They no longer needed the toys to play with. Toys did not trigger feelings any more, and Kate did not feel overwhelmed now when the 'children' came out. She still felt some lack of confidence when they did come out, however, if the 'teenagers' came out she felt more confident. Kate as an adult was also becoming more confident and assertive, and she was dealing with her son a lot better, although he was still receiving treatment, and had been diagnosed with ADHD (Attentional Deficit Hyperactive Disorder).

Kate's mother was now talking to the 'children' (at least recognising when any one of them came out) and apologising for letting them down. She also apologised to adult Kate for not believing her and supporting her when she had breast cancer. She also offered Kate and her husband to share their house temporarily which was near to the place where Kate and her husband were going to move.

Kate now felt she was ready to end the therapy as she felt she was becoming integrated and she knew how to deal with anymore children who might reveal themselves. She considered that she had shared the pain of all her 'children'. It had given her more strength and she felt able to deal with difficult situations, particularly with her own health issues, her family and her son's abuse and treatment.

Kate's Own Conclusion

Kate said that she had felt that every stage in the therapy, when a child state emerged, was like a railway track to follow. As she follows it, it comes to an end as a pathway, which gives her more choices and pathways in her life. She said she would continue to use all the strategies she learnt from the therapy. She realised she had to go along with each child state of her past as it emerged, and use grounding techniques and the procedure she worked out for herself as described above, until she, the adult, felt in control.

Regarding the hypnotic interventions, she felt the safe remembering technique with the Bubble enabled her to 'change history', meaning that she no longer had to be haunted by the abusive past. The safe remembering technique was used twice; once to resolve the traumas of rape by her first husband, and again when she was with her abusive uncle in the park at age 9. The use of the Bubble to keep her 'children' safe, and enabling her to keep in control, so she as an adult was not overwhelmed by the traumatised child states, she also found invaluable. Most of the memory integration she did herself, and was just gently guided by the therapist.

Comments on Kate's Therapy

Kate's hypnotic skills were utilised throughout the therapy to great advantage; not just to facilitate integration of the child states, which held the traumatic memories, but also to help her through the various physical illnesses she had to suffer. The hypnotic procedures were quite flexible and could be modified to suit her needs at the time, and most of the modifications were her own innovations. There were not many formal hypnotic inductions and the guidelines for treating DID were adhered to.

The psychotherapy lasted for a period of about six years. During this time she had a one year break from it, when she and her husband went to Scotland. There were also breaks in the therapy when she had to have treatment or surgery for her physical illnesses. These breaks were periods of several weeks. In spite of these interruptions, she was able to carry out her homework assignments from the psychotherapy and return to it without any major relapse.

Kate did not have much support from the members of her dysfunctional family of the past, until her mother and father were seen by the therapist. She was a highly motivated and committed client, who achieved a considerable degree of integration, in spite of the set-backs with her physical health and her son's problems.

In the experience of the present author and colleagues, these therapeutic approaches with hypnosis appear to have been very effective and well accepted by the clients. However, as rightly pointed out in Chapter 1, hypnosis in the treatment of trauma may be used to modulate and integrate traumatic memories, but systematic group, as well as single-case studies, need to be conducted before we can reach a definite conclusion as to the efficacy of hypnosis compared to other approaches in the treatment of trauma. Other important factors would be length of treatment with and without hypnosis, and contraindications if any. More research is needed in this promising field.

REFERENCES

Ainsworth MDS (1985) Patterns of infant-mother attachment: antecedents and effects on development. *Bulletin of the New York Academy* 61: 771–91.

Ainsworth MDS, Blehar MC, Waters E, Wall S (1978) *Patterns of Attachment: A Psychological Study of the Strange Situation*. Hillsdale, NJ: Erlbaum.

Alden P (1995) Back to the past: Introducing the 'Bubble'. *Contemporary Hypnosis* 12: 59–68.

Alexander PC (1992) Application of attachment theory to the study of sexual abuse. *Journal of Consulting and Clinical Psychology* 60: 185–95.

Allen JG (2001) *Traumatic Relationships and Serious Mental Disorders*. New York: J Wiley & Sons.

American Psychiatric Association (1994) *Diagnostic and Statistical Manual of Mental Disorders DSMIV*. Washington DC.

American Society of Clinical Hypnosis (1994) *Clinical Hypnosis and Memory Guidelines for Clinicians and for Forensic Hypnosis*. American Society of Clinical Hypnosis Press.

Andrews B (1995) Bodily shame as a mediator between abusive experiences and depression. *Journal of Abnormal Psychology* 104: 277–85.

Andrews B, Brewin CR, Ochera J, Morton J, Bekerian DA, Davies GM et al. (2000) The timing, triggers and qualities of recovered memories in therapy. *British Journal of Clinical Psychology* 39: 11–26.

Banyai EA, Hilgard ER (1976) A comparison of active-alert hypnotic induction and traditional relaxation induction. *Journal of Abnormal Psychology* 85: 218–24.

Barach PM (1991) Multiple personality disorder as an attachment disorder. *Dissociation* 4: 117–23.

Barber TX (1969) *Hypnosis: A Scientific Approach*. New York: Van Nostrand Reinhold.

Barber TX, Spanos NP, Chaves JF (1974) *Hypnosis, Imagination and Human Potentialities*. Elmsford, NY: Pergamon Press.

Bartlett FC (1932) *Remembering: A Study in Experimental and Social Psychology*. Cambridge: Cambridge University Press.

Bass E, Davis L (1988) *The Courage to Heal: A Guide for Women Survivors of Child Sexual Abuse*. New York: Harper & Row.

Beahrs JO (1982) *Unity and Multiplicity*. New York: Brunner/Mazel.

Belicki K, Correy B, Bancock A, Cuddy M, Dunlop A (1994) *Reports of Sexual Abuse: Facts or Fantasies?* Unpublished Manuscript. Brock University, St Catherines, Ontario.

Bell L (2002) How accurately does DSM IV measure borderline personality disorder? *Clinical Psychology* 15: 16–17.

Bell L (2003) *Managing Intense Emotions and Overcoming Self-Destructive Habits*. Hove and New York: Brunner-Routledge.

Bernstein E, Putman FW (1986) Development, reliability and validity of a dissociation scale. *Journal of Nervous and Mental Diseases* 102: 280–6.

Bliss EL (1986) *Multiple Personality, Allied Disorders and Hypnosis*. New York: Oxford University Press.

Blizard RA (2001) Masochistic and sadistic ego-states: dissociative solutions to the dilemma of attachment of an abusive caretaker. *Journal of Trauma and Dissociation* 2(4): 37–58.

Blizard RA (2003) Disorganised attachment, development of dissociated self states and a relational approach to treatment. *Journal of Trauma and Dissociation* 4(3): 27–50.

Bloom PB (1994) Clinical guidelines in using hypnosis in uncovering memories of sexual abuse. *International Journal of Clinical and Experimental Hypnosis* 42: 173–8.

Blume ES (1990) *Secret Survivors: Uncovering Incest and its After-effects in Women*. New York: J Wiley & Sons.

Bolen JD (1993) The impact of sexual abuse on women's health. *Psychiatric Annals* 23: 446–53.

Bower GH (1981) Mood and memory. *American Psychologist* 36: 129–48.

Bowlby J (1973) *Attachment and Loss: Vol. 2 Separation*. New York: Basic Books.

Bowlby J (1988). Development psychiatry comes of age. *American Journal of Orthopsychiatry* 145: 1–10.

Bremner JD, Randall P, Scott TM, Bronen RA, Seibyl JP, Southwick SM (1995) MRI-based measure of hippocampal volume in patients with PTSD. *American Journal of Psychiatry* 152: 973–81.

Brende JO (1985) The use of hypnosis in posttraumatic conditions. In WE Kelly (ed.) *Post Traumatic Stress Disorder and the War Veteran Patient*. New York: Brunner/Mazel.

Breuer J, Freud S (1893–95) Studies on hysteria. In J Strachey (ed & trans.) *The Standard Edition of the Complete Psychological Works of Sigmund Freud, vol. 2*. Norton: New York Press.

Brewin CR, Andrews B (1997) Reasoning about repression: inferences from clinical and experimental data. In MA Conway (ed.) *Recovered Memories and False Memories*, 192–205. Oxford: Oxford University Press.

Brewin CR, Andrews B (1998) Recovered memories of trauma: phenomenology and cognitive mechanisms. *Clinical Psychology Review* 18: 949–70.

Brewin CM, Andrews B, Gotlieb I (1993) 1. Psycho-pathology and early experience: a re-appraisal of retrospective reports. *Psychological Bulletin* 113: 82–98.

Briere J (1992) *Child Abuse Trauma: Theory and Treatment of the Lasting Effects*. Newburg Park, CA: Sage.

Briere J (1996) A self-trauma model for treating adult survivors of severe child abuse. In J Briere, L Berliner, J Bulkley, C Jenny, T Reid (eds) *The APSA Handbook on Child Maltreatment*. Thousand Oakes, CA: Sage.

Briere J (2002) *Multiscale Dissociation Inventory (MDI)*. Odessa FL: Psychological Assessment Resources.

Briere J, Runtz M (1987) Post sexual abuse trauma: data and implications for clinical practice. *Journal of Interpersonal Violence* 2: 367–79.

Briere J, Conte J (1993) Self-reported amnesia for abuse in adults molested in childhood. *Journal of Traumatic Stress* 6: 21–31.

Briere J, Weathers FW, Runtz M (2005) Is dissociation a multi-dimensional construct? Data from the multiscale inventory. *Journal of Traumatic Stress* 18(3): 221–3.

British Psychological Society (1995) *Recovered Memories: The Report of the Working Party of The British Psychological Society.* Leicester: BPS Publications.

Brown D (1995) Pseudo Memories: The Standard of Science and the Standard of Care in Trauma Treatment. *American Journal of Clinical Hypnosis* 37: 1–24.

Brown D, Scheflin AW, Hammond DC (1998) *Memory, Trauma, Treatment and the Law.* New York: WW Norton & Co.

Brown DP, Fromm E (1986) *Hypnotherapy and Hypnoanalysis.* Hillsdale, NJ: Erlbaum.

Brown RJ, Antonova E, Langley A, Oakley DA (2001) The effects of absorption and reduced critical thought on suggestibility in a hypnotic context. *Contemporary Hypnosis* 18(2): 62–72.

Bullard TE (1987) *UFO Abductions: The Measure of Mystery.* Mount Rainier MO: Fund for UFO Research.

Burbach DJ, Borduin CM (1986) Parent–child relations and the etiology of depression: a review of methods and findings. *Clinical Psychology Review* 6: 133–53.

Burgess RL, Youngblade LM (1988) Social incompetence and the intergenerational transmission of abusive parental practices. In GT Hotalin, D Finkelhor, JT Kirkpatrick, MA Strauss (eds), *Family Abuse and Its Consequences: New Directions in Research*, 38–60. Newbury Park, CA: Sage.

Cameron C (1994) Women survivors confronting their abusers: Issues, decisions and outcomes. *Journal of Childhood Sexual Abuse* 3: 7–35.

Cameron C (1996) Comparing amnesic and non-amnesic survivors of childhood sexual abuse: a longitudinal study. In K Pezdek, WP Banks (eds) *The Recovered Memory/False Memory Debate*, 41–68. New York: Academic Press.

Cardena E (1994) The domain of dissociation. In SJ Lynn, Rhue JW (eds) *Dissociation.* New York: Guilford Press.

Cardena E (2000) Hypnosis in the treatment of trauma: a promising, but not fully supported, efficacious intervention. *International Journal of Experimental and Clinical Hypnosis* 48(2): 225–38.

Cardena E, Spiegel D (1993) Dissociative reactions to the San Francisco Bay area earthquake of 1989. *American Journal of Psychiatry* 150(3): 474–8.

Cardena E, Lynn JL, Krippner S (2000) *Varieties of Anomalous Experience.* Washington DC: American Psychological Association.

Carlson EB (1997) *Trauma Assessment: A Clinician's Guide.* New York: Guilford Press.

Carlson EB, Putnam FW (1993) An update to the dissociative experiences scale. *Dissociation* 6: 16–27.

Carlson EB, Furby L, Armstrong J, Shlaes J (1998) A conceptual framework for the long-term psychological effects of traumatic childhood abuse. *Child Maltreatment* 2(3): 272–95.

Christo G (1997) Child sexual abuse: psychological consequences. *The Psychologist* 10(5): 205–9.

Chu JA (1998) Rebuilding shattered lives: the responsible treatment of complex post-traumatic stress and dissociative disorders. New York: J Wiley & Sons.

Chu JA, Dill DL (1990) Dissociative symptoms in relation to childhood physical and sexual abuse. *American Journal of Psychiatry* 147: 887–92.

Clark MS, Milberg S, Ross J (1983) Arousal cues arousal-related material in memory: implications for understanding effects of mood on memory. *Journal of Verbal Learning and Verbal Behaviour* 22: 633–49.

Cole PM, Putnam FW (1992) Effect of Incest on self and social functioning: a developmental psychopathology perspective. *Journal of Consulting and Clinical Psychology* 60: 174–84.

Conway MA (1995) *Flashbulb Memories*. Hillsdale, NJ: Erlbaum.

Conway MA (ed.) (1997) *Recovered Memories and False Memories*. Oxford: Oxford University Press.

Coons PM (1994) Confirmation of childhood abuse in child and adolescent cases of multiple personality disorder and dissociative disorder not otherwise specified. *Journal of Nervous and Mental Disease* 182: 461–4.

Coulton CJ, Korbin JE, Su M, Chow J (1995) Community level factors and child maltreatment rates. *Child Development* 66: 1262–76.

Courtois CA (1997) Delayed memories of child sexual abuse: critique of the controversy and clinical guidelines. In MA Conway (ed.) *Recovered Memories and False Memories* 206–29. Oxford: Oxford University Press.

Crawford HJ, Knebel T, Vendemia MC (1998) The nature of hypnotic analgesia: neurophysiological foundation and evidence. *Contemporary Hypnosis* 15: 22–33.

Crittenden P (1983) The relationship of quality of network support to quality of child rearing and child development. Paper presented at the Forum for Developmental Research, Richmond VA.

Croft RJ, Williams JD, Haenschel C, Gruzelier JH (2002) Pain perception, 40Hz oscillations and hypnotic analgesia. *International Journal of Psychophysiology* 46: 101–8.

Damasio A (2000) *The Feeling of What Happens: Body, Emotion and the Making of Consciousness*. Random House, London.

Davidson RJ, Tomarken AJ (1989) Laterality and emotion: an electrophysiological approach. In F Baller, J Grafman (eds) *Handbook of Neuropsychology*. 3: 419–41. Amsterdam: Elsevier.

Davies JM, Frawley MG (1994) *Treating the Adult Survivor of Childhood Sexual Abuse: A Psycho-analytic Perspective*. New York: Basic.

De Shazer S (1985) *Keys to Solution in Brief Therapy*. New York: Norton.

Degun MD, Degun GS (1983) Covert sensitisation with the use of hypnosis. *British Journal of Experimental and Clinical Hypnosis* 1(1): 27–32.

Degun MD, Degun GS (1988) The use of hypnotic dream suggestion in psychotherapy. In M Heap (ed.) *Hypnosis: Current Clinical, Experimental and Forensic Practices* 21: 221. London: Croom Helm.

Degun MD, Degun GS (1991) Hypnotherapy and sexual problems. In M Heap, W Dryden (eds) *Hypnotherapy: A Handbook*. Milton Keynes: Open University Press.

Degun-Mather MD (1997) Group therapy and hypnosis for the treatment of bulimia nervosa. In BJ Evans, GJ Corman, GD Burrows (eds) *Hypnosis for Weight-management and Eating Disorders: A Clinical Handbook*. Published by the Australian Journal of Clinical and Experimental Hypnosis.

Degun-Mather MD (2003) Ego-state therapy in the treatment of a complex eating disorder. *Contemporary Hypnosis* 20(3): 165–73.

Dolan YM (1991) *Resolving Sexual Abuse: Solution-Focused Therapy and Ericksonian Hypnotherapy for Adult Survivors*. New York: W.W. Norton & Co.

Dolan YM (1998) *One Small Step: Moving beyond Trauma and Therapy to a Life of Joy*. Watsonville, CA: Papier Mache Press.

Dywan J, Bowers K (1983) The use of hypnosis to enhance recall. *Science* 222: 184–5.

Elliott D, Briere J (1995) Epidemiology of memory and trauma. Paper presented at the annual meeting of the International Society of Traumatic Stress Studies, Chicago.

Ennis CZ, McNeilly CL, Corkery JM, Gilbert MS (1995) The debate about delayed memories of child sexual abuse: a feminist perspective. *The Counselling Psychologist* 23: 181–279.

Ensink BJ (1992) *Confusing Realities: A Study of Child Sexual Abuse and Psychiatric Symptoms*. Amsterdam: VU University Press.

Erdelyi MH (1996) *The Recovery of Unconscious Memories: Hypermnesia and reminiscence*. Chicago: University of Chicago Press.

Erickson MH, Rossi EL (1980) The February man: facilitating new identity in hypnotherapy. In EL Rossi (ed.). *The Collected Papers of Milton H. Erickson on Hypnosis, Vol. 4*, 525–42. New York: Irvington.

Evans F (2000) The domain of hypnosis: a multifactorial model. *American Journal of Clinical Hypnosis* 43: 1–16.

Everill JT, Waller G (1995) Reported sexual abuse and eating psychopathology: a review of the evidence for a causal link. *International Journal of Eating Disorders* 18(1): 1–11.

Eysenck HJ, Furneaux WD (1945) Primary and secondary suggestibility: an experimental and statistical study. *Journal of Experimental Psychology* 35: 485–503.

Fairbairn WRD (1952) Steps on the development of an object-relations theory of the personality. In WRD Fairburn, *Psychoanalytic Studies of the Personality*, 152–61. London: Routledge & Kegan Paul (original work published 1949).

Farvolden P, Woody EZ (2004) Hypnosis, memory, and frontal executive functioning. *International Journal of Clinical and Experimental Hypnosis* 52: 3–26.

Feldman CM (1997) Childhood precursors of adult interpersonal violence. *Clinical Psychology: Science and Practice* 4: 307–34.

Feldman M (1994) Projective identification in phantasy and enactment. *Psychoanalytic Inquiry* 14: 423–40.

Feldman-Summers S, Pope KS (1994) The experience of forgetting childhood abuse: a national survey of psychologists. *Journal of Consulting and Clinical Psychology* 62: 636–9.

Fellows BJ, Richardson J (1993) Relaxed and alert hypnosis: an experimental comparison. *Contemporary Hypnosis* 10: 49–54.

Finkelhor D (1987) The trauma of child sexual abuse: two models. *Journal of Interpersonal Violence* 2(4): 348–66.

Fivush R, Edwards VJ (2004) Remembering and forgetting childhood sexual abuse. *Journal of Child Sexual Abuse* 13(2): 1–20.

Flisher AJ, Kramer RA, Hoven CW, Greenwald S, Alegria M, Bird HR et al. (1997) Psychosocial characteristics of physically abused children and adolescents. *Journal of the American Academy of Child and Adolescent Psychiatry* 36: 123–31.

Foa EB (1995) *Postraumatic Stress Diagnostic Scale*. Minneapolis: National Computer Systems.

Foa EB, Kozak MJ (1986) Emotional processing of fear: exposure to corrective information. *Psychological Bulletin* 99: 20–35.

Foa EB, Molnar C, Cashman L (1995) Change in rape narratives during exposure therapy for posttraumatic stress disorder. *Journal of Traumatic Stress* 8: 675–90.

Foa EB, Steketee G, Rothbaum BO (1998) Behavioural/cognitive conceptualisation of post traumatic stress disorder. *Behaviour Therapy* 20: 155–76.

Fraser GA (1991) The dissociative table technique: a strategy for working with ego-states in dissociative disorders and ego-state therapy. *Dissociation: Progress in the Dissociative Disorders* 4: 205–13.

Fraser GA (1993) Special treatment technique to access the inner personality system of multiple personality patients. *Dissociation: Progress in the Dissociative Disorders* 6: 193–8.

Fraser GA (2003) Fraser's 'dissociative table technique' revisited, revised: a strategy for working with ego-states in dissociative disorders and ego-state therapy. *Journal of Trauma and Dissociation* 4(4): 5–28.

Frederick C (2005) Selected topics in ego-state therapy. *International Journal of Clinical and Experimental Hypnosis* 53(4): 339–429.

Frederick C, McNeal S (1999) *Inner Strengths: Contemporary Psychotherapy and Hypnosis for Ego-strengthening*. Mahwah, NJ: Lawrence Erlbaum Associates.

Freud S (1964) The dissection of the psychical personality. In J Strachey (ed. & trans.) *The Standard Edition of the Complete Psychological Works of Sigmund Freud* 22: 57–80. London: Hogarth Press (original work published 1933).

Freyd J (1996) *Betrayal Trauma: The Logic of Forgetting Childhood Abuse*. Cambridge, MA: Harvard University Press.

Freyd J, DePrince AP, Zurbriggen EL (2001) Self-reported memory for abuse depends upon victim-perpetrator relationship. *Journal of Trauma and Dissociation* 2(3): 5–16.

Friederick M, Trippe RH, Özcan M, Weiss T, Hecht H, Miltner WHR (2001) Laser-evoked potentials to noxious stimulation during hypnotic analgesia and distraction of attention suggest different brain mechanisms of pain control. *Psychophysiology* 38: 768–76.

Garbarino J (1981) Child abuse and juvenile delinquency: the developmental impact of social isolation. In RJ Hunner, YE Walker (eds) *Exploring the Relationship between Child Abuse and Delinquency*, 115–27. Montclair, NJ: Allanheld Osmun.

Garry M, Loftus EF, Brown SW (1994) Memory: a river runs through it. *Consciousness and Cognition* 3: 438–51.

Gibson HB, Heap M (1991) *Hypnosis in Therapy*. London: Lawrence Erlbaum Associates.

Gray JF (1982) *The Neuropsychology of Anxiety: An Enquiry into the Functions of the Septohippocampal System*. New York: Oxford University Press.

Groth-Marnat G, Schumacher JF (1990) Hypnotisability, attitudes towards eating and concern with body size in a female college population. *American Journal of Clinical Hypnosis* 32(3): 201–7.

Gruzelier JH (1998) A working model of the neurophysiology of hypnosis: a review of the evidence. *Contemporary Hypnosis* 15: 3–21.

Gruzelier JH (2000) Redefining hypnosis: theory, methods and integration. *Contemporary Hypnosis* 17: 51–70.

Gruzelier JH (2005) Altered states of consciousness and hypnosis in the twenty-first century. *Contemporary Hypnosis* 22(1): 1–7.

Gruzelier JH, Warren K (1993) Neuropsychological evidence of reductions on left frontal tests with hypnosis. *Psychological Medicine* 23: 93–101.

Gudjonsson GH (1992) *The Psychology of Interrogations, Confessions and Testimony*. Chichester: J Wiley & Sons.

Gudjonsson GH, Clark NK (1986) Suggestibility in police interrogation: a social psychological model. *Social Behaviour* 1: 83–104.

Hall RCW, Tice L, Beresford TP, Wooley B, Hall AK (1989) Sexual abuse in patients with anorexia nervosa and bulimia. *Psychosomatics* 30: 79–88.

Hammond CD (ed.) (1990) *Handbook of Hypnotic Suggestions and Metaphors*. An American Society of Clinical Hypnosis Book. New York: WW Norton & Co.

Heap M, Aravind KK (2002a) *Hartland's Medical and Dental Hypnosis* (4th edn). Churchill Livingstone, Edinburgh.

Heap M, Aravind KK (2002b) Hypnotic procedures in psychodynamic therapy. In M Heap, KK Aravind. *Hartland's Medical and Dental Hypnosis*. (4th edn). Churchill Livingstone, Edinburgh.

Herman JL (1992) *Trauma and Recovery*. New York: Basic Books.

Herman JL (1996) Crime and memory. In CB Strozier, M Flynn (eds) *Trauma and Self.* Rowman & Littlefield, Lanham, MD.

Herman JL, Schatzow E (1987) Recovery and verification of memories of childhood sexual trauma. *Psycho-analytic Psychology* 4: 1–14.

Herman JL, Perry C, Van der Kolk BA (1989) Childhood trauma in borderline personality disorder. *American Journal of Psychiatry* 146: 490–5.

Herzberger S, Potts D, Dillon M (1981) Abusive and non-abusive parental treatment from the child's perspective. *Journal of Consulting and Clinical Psychology* 49: 81–90.

Hilgard E (1986) *Divided Consciousness: Multiple Controls in Human Thought and Action* (rev. edn). New York: J Wiley & Sons.

Hilgard E (1991) A neodissociation interpretation of hypnosis. In SJ Lynn, JW Rhue (eds) *Theories of Hypnosis: Current Models and Perspectives*, 83–104. New York: Guildford Press.

Hilgard JR (1970) *Personality and Hypnosis: A Study of Imaginative Involvement.* Chicago: University of Chicago Press.

Holmes EA, Brown RJ, Mansell W, Pasco Fearon R, Hunter ECM, Frasquillo F et al. (2005) Are there two qualitatively distinct forms of dissociation? A review and some clinical implications. *Clinical Psychology Review* 25: 1–23.

Holmes J (1993) *John Bowlby and Attachment Theory.* Routledge, London and New York.

Hooper D, Dryden W (eds) (1994) *Couple Therapy: A Handbook.* Milton Keynes: Open University Press.

Horowitz MJ (1976) *Stress Response Syndromes.* New York: Aronson.

Horowitz MJ (1986) *Stress Response Syndromes* (2nd edn). Northvale, NJ: Aronson.

Horowitz MJ (1991) Person schemas. In MJ Horowitz (ed.) *Person Schemas and Maladaptive Interpersonal Patterns,* 13–31. Chicago: University of Chicago Press.

Hull CL (1933) *Hypnosis and Suggestibility.* New York: Appleton-Century-Crofts.

Ibbotson G (2005) *The Cinema Technique.* Personal communication.

International Society for the Study of Dissociation (1994) *Guidelines for Treating Dissociative Identity Disorder (Multiple Personality Disorder) in Adults.* Skakie, IL: ISSD.

International Society for Traumatic Stress Studies (1998) *Childhood Trauma Remembered: A Report on the Current Scientific Knowledge Base and its Applications.* Northbrook, IL: ISTSS.

Janet P (1907) *The Major Symptoms of Hysteria.* New York: Macmillan.

Janet P (1909) *Les Nervoses.* Paris: Flammarion.

Janoff-Bulman R (1992) Shattered assumptions. *Towards a New Psychology of Trauma.* New York: The Free Press.

Jehu D (1979) *Sexual Dysfunctions – A Behavioural Approach.* Chichester: J Wiley & Sons.

Jehu D (1988) *Beyond Sexual Abuse: Therapy with Women who were Childhood Victims.* Chichester: J Wiley & Sons.

Jones BP (1993) Repression: the evolution of a psychoanalytic concept from the 1890s to the 1990s. *Journal of the American Psychoanalytic Association* 41: 63–93.

Kallio S, Revonsuo A, Hamalainen H, Gruzelier JH (2001) Anterior brain functions and hypnosis: a test of the frontal hypothesis. *International Journal of Clinical and Experimental Hypnosis* 49: 95–108.

Kaplan HS (1974) *The New Sex Therapy.* New York: Brunner/Mazel.

Kaufman JL (1991) Depressive disorders in maltreated children. *American Journal of Child and Adolescent Psychiatry* 30: 257–65.

Kennerley H (1996) Cognitive therapy of dissociative symptoms associated with trauma. *British Journal of Clinical Psychology* 35: 325–40.

Kennerley H, Whitehead L, Butler G (personal communication) *Survivors of Sexual Abuse: Recovery Workbook* (unpublished).

Kihlstrom JF (1984) Conscious, subconscious, unconscious: a cognitive approach. In KS Bowers, D Meichenbaum (eds) *The Unconscious Reconsidered*, 149–211. New York: J Wiley & Sons.

Kihlstrom JF (1994) One hundred years of hysteria. In SJ Lynn, JW Rhue (eds) *Dissociation: Clinical and Theoretical Perspectives*, 365–94. New York: Guilford.

Kihlstrom JF (2003) The fox, the hedgehog and hypnosis. *International Journal of Clinical and Experimental Hypnosis* 51: 166–89.

Kim JJ, Fanselow MS (1992) Modality-specific retrograde amnesia of fear. *Science* 256(5057): 675–7.

Kirsch I (1990) *Changing Expectations: A Key to Effective Psychotherapy*. Pacific Grove, CA: Brooks/Cole.

Kirsch I (1991) The social learning theory of hypnosis. In SJ Lynn, RW Rhue (eds) *Theories of Hypnosis: Current Models and Perspectives*, 446–59. New York: Guilford Press.

Kirsch I, Lynn SJ, Rhue JW (1993) Introduction to clinical hypnosis. In JW Rhue, SJ Lynn, I Kirsch (eds) *Handbook of Clinical Hypnosis*, 3–22. Washington DC: American Psychological Association.

Kirsch I, Montgomery G, Sapirstein G (1995) Hypnosis as an adjunct to cognitive-behavioural therapy: a meta-analysis. *Journal of Consulting and Clinical Psychology* 63: 214–20.

Klein M (1975) Some theoretical conclusions regarding the emotional life of the infant. In *The Writings of Melanie Klein* 3: 61–93. London: Hogarth Press (original work published 1952).

Kluft RP (1992) A specialist perspective on multiple personality disorder. *Psychoanalytic Inquiry* 12(1): 112–23.

Kluft RP (1993) Multiple personality disorder. In D Spiegel (ed.). *Dissociative Disorders: A Clinical Review*. Lutherville, MD: Sidran Press.

Kolb LC (1988) Recovery of memory and repressed fantasy in combat-induced post traumatic stress disorder of Vietnam veterans. In HM Pettinati (ed.). *Hypnosis and memory*, 265–74. Guilford Press, New York.

Koverola C, Pound J, Heger A, Lytle C (1993) Relationship of child sexual abuse to depression. *Child Abuse and Neglect* 17: 393–400.

Krippner S (2005) Trance and trickster: hypnosis as a liminal phenomenon. *International Journal of Clinical and Experimental Hypnosis* 53(2): 97–118.

Kristiansen CM, Felton KA, Hovdestad WE, Allard CB (1995) *The Ottawa Survivor's Study: A summary of the findings*. Unpublished manuscript.

Kuehn LL (1974) Looking down a gun barrel: person perception and violent crime. *Perceptual and Motor Skills* 39: 1159–64.

Lang PJ (1979) A bioinformational theory of emotional imagery. *Psychophysiology* 16: 495–512.

Lawrence JR, Perry C (1981) The 'hidden observer' phenomenon in hypnosis: some additional findings. *Journal of Abnormal Psychology* 90: 334–44.

Layden MA, Newman CF, Freeman A, Byers-Morse S (1993) *Cognitive Therapy of Borderline Personality Disorder*. Needham Heights, MA: Allyn & Bacon.

Le Doux JE (1992) Emotion as memory: anatomical systems underlying indelible neural traces. In SA Christiansen (ed.) *Handbook of Emotion and Memory*, 269–88. Hillsdale, NJ: Erlbaum.

Lewis DO, Shanock SS, Pincus JH, Glaser GH (1979) Violent juvenile offenders: psychiatric, neurological, psychological and abuse factors. *Journal of the American Academy of Child Psychiatry* 18: 307–19.

Lex BW (1979) The neurobiology of ritual trance. In EG d'Aguilli, CD Lauflin, J MacManis (eds) *The Spectrum of Ritual*. New York: Columbia University Press.

Lightstone J (2004) Dissociation and compulsive eating. *Journal of Trauma and Dissociation* 5(4): 17–32.

Loftus EF, Polensky S, Fullilove MT (1994) Memories of childhood sexual abuse: remembering and repressing. *Psychology of Women Quarterly* 18: 67–84.

Lynn SJ, Rhue JW (1988) Fantasy proneness: hypnosis, developmental antecedents and psychopathology. *American Psychologist, 43*, 35–44.

Lynn, SJ, Rhue JW (eds) (1991) *Theories of Hypnosis: Current Models and Perspectives.* New York: Guilford Press.

McClure MB (1990) *Reclaiming the Heart: A Handbook of Help and Hope for Survivors of Incest.* Warner Books, New York.

McCranie EJ, Crasilneck HB, Teter HR (1955) The electroencephalogram in hypnotic age regression. *Psychiatric Quarterly* 29: 85–8.

McNally RJ (2003) *Remembering Trauma.* Cambridge, Massachusetts and London, England: Belknap Press of Harvard University Press.

Main M (1995) Recent studies in attachment; overview with selected implications for clinical work. In S Goldberg, R Muir, J Kerr (eds) *Attachment Theory; Social, Developmental, and Clinical Perspectives*, 407–74. Hillsdale NJ: Analytical Press.

Main M, Solomon J (1986) Discovery of an insecure – disorganised/disoriented attachment pattern: procedures, findings and implications for the classification of behaviour. In TB Brazelton, MW Yogman (eds) *Affective Development in Infancy*, 95–124. Norwood, NJ: Ablex.

Maltz W (1988) Identifying and treating the sexual repercussions of incest: a couples therapy approach. *Journal of Sex and Marital Therapy* 14(2): 142–72.

Marmar CR, Weiss DS, Pynoos RS (1995) Dynamic psychotherapy of post traumatic stress disorder. In MJ Friedman, DS Charney, AY Deutch (eds) *Neurological and Clinical Consequences of Stress: From Normal Adaptation to Post Traumatic Stress Disorder*, 495–506. Philadelphia: Lippencott-Raven.

Martinez-Taboas A (1991) Multiple personality in Puerto Rico: analysis of 15 cases. *Dissociation* 4: 189–92.

Melchert TP (1996) Childhood memory and a history of different forms of abuse. *Professional Psychology Research and Practice* 27: 438–46.

Mesulam MM (1998) From sensation to cognition. *Brain* 121: 1013–52.

Mollon P (1996) *Multiple Selves, Multiple Voices. Working with Trauma, Violation and Dissociation.* Chichester: J Wiley & Sons.

Mollon P (1998*) Remembering Trauma: A Psychotherapists Guide to Memory and Illusion.* Chichester: J Wiley & Sons.

Muntaha S (2004) Asian women and self-harm: a coping strategy. *Clinical Psychology* 42: 13–15.

Naish PLN (2001) Hypnotic time perceptions: busy beaver or tardy timekeeper? *Contemporary Hypnosis* 18(2): 87–99.

Nijenhuis ERS (1999) *Somatoform Dissociation: Phenomena, Measurement and Theoretical Issues.* The Netherlands: Van Gorcum.

Nijenhuis ERS (2000) Somatoform dissociation: major symptoms of dissociative disorders. *Journal of Trauma and Dissociation* 1(4): 7–32.

Nijenhuis ERS, Van der Hart O (1999) Forgetting and re-experiencing trauma: from anaesthesia to pain. In JM Goodwin, R Attias (eds) *Splintered Reflections: Images of the Body in Trauma*, 39–65. New York: Basic Books.

Nijenhuis ERS, Spinhoven P, Van Dyck R, Van der Hart O, Vanderlinden J (1997) The development of the Somatoform Dissociation Questionnaire (SDQ20). *Journal of Nervous and Mental Disease* 184: 688–94.

Nijenhuis E, Van Engen A, Kusters I, Van der Hart O (2001) Peritraumatic somatoform dissociation in relation to recall of childhood sexual abuse. *Journal of Trauma and Dissociation* 1(3): 49–68.

O'Hanlon B, Bertolino B (1998) *Even from a Broken Web*. New York: J Wiley & Sons.

Oakley D, Alden P, Degun-Mather M (1996) The use of hypnosis in therapy with adults. *The Psychologist* 9(11): 502–5.

Orne MT (1951) The mechanism of hypnotic age regression: an experimental study. *Journal of Abnormal and Social Psychology* 46: 213–25.

Orne MT (1961) The potential uses of hypnosis in interrogation. In AD Biderman, H Zimmer (eds) *The Manipulation of Human Behaviour*, 169–215. New York: J Wiley & Sons.

Orne MT (1962) On the social psychology of the psychological experiments: with particular reference to demand characteristics and their implications. *American Psychologist* 17: 776–83.

Orne MT, Soskis DA, Dinges DG, Orne EC (1984) Hypnotically induced testimony and the criminal justice system. In GL Wells, EF Loftus (eds) *Advances in the Psychology of Eyewitness Testimony*, 171–213. New York: Cambridge University Press.

Orne MT, Whitehouse WG, Dinges DF, Orne EC (1988) Reconstructing memory through hypnosis: forensic and clinical applications. In HM Pettinati. *Hypnosis and Memory*. New York: Guildford Press.

Owens JH (2003) *Magic Carpet Script*. Personal communication. Unpublished.

Pendergrast M (1996) *Victims of Memory: Incest Accusations and Shattered Lives*. London: Harper Collins.

Pennebaker JW, Beall SK (1986) Confronting a traumatic event: toward an understanding of inhibition and disease. *Journal of Abnormal Psychology* 95: 274–81.

Perez C, Widom C (1994) Childhood victimisation and long term intellectual and academic outcomes. *Child Abuse & Neglect* 18: 617–33.

Perry C (1995) The false memory syndrome (FMS) and disguised hypnosis. *Hypnos: Swedish Journal of Hypnosis in Psychotherapy and Psychosomatic Medicine* 22: 189–97.

Perry C (2000) Hypnosis and the elicitation of repressed and/or dissociated memories. *Hypnos: Swedish Journal of Hypnosis in Psychotherapy and Psychosomatic Medicine* 27(3): 124–30.

Perry C, Walsh B (1978) Inconsistencies and anomalies of response as a defining characteristic of hypnosis. *Journal of Abnormal Psychology* 87: 574–77.

Pettinati HM (1988) Hypnosis and memory: integrative summary and future directions. In HM Pettinati (ed.) *Hypnosis and Memory*. New York: Guilford Press.

Phillips M, Frederick C (1992) The use of hypnotic age progressions as prognostic, ego-strengthening and integrating techniques. *American Journal of Clinical Hypnosis* 35(2): 99–108.

Phillips RG, Le Doux JE (1992) Differential contribution of amygdala and hippocampus to cued and contextual fear conditioning. *Behavioral Neuroscience* 106: 274–85.

Piper A (2004) The persistence of folly: a critical examination of dissociative identity disorder. *The Canadian Journal of Psychiatry* 49: 592–600.

Pope HG, Hudson JI (1995) Can memories of childhood sexual abuse be repressed? *Psychological Medicine* 25: 121–6.

Pope KS, Brown LS (1996) *Recovered Memories of Abuse*. Washington DC: American Psychological Association.

Putnam FW (1988) The switch process in multiple personality disorder and other state-change disorders. *Dissociation* 1: 24–32.

Putnam FW (1989) *Diagnosis and Treatment of Multiple Personality Disorder*. New York: Guilford.

Putnam FW, Loewenstein RJ (1993) Treatment of multiple personality disorder: a survey of current practices. *American Journal of Psychiatry* 150: 1048–52.

Putnam FW, Guroff JJ, Silberman EK, Barban L, Post RM (1986) The clinical phenomenology of multiple personality disorder: review of 100 recent cases. *Journal of Clinical Psychiatry* 47: 285–93.

Putnam WH (1979) Hypnosis and distortions in eyewitness memory. *International Journal of Clinical and Experimental Hypnosis* 27: 437–48.

Rainer D (1983) *Eyewitness Testimony: Does Hypnosis enhance Accuracy, Distortion and Confidence?* Unpublished doctoral dissertation. University of Wyoming.

Rainville P, Price DD (2003) Hypnosis phenomenology and the neurobiology of consciousness. *International Journal of Clinical and Experimental Hypnosis* 51(2): 105–29.

Rauch SL, Van der Kolk BA, Fisler RE, Alpert NM, Orr SP, Savage CR et al. (1996) A symptom provocation study of post traumatic stress disorder using position emission tomography and script driven imagery. *Archives of General Psychiatry* 53 (May): 380–7.

Resnick HS, Yehuda R, Acierno R (1997) Acute post rape plasma cortisol, alcohol uses and PTSD symptom profile among recent rape victims. *Annals of the New York Academy of Sciences* 821: 433–6.

Rodeghier M, Goodpaster J, Blatterbauen S (1991) Psychosocial characteristics of abductees. Result from the CUFOS abduction project. *Journal of UFO Studies* 3: 59–90.

Roe CM, Schwartz MF (1996) Characteristics of previously forgotten memories of sexual abuse: a descriptive study. *Journal of Psychiatry and Law* 24: 189–206.

Root MP, Fallon P (1988) The incidence of victimisation experiences in a bulimic sample. *Journal of Interpersonal Violence* 3: 161–73.

Rorty M, Yager J (1996) Speculations on the role of childhood abuse in the development of eating disorders among women. In MF Schwartz, L Cohn (eds) *Sexual Abuse and Eating Disorders*. New York: Brunner/Mazel.

Ross CA, Heber S, Norton GR, Anderson G (1989) Differences between multiple personality disorder and other diagnostic groups on structured interview. *Journal of Nervous and Mental Disease* 179(8): 487–91.

Ross CA, Norton GR, Wozney K (1989) Multiple personality disorder: an analysis of 236 cases. *Canadian Journal of Psychiatry* 34: 413–18.

Rothschild B (2000) The body remembers. In: *The Psychophysiology of Trauma and Trauma Treatment*. New York: WW Norton.

Sanders B, Becker-Lausen E (1995) The measurement of psychological maltreatment: early data on the Child Abuse and Trauma Scale. *Child Abuse and Neglect* 19: 315–23.

Sanders GS, Simmons WL (1983) Use of hypnosis to enhance eyewitness accuracy: does it work? *Journal of Applied Psychology* 68: 70–7.

Sanders S (1986) The Perceptual Alteration Scale: a scale measuring dissociation. *American Journal of Clinical Hypnosis* 29(2): 95–102.

Sapolsky RM, Hideo E, Rebert CS, Finch CE (1990) Hippocampal damage associated with prolonged glucocorticoid exposure in primates. *Journal of Neuroscience* 10: 2897–902.

Sarbin TR (1950) Contributions to role-taking theory: 1. Hypnotic behaviour. *Psychological Review* 57: 255–70.

Scaer RC (2001) *The Body Bears the Burden: Trauma, Dissociation and Disease*. New York: Haworth Press.

Schmucker MR, Dancu C, Foa EB, Niederee JL (1995) Imagery rescripting: a new treatment for survivors of childhood sexual abuse suffering from posttraumatic stress. *Journal of Cognitive Psychotherapy: An International Quarterly* 9(1): 3–17.

Schore AN (1994) *Affect Regulation and the Origin of the Self: The Neurobiology of Emotional Development.* Hillsdale, NJ: Lawrence Erlbaum Associates.

Schore AN (2001) The effects of relational trauma on right brain development, affect regulation and infant mental health. *Infant Mental Health Journal* 22: 201–69.

Schore AN (2003) Early relational trauma, disorganised attachment, and the development of a predisposition to violence. In MF Solomon, DJ Siegel (eds) *Healing Trauma: Attachment, Mind, Body and Brain,* 107–67. New York, London: W.W. Norton.

Schwartz MF, Cohn L (eds) (1996) *Sexual Abuse and Eating Disorders.* New York: Brunner/Mazel.

Shalev AY, Peri T, Canetti L, Schreiber S (1996) Predictors of PTSD in injured trauma survivors: a prospective study. *American Journal of Psychiatry* 153: 219–25.

Sheehan PW, Grigg L, McCann T (1984) Memory distortion following exposure to false information in hypnosis. *Journal of Abnormal Psychology* 93: 259–65.

Sinason V (ed.) (2002) *Attachment, Trauma, and Multiplicity: Working with Dissociative Identity Disorder.* East Sussex: Brunner-Routledge.

Sjorberg BM, Hollister LE (1965) The effects of psychomimetic drugs on primary suggestibility. *Psychopharmacologia* 8: 251–62.

Smith M, Bentovim A (1994) Sexual abuse. In M Rutter, E Taylor, J Hersov (eds) *Child and Adolescent Psychiatry: Modern Approaches* (3rd edn). Oxford: Blackwell Science.

Smolak L, Murnen SK (2002) A meta-analysis of the relationship between child sexual abuse and eating disorders. *International Journal of Eating Disorders* 31: 136–50.

Spanos NP (1991) A sociocognitive approach to hypnosis. In SJ Lynn, JW Rhue (eds) *Theories of Hypnosis: Current Models and Perspectives,* 324–61. New York: Guilford Press.

Spanos NP (1996) *Multiple Identities and False Memories.* Washington DC: American Psychological Association.

Spanos NP, Menary E, Gabora NJ, Dubreuil SC, Dewhirst B (1991) Secondary identity enactments during hypnotic past life regression: A socio-cognitive perspective. *Journal of Personality and Social Psychology* 61: 308–20.

Spiegel D (1984) Multiple personality as a post traumatic stress disorder. *Psychiatric Clinics of North America* 7: 101–10.

Spiegel D (1993) Hypnosis in the treatment of post traumatic stress disorders. In JW Rhue, SJ Lynn, I Kirsch (eds) *Handbook of Clinical Hypnosis,* 493–508. Washington DC: American Psychological Association.

Spiegel D (1996) Hypnosis in the treatment of posttraumatic stress disorder. In SJ Lynn, I Kirsch, JW Rhue (eds) *Casebook of Clinical Hypnosis,* 99–111. Washington DC: American Psychological Association.

Spiegel D (1998) Hypnosis and implicit memory: automatic processing and explicit content. *American Journal of Clinical Hypnosis* 40(3): 231–40.

Spiegel D (2001) Hypnosis, dissociation and trauma. In GD Burrows, RO Stanley, PB Bloom (eds) *International Handbook of Clinical Hypnosis,* 143–58. Chichester: J Wiley & Sons.

Spiegel D (2003) Hypnosis and traumatic dissociation: therapeutic opportunities. *Journal of Trauma and Dissociation* 4(3): 73–90.

Spiegel D (2005) Multi-levelling the playing field: altering our state of consciousness to understand hypnosis. *Contemporary Hypnosis* 22(1): 31–3.

Spiegel D, Cardena E (1990) New uses of hypnosis in the treatment of post traumatic stress disorder. *Journal of Clinical Psychiatry* 51 (Suppl.): 39–43.

Spiegel H, Spiegel D (1978) *Trance and Treatment: Clinical Uses of Hypnosis.* New York: Basic Books.

Spence SH (1991) *Psychosexual Therapy: A Cognitive-Behavioural Approach.* London: Chapman & Hall.

Starr RH (Jr), Wolfe DA (1991) *The Effects of Child Abuse and Neglect: Issues and Research.* London: New York: Guilford Press.

Steele K, van der Hart O, Nijenhuis ERS (2001) Dependency in the treatment of complex post traumatic stress disorder and dissociative disorders. *Journal of Trauma and Dissociation Vol. 2,* No. 4: 79–116.

Steele K, Van der Hart O, Nijenhuis ERS (2005) Phase-oriented treatment of structural dissociation in complex traumatisation: overcoming trauma-related phobias. *Journal of Trauma and Dissociation* 6(3): 11–53.

Stein C (1963) The clenched fist technique as a hypnotic procedure in clinical psychotherapy. *American Journal of Clinical Hypnosis* 6: 113–19.

Stein MB, Koverola C, Hanna C, Torchia MG, McClarty B (1997) Hippocampal volume in women victimised by childhood sexual abuse. *Psychological Medicine* 27(4): 951–9.

Stoyva JM (1967) Post hypnotically suggested dreams and the sleep cycle. In C Scott Moss (ed.) *The Hypnotic Investigation of Dreams* 255–68.

Straker G, Watson D, Robinson T (2002) Trauma and disconnection: a transtheoretical approach. *International Journal of Psychotherapy* 7(2): 145–58.

Straus MA, Gelles RJ, Steenmetz SK (1980) *Behind Closed Doors: Violence in the American Family.* New York: Anchor Press.

Stuss DT, Alexander MP (1999) Affectively burnt in: a proposed role of the right frontal lobe. In E Tulving (ed.) *Memory, Consciousness and the Brain: The Talin Conference,* 215–27. Philadelphia: Psychology Press.

Swica Y, Lewis DO, Lewis M (1996) Child abuse and dissociative identity disorder/multiple personality disorder: the documentation of childhood maltreatment and the corroboration of symptoms. *Child and Adolescent Psychiatric Clinics of North America* 5: 431–47.

Tarnoplosky A (2003) The concept of dissociation in early psychoanalytic writers. *Journal of Trauma and Dissociation* 4(3): 7–25.

Tart CT (1972) Scientific foundations for the study of altered states of consciousness. *Journal of Transpersonal Psychology* 3: 93–124.

Terr L (1988) Case study: what happens to early memories of trauma? A study of twenty children under age five at the time of the documented traumatic events. *Journal of The American Academy of Child and Adolescent Psychiatry* 27: 96–104.

Terr L (1991) Childhood traumas: an outline and overview. *American Journal of Psychiatry* 148: 10–20.

Tillman JG, Nash MR, Lerner PM (1994) Does trauma cause dissociative pathology? In SJ Lynn, JW Rhue (eds) *Dissociation: Clinical and Theoretical Perspectives.* New York: Guilford Press.

Torem MS (1992) Back from the future: a powerful age progression technique. *American Journal of Clinical Hypnosis* 35(2): 81–8.

Toth S, Manly JT, Cicchetti D (1992) Child maltreatment and vulnerability to depression. *Development and Psychopathology* 4: 97–112.

Treuer T, Koperdak M, Rozsa S, Furedi J (2005) The impact of physical and sexual abuse on body image in eating disorders. *European Eating Disorders Review* 13(2): 106–11.

Van der Hart O, Brown P (1992) Abreaction re-evaluated. *Dissociation* 3: 127–40.

Van der Kolk BA (1994) The body keeps the score: memory and evolving psychobiology of posttraumatic stress. *Harvard Review of Psychiatry* 1(5): 253–65.

Van der Kolk BA (1996) Trauma and memory. In BA Van Der Kolk, AC McFarlane, L Weisaeth (eds) *Traumatic Stress: The Effects of Overwhelming Experience on Body, Mind and Society.* New York: Guilford Press.

Van der Kolk BA (2000a) The assessment and treatment of complex PTSD. In R Yehuda (ed.) *Traumatic Stress.* American Psychiatric Press, Washington, DC.

Van der Kolk BA (2000b) Post traumatic stress disorder and the nature of trauma. *Dialogues in Clinical Neuroscience* 2(1): 7–22.

Van der Kolk BA (2000c) *PTSD Masterclass.: The Black Hole of Trauma.* North East Essex Mental Health Trust.

Van der Kolk BA (2003) Post traumatic stress disorder and the nature of trauma. In MF Solomon, DJ Siegel (eds) *Healing Trauma: Attachment, Mind, Body and Brain,* 168–95. New York: WW Norton & Co.

Van der Kolk BA, Fisler RE (1994) Childhood abuse and neglect and loss of self-regulation. *Bulletin of the Menninger Clinic* 58(2): 145–68.

Van der Kolk BA, Fisler RE (1995) Dissociation and the fragmentary nature of traumatic memories: overview and exploratory study. *Journal of Traumatic Stress* 8: 505–25.

Van der Kolk BA, McFarlane AC, Weisaeth L (1996) *Traumatic Stress: The Effects of Overwhelming Experience on Mind, Body, and Society.* New York: Guilford Press.

Van der Kolk BA, Pelcovitz D, Roth S, Mandel FS, McFarlane A, Herman JL (1996) Dissociation, somatisation, and affect dysregulation: the complexity of adaptation to trauma. *American Journal of Psychiatry* 153: 83–93.

Van der Kolk BA, Van der Hart O, Marmar CR (1996) Dissociation and information processing in post traumatic stress disorder. In BA Van der Kolk, AC McFarlane, I Weisaeth (eds) *Traumatic Stress: The Effects of Overwhelming Experience in Mind and Body,* 303–27. New York: Guilford Press.

Vanderlinden J, Vandereycken W, Probst M (1995) Dissociative symptoms in eating disorders: a follow-up study. *European Eating Disorders Review* 3: 174–84.

Vanderlinden J, Vandereycken W (1997) *Trauma, Dissociation, and Impulse Dyscontrol in Eating Disorders.* New York: Brunner/Mazel.

Vermetten E, Bremner JD (2004) Functional brain imaging and the induction of traumatic recall: a cross correlational review between neuroimaging and hypnosis. *International Journal of Clinical and Experimental Hypnosis* 52(3): 280–312.

Viatl D, Gruzelier J, Jamieson G, Lehmann D, Ott U, Sammer G et al. (2005) Psychobiology of altered states of consciousness. *Psychological Bulletin* 131(1): 98–127.

Vingoe F (1987) When is a placebo not a placebo? That is the question. *British Journal of Experimental and Clinical Hypnosis* 4: 165–7.

Waller G, Hamilton K, Elliott P, Lewendon J, Stopa L, Waters A et al. (2000) Somatoform dissociation, psychological dissociation, and specific forms of trauma. *Journal of Trauma and Dissociation* 1(4): 81–98.

Waller NG, Putnam FW, Carlson EB (1996) Types of dissociation and dissociative types: a taxometric analysis of dissociative experiences. *Psychological Methods* 1: 300–21.

Watkins HH (1980) The silent abreaction. *International Journal of Clinical and Experimental Hypnosis, Vol. XXV111,* 2, 101–112.

Watkins J.G. (1971) The Affect Bridge: A Hypnoanalytic Technique. *International Journal of Clinical and Experimental Hypnosis* 19(1): 21–7.

Watkins JG, Watkins HH (1997) *Ego-states. Theory and Therapy.* New York: WW Norton & Co.

Wenninger K, Heiman JR (1998) Relating body image to psychological and sexual functioning in child sexual abuse survivors. *Journal of Traumatic Stress* 11(3): 543–62.

Whalen JE, Nash MR (1996) Hypnosis and dissociation: theoretical, empirical and clinical perspectives. In KL Michelson, WJ Ray (eds) *Handbook of Dissociation: Theoretical, Empirical and Clinical Perspectives,* 191–206. New York: Plenum.

Widom CS (1989) Does violence beget violence? a critical examination of the literature. *Psychological Bulletin* 106: 3–28.

Widom CS (1993) Child abuse and alcohol use and abuse. In SE Martin (ed) *Alcohol and Interpersonal Violence: Fostering Interdisciplinary Research.* NIAAA Research Monograph No. 24 NIH Publication No.93–3496, 291–314. Rockville MD: National Institute of Health.

Widom CS (1997) Accuracy of adult recollections of childhood victimisation. Part 2: Childhood sexual abuse. *Psychological Assessment* 9: 34–46.

Williams JD, Gruzelier JH (2001) Differentiation of hypnosis and relaxation by analysis of narrow band theta and alpha frequencies. *International Journal of Clinical and Experimental Hypnosis* 49: 185–286.

Williams L (1994) Recall of childhood trauma: a prospective study of womens' memories of child sexual abuse. *Journal of Consulting and Clinical Psychology* 62: 1167–76.

Williams LM (1995) Recovered memories of abuse in women with documented child sexual victimisation histories. *Journal of Traumatic Stress* 8: 649–73.

Williams TL, Gleaves DH (2003) Childhood sexual abuse, body image and disordered eating: a structural modelling analysis. *Journal of Trauma and Dissociation* 4(4): 91–108.

Williamson A (2005) *The Time Road Metaphor.* Personal communication.

Wilson SC, Barber TX (1978) The Creative Imagination Scale as a measure of hypnotic responsiveness: applications to experimental and clinical hypnosis. *American Journal of Clinical Hypnosis* 20: 235–49.

Wolfe DA (1999) *Child Abuse: Implications for Child Development and Psychopathology,* 2nd edn. Thousand Oaks, CA: Sage.

Yellowlees A (1997) *Working with Eating Disorders and Self-esteem.* Dunstable and Dublin: Folens.

Young L (1992) Sexual abuse and the problem of embodiment. *Child Abuse and Neglect* 16: 89–100.

Yuille JC, McEwan H (1985) Use of hypnosis as an aid to eyewitness memory. *Journal of Applied Psychology* 70: 389–400.

Zelikovsky N, Lynn SJ (1994) The after-effects and assessment of physical and psychological abuse. In SJ Lynn, JW Rhue (eds) *Dissociation: Clinical and Theoretical Perspectives,* 190–214. New York: Guilford Press.

Zelikovsky N, Lynn SJ (2002) Childhood psychological and physical abuse: psychopathology dissociation and Axis 1 diagnosis. *Journal of Trauma and Dissociation* 3(3): 27–58.

INDEX